ISLAM and DEVELOPMENT

Contemporary Issues in the Middle East

With contributions from

Hossein Askari
Mangol Bayat
Daniel Crecelius
Lucy E. Creevey
John Thomas Cummings
John L. Esposito
Yvonne Haddad
Michael C. Hudson
Fred R. von der Mehden
Akbar Muhammad
Ahmad Mustafa
James P. Piscatori
John Alden Williams

ISLAM and DEVELOPMENT

Religion and Sociopolitical Change

Edited by

JOHN L. ESPOSITO

SYRACUSE UNIVERSITY PRESS

1980

ACKNOWLEDGMENTS

It would not be possible to name all those who have been consulted during the preparation of this volume. However, there are a number who deserve special mention. The original idea for this volume was an outgrowth of a panel, "Islam and Politics," which I developed for the Islamic Studies Group of the American Academy of Religion. Ismail R. al-Faruqi, my good friend and teacher, has throughout the years made me aware of dimensions of Islam that transcend books. I have been fortunate enough to have several excellent typists: Elizabeth Stebbins, Lorna Mattus, and Jean Heffernan. Gary Regele-De Angelis was especially helpful in reviewing the completed volume. The College of the Holy Cross has provided financial assistance over the years for my research.

Finally, I am especially endebted to my parents and Jean, whose encouragement on this and other projects has been immeasurable.

JLE

Chapter 3 is a revised version of a chapter that first appeared under the same title in *Religion and Political Modernization,* edited by Donald Eugene Smith (New Haven: Yale University Press, 1974).

Library of Congress Cataloging in Publication Data
Main entry under title:

Islam and development.

   (Contemporary issues in the Middle East)
   Includes bibliographical references and index.
   1. Islam—20th century—Addresses, essays, lectures.
2. Islam and politics—Addresses, essays, lectures.
3. Islamic countries—Politics and government—
Addresses, essays, lectures. I. Esposito, John L.
II. Askari, Hossein. III. Series: Contemporary
issues in the Middle East series.
BP163.I735   909'.097671   80-25119
ISBN 0-8156-2229-5
ISBN 0-8156-2230-9 (pbk.)

CONTENTS

CONTRIBUTORS

HOSSEIN ASKARI is Professor of International Business and Middle Eastern Studies, University of Texas at Austin.

MANGOL BAYAT is Assistant Professor of History, Harvard University.

DANIEL CRECELIUS is Professor of History, California State University, Los Angeles.

LUCY E. CREEVEY is Associate Professor and Director of Urban Planning, University of Pennsylvania.

JOHN THOMAS CUMMINGS is Assistant Professor of International Business, University of Texas at Austin.

JOHN L. ESPOSITO is Associate Professor and Chairman, Department of Religious Studies, College of the Holy Cross, Worcester, Massachusetts.

YVONNE HADDAD is at the MacDonald Center, Hartford Seminary Foundation, Hartford, Connecticut.

MICHAEL C. HUDSON is Director, Center for Contemporary Arab Studies, Georgetown University, Washington, D.C.

FRED R. VON DER MEHDEN is Professor of Political Science, Rice University, Houston, Texas.

AKBAR MUHAMMAD is Associate Professor of History and Chairman, Department of Afro-American and African Studies, State University of New York at Binghamton.

AHMAD MUSTAFA is a Ph.D. candidate in the School of Business and Management, University of Texas at Austin.

JAMES P. PISCATORI is a Senior Fellow at the Royal Institute of International Affairs, London.

JOHN ALDEN WILLIAMS is Professor of History and Middle Eastern Studies, University of Texas at Austin.

INTRODUCTION

$\mathcal{T}$HE ISLAMIC WORLD stretches from North America to Southeast Asia and includes some forty independent states in which Muslims constitute a majority of the population. Islam has approximately 750 million adherents and, therefore, is the second largest of the world's religions.

A distinctive feature of the Islamic tradition is the belief that Islam is a total, comprehensive way of life. Religion has an integral, organic relationship to politics and society. This Islamic ideal is reflected in the development of Islamic law which was a comprehensive law, encompassing a Muslim's duties to God (worship, fasting, pilgrimage) and duties to one's fellow man (family, commercial, and criminal laws). Therefore, the Islamic tradition provided a normative system in which religion was integral to all areas of Muslim life — politics, economics, law, education, and the family.

In the twentieth century Muslim countries have faced formidable political and social challenges: the struggle for independence from colonial dominance, the formation and development of independent nation states with all the pressures and problems of modernization, the Arab-Israeli conflict, and more recently, the emergence of the oil-producing states as a major world economic power bloc. The history of Islam in the modern period reflects the continued interaction of the Islamic tradition with the forces of change.

While Islam may be acknowledged as a significant force in the precolonial period and to varying degrees during the twentieth-century independence movements, the strength and interaction of Islam in sociopolitical change has often been overlooked or underestimated. For most observers, Islam was simply an obstacle to change, an obstacle whose relevance to the political and social order would increasingly diminish.

Present political events in the Muslim world have therefore caught most analysts off guard; suddenly, experts (academic and government) and the media alike have become aware of a phenomenon labeled variously as the "Islamic resurgence," "militant Islam," or the "Islamic revival." The Iranian revolution, the seizure of the mosque at Mecca, the attempt to introduce an Islamic system (Nizam-i-Islam) in Pakistan, as well as reports from many Muslim countries regarding increased public observance of Muslim practices (mosque attendance, Islamic dress, fasting during Ramadan, etc.) have contributed to a sense that Islam has reappeared and, inexplicably, has become a significant factor in sociopolitical change. Many deep-rooted myths or assumptions about Islam have been challenged — among them that Islam is a static, monolithic structure and outlook on life whose tradition has little import or relevance for the present contemporary world; that modernization means following the path of Westernization and secularization as manifested in the development of the West; that the spheres of religion and politics must necessarily be separate in a modern system of government.

This book seeks to provide some perspective and insight into the complex and living role of Islam in sociopolitical change. Specialists from several disciplines (history, political science, economics, and Islamic studies) explore the interaction of religious tradition and modernity in the modern Muslim world (Africa, the Middle East, South and Southeast Asia) and its effects upon political and socioeconomic development.

Michael C. Hudson notes in the first chapter, "Islam and Political Development," that Islamic resurgence brings into sharper focus a fundamental disagreement between the apparent desires of many Muslims (for whom political development is unthinkable without Islam) and the conventional wisdom of Western social science (which has maintained that Islam is at best an impediment to political development).

Western perceptions (or misperceptions) have too often been rooted in negative cultural stereotypes and biases. This has been compounded by distinctive differences between Islamic and Western social scientific world views — the former God centered and normative and the latter man centered, rooted in a postclassical nineteenth-century positivist, empirical tradition. As Hudson asserts, given different societies and cultures and thus their differing ideals, "there are no grounds for predicting a unilinear trend toward a universal condition of political development on the normative level."

Similarly, given the richness, diversity, and flexibility of the Islamic tradition, the question is not, according to Hudson, "Is Islam compatible with political development?" but rather "How much and what

kinds of Islam are compatible with (or necessary for) political development in the Muslim world?" Hudson sees a broad spectrum of roles for
Islam ranging from more fundamentalist religious states like Iran to that
of modern Egypt.

A common assumption in development theory has been that
modernization weakens religious tradition as it fosters the process of secularization. The reality in many Muslim countries contradicts this facile
presupposition. While modernization has often meant the curtailment of
the traditional power and influence of the religious establishment (*ulama*)
as government advisers and protectors of the law, religion itself has not
been weakened appreciably. As several chapters demonstrate, in many
Muslim countries (among them Iran, Egypt, and Malaysia) it is the young
university educated Muslims who are using their newly acquired knowledge and skills to develop Islamic responses to political and social problems and to organize movements to implement them. Hudson correctly
concludes that the Islamic resurgence is not so much the product of mass
alienation or rejection of modernization as the re-emergence of Islam as
an important component of political ideology. Islam is an instrument espoused both by incumbent governments and opposition forces as they
respond to the political exigencies of their countries and try to obtain legitimation and mass support for their programs and policies.

Religion is not only organically related to politics but also is integral to the economic structure of an Islamic state. The Quran, the example of the Prophet Muhammad, and Islamic history attest to this fact. Oil
wealth, as well as the political resurgence of Islam, have reawakened interest in the potential impact of Islam on economic development. Are Islamic states or more Islamic forms of government antithetical to viable
modern economics? What effects would Islamic prescriptions have in the
areas of taxation, interest, insurance, etc.? John Thomas Cummings,
Hossein Askari, and Ahmad Mustafa in "Islam and Modern Economic
Change" provide a chapter which complements Hudson's. They focus on
the resources of traditional Islamic economics, its compatibility with
Western capitalist thought, and its relationship to current socioeconomic
change in the Middle East.

Islam addresses itself to many aspects of economic development
—private ownership, taxation, interest, income distribution, etc. However, all economic thought was subject to the Islamic ethical norms set
forth in the teachings of the Quran, Muhammad, and Islamic law. The result, according to Cummings and his colleagues, is an economic tradition
which constitutes an alternative approach to laissez faire capitalism and
Marxist socialism. "If Western countries can evolve economic systems of

a hybrid nature," they ask, "might not Islamic countries do the same?" They maintain that Islamic principles of economics do not necessarily preclude rapid economic growth. On the contrary, Islamic principles advocate factors which are generally regarded as essential to economic progress — private property, profit incentive, hard work, and eternal reward for economic success.

Egypt has long been regarded as among the leading modern Muslim states, in part because it was considered very much a Westernized secular state. The case studies of Daniel Crecelius and John Alden Williams reveal the fallacies of such an oversimplification.

Daniel Crecelius' "The Course of Secularization in Modern Egypt" provides an excellent example of the complexity of change and the failure of accepted development theories to explain adequately modern Egypt's "retreat from secularism" in the twentieth century. As he notes, studies of Islam and modernization have not made clear distinctions between the ideas and policies of a relatively small Western-oriented elite leadership and their actual impact on Muslim society. The result has been a failure to appreciate adequately the presence and hold of Islam on a majority of the population — educated and uneducated — and therefore to foresee the influence that religion and religious issues will bring to bear on contemporary politics.

From the early nineteenth century, Crecelius points out, secularization in Egypt "appeared to be a unilinear force leading toward a predictable goal." Muhammad Ali Pasha (1805–49) had put Egypt on the path of modernization, and under successive governments Egypt adopted Western secular models in her social and political development. Since the religious leadership (*ulama*) was seen as an obstacle to change, its power was curtailed and neutralized through a process of differentiation between religious and secular institutions, a pattern followed in many other Muslim states. Thus parallel state structures such as secular legal codes, courts, and modern Western-oriented schools were introduced. Instead of a frontal attack, Egypt developed a system which enabled the political leadership to weaken and control the religious establishment and its institutions.

After the revolution of 1952, Egypt under Nasser appeared to continue along a secular path; the *shariah* courts were abolished and religious endowments *(waqfs)* nationalized. However, by the late 50s and early 60s Islam progressively re-emerged as a significant factor in Egyptian politics. The Nasser regime harnessed Islamic beliefs and symbols to legitimate and gain widespread support for its socialist ideology, policies, and programs such as land reform, birth control, and foreign policy. This trend continues under Anwar Sadat. Crecelius concludes from the Nasser and Sadat years that the "very essence of a secular state appears to be missing in Egypt today."

During the twentieth century, a major area of Islamic social reform has concerned the role and status of Muslim women. Among the major reforms undertaken have been: the elimination of the veil; the reform of family laws (marriage, divorce, and inheritance); and the expansion of educational and occupational opportunities. However, observers of the Islamic revival have noted what seems to be a reversal in this process as symbolized by a return to Islamic dress. Two chapters explore the meaning and implications of this phenomenon in Egypt and Iran.

John Alden Williams' "Veiling in Egypt as a Political and Social Phenomenon" focuses on the motives and issues underlying an apparently inexplicable regression. Egypt has led the Islamic world in improving the status of women. Yet today middle-class Egyptian women, the very strata of society that fought for and benefitted most from reforms, are donning Islamic dress. Is this simply a rejection of modernization in favor of Islamic fundamentalism? Williams rejects such a conclusion. Rather, he sees its origin in a return to Islamic values. Faced with acute socioeconomic problems, disenchanted with Western and Marxist models, some women turn to their Islamic tradition for a greater sense of identity and authenticity. As Williams perceptively notes: "modernization is not being questioned; false models and false friends are being questioned." Therefore, this experiment is neither a rejection of modernity nor an unquestioning appropriation of the past. Rather, it is an attempt to develop a more indigenous, Islamic response in the midst of social disruption and a sense of spiritual malaise.

Analysis of Iran's revolution of 1978–79 poses many questions for those who would seek to understand its Islamic character and dimensions. In "Islam in Pahlavi and Post-Pahlavi Iran: A Cultural Revolution?" Mangol Bayat provides a historical perspective on those fundamental political beliefs and institutions of Shii Islam which have a direct bearing on Iran's Islamic revolution. Bayat argues that in pre-Pahlavi Iran the relationship of Shii Islam to the state was not uniform but rather took on various configurations. Moreover, though the *ulama* progressively institutionalized their religious authority, they were far from a uniform, cohesive group: "Internal factions, divergence of religious outlook, conflicts of interests . . . seriously divided their ranks." This situation changed during the modern period due to the secularizing reforms and anticlerical policies implemented by the Pahlavi dynasty which emphasized a Persian (pre-Islamic) heritage to establish its imperial identity and undertook modern reforms in law and education, based primarily upon Western models. Such policies put the *ulama* on the defensive and resulted in the 1960s and 70s in their emergence "as a distinct, socially defined, ideologically cohesive class of its own . . . [their revolt] was more than just a revolution for the sake of religion. It was a social and cultural revolution as well."

Of equal significance is the emergence of a lay Islamic ideology among the professional classes which was to add further to the religious undertone of the nationalist movement and the revolution. The reformist thought of Mihdi Bazargan and especially Ali Shariati provided an indigenously rooted and thus culturally authentic alternative for those who found themselves economically and culturally alienated. While the exigencies of the revolution called for unity, Bayat demonstrates that there are profound differences between Shariati's writings and the views of the Ayatollah Khomeini and other traditional religious leaders. This divergence between clerical leaders and lay Islamic ideologists is critical both for the future of Islam and of Iran.

The Arab-Israeli conflict is a root cause for continued instability in the Middle East. Resolution of the Palestine problem in general and the status of the holy city of Jerusalem in particular are a *sine qua non* for peace. Yvonne Haddad in "The Arab-Israeli Wars, Nasserism, and the Affirmation of Islamic Identity" examines the ways in which the wars and Nasser's response during this period to the political realities of Egypt and the Arab world contributed to a reaffirmation of Islamic identity in Arab politics.

As Haddad observes, the existence and prosperity of the state of Israel is a direct challenge to the Arab/Islamic view of the historical process. The loss of Jerusalem in 1967, the third most holy city (after Mecca and Medina) in Islam, intensified the religious significance of the conflict. For most Muslims, Israel stands as a symbol of Western power, a continuation of colonialism and imperialism, and a reminder of Muslim impotence. Nasser was able to shrewdly seize upon these concerns and use Islam in responding not only to the Palestine problem but also in legitimating his rule and policies within Egypt as well as establishing his position as a popular Arab nationalist leader abroad.

Haddad analyzes the identity crisis precipitated by the disastrous Arab defeat in the 1967 war and reflected in the postwar period of self-examination as well as its reversal as a result of the Arab (psychological) "victory" in the 1973 war with its use of Islamic symbols, slogans, and language which underscored the Islamic character of the battle and victory. She also demonstrates how Nasser progressively turned to Islam politi-

cally so that in the end the state's traditional function to protect and propagate Islam was replaced by the control and manipulation of religion to
legitimate and win mass support for Nasser's Arab nationalism and socialism and his desire to emerge as a pan-Arab leader.

Saudi Arabia and Pakistan provide the two major examples of
formal Islamic states. Therefore, they illustrate some of the questions and
problems which other Muslim states may encounter in seeking to establish more Islamic political and social orders.

Until the Iranian revolution, Saudi Arabia was the first nation to
come to mind when speaking of an Islamic state. While its oil wealth and
emergence as a major world economic power have heightened interest
and coverage of Saudi politics and society, all too often an appreciation
of its Islamic character has rarely gone beyond stereotypical images and
stories of the status of women or Islamic criminal punishments. James P.
Piscatori in "The Roles of Islam in Saudi Arabia's Political Development"
demonstrates how "Islam is an abiding, if not also central, reality in Saudi
Arabia."

'Islam has given life and form to the Saudi state from its mid-
eighteenth century origins to the present. The strength and pervasiveness
of its presence may be seen at every level — political, judicial, and socioeconomic. Under Muhammad ibn Saud and Muhammad ibn Abd al-
Wahhab, Islam became the cohesive force by which the temporal and
spiritual were joined in a religio-political movement. In the Quran and the
sharia the Saud family has found legitimation for their monarchy and a
fairly broad framework within which to govern and rule without benefit
of a constitution or national assembly. Furthermore, Islam has served as
an important factor in national decision making. Thus successive governments here obtained *fatwas* (formal legal opinions) from the *ulama* in order to provide an Islamic rationale and thus legitimation for actions and
policies undertaken by the royal family — from justification of the transfer of power to Faysal in 1964, to validation of the government's actions
in ending the seizure of the Grand Mosque in 1979.

Despite popular assumptions to the contrary, while respecting
traditional beliefs and values, Saudi Arabia has been able to effect substantive change and reform. Piscatori discusses some of these changes
and, more importantly, analyzes those factors which have enabled this
Muslim society to use Islam to facilitate reforms: from the early acceptance of radio and photography to modern education for women as well
as substantive legal reforms. The result has been a blending of the traditional and the modern as reflected, for example, in the Saudi legal system.
Unlike most states in the Islamic world where civil courts and laws pre-

dominate and the *sharia* is restricted to family law, in Saudi Arabia *sharia* courts exercise jurisdiction in all spheres of life (civil, criminal, and family). However, the judicial system also includes such additions as an appellate court system. Moreover, Saudi law incorporates both traditional *sharia* regulations including the Quran-prescribed penalties *(hudud)* for theft, drinking, and adultery, and royally decreed modern laws governing such areas as mining, commerce, and social insurance.

While Islam has served the Saud family well, its role in the future political and social development of Saudi Arabia bear watching. The continued pressures of rapid change, the compromises necessitated in modernizing, and discontent over the maldistribution of wealth and corruption pose a serious challenge to the future of Islam and the Saud dynasty.

Islam provided the *raison d'etre* for the partitioning of India and the establishment of Pakistan as a separate nation state in 1947. In "Pakistan: Quest for Islamic Identity," I examine Pakistan's attempt to translate her Islamic aspiration into a political and social reality. While Islam had been used to mobilize and unite Muslims during the independence movement, little consensus existed about such fundamental questions as: "What does it mean to say that Pakistan is a modern Islamic state? How is its Islamic character to be reflected in the ideology and institutions of the state?" A review of the period from 1947–70 reveals limited results. Political instability and sharp differences between traditionalists and modernists produced an ad hoc, piecemeal approach whose compromises contributed little to the development of a consistent Islamic ideology which could serve as a basis for national unity amidst Pakistan's vast linguistic and regional divisions.

In the 1970s Islam re-emerged as a major component in Pakistan's political development. Islamic slogans and symbols were used by a coalition of opposition forces against the Bhutto government. Moreover, a commitment to the introduction and enforcement of an Islamic system *(Nizam-i-Islam)* has become the chief means of the present ruler, General Zia-ul-Haq to legitimate his coup and continued rule. Islamic political, legal, and social reforms have been introduced. A careful examination of these changes and an analysis of the problems and issues which they raise reveals the continued limitations of Pakistan's approach to Islamic self-definition. Furthermore, Pakistan's example may have implications for other Muslim countries who seek greater Islamization of their political and social systems.

Malaysia and Nigeria are predominantly Muslim countries with significant non-Muslim populations. If Islamic ideology and identity were emphasized in such nations, what would be the effects on national unity and the status of minorities? While historically non-Muslims often enjoyed more freedom and rights under Muslim rule than afforded by other governments, their status as *dhimmi* ("protected ones"), if judged by today's standards, would inevitably still be regarded as second class. Malaysia (as a Muslim state) and Nigeria (as a secular state) have responded differently to the problems of minority status, national unity, and nation building; the Malay government has responded with economic policies and ties to other Middle Eastern countries, Nigeria with education.

In "Islamic Resurgence in Malaysia," Fred R. von der Mehden examines the renewed emphasis on the identity of Malay ethnicity and Islam and its impact on Malaysian society. While the majority of the population (55 percent) is Malay Muslim, the Chinese constitute the largest (38 percent) and most influential minority. Malay Muslims have dominated the political and administrative structures; however, the Chinese have in an equal fashion, dominated the economic sector. This imbalance has generated serious communal tensions and conflicts. Von der Mehden dates the beginnings of the resurgence of Islam in Malaysia to the government's response to communal riots in May 1969 between Malays and Chinese. Under the constitution Islam is the state religion, but all minorities enjoy equal rights. Historically, the Malay Muslim-dominated government had pursued a "politics of accommodation." While continuing to espouse this policy, the government began a major tilt toward the Malay Muslim community in order to improve its economic status. This included policies such as subsidies and job quota systems as well as a significant increase in government support for Islamic causes and activities. The process of Islamic revival has been further enhanced by closer ties with the Middle East and the growth and impact of Islamic missionary movements. The latter are especially important since their goals are not only the conversion of non-Muslims but also religious renewal among Malay Muslims. A distinctive feature of a number of these Islamic movements is the leadership exercised by modern, educated university professors and students: "some observers believe that some 80 percent of the Malay university students are part of one of the many Dakwah organizations." This phenomenon demonstrates the ability of modernization to contribute to Islamic renewal rather than to weaken religion through secularization. Von der Mehden assesses the sociopolitical implications of the Islamic resurgence in Malaysia. Is an Islamic revolution likely?

Education is an important element in sociopolitical change for it can bridge the gap between tradition and modernity. Akbar Muhammad in "Islam and National Integration through Education in Nigeria" discusses the special significance of educational reform in Nigeria since it is a major instrument in the implementation of "Nigerianization." Unlike Malaysia, Nigeria has chosen a secular path to build a pluralistic society.

Muslims constitute the largest religious community in Nigeria. Like Malaysia, Nigeria is faced with building a nation in a multiethnic (more than 250 groups) and a multireligious context. Muhammad examines the factors in Nigeria's history which have fostered the development of a strong sense of Islamic identity and community. Northern Nigeria was (and is) predominantly Muslim in contrast to the Christian and animist South. British administrative policy tended to reinforce the North's sense of separateness and difference — politically, legally, and educationally.

The most important factor in building and reinforcing Nigerian Muslim identity is the traditional Islamic education system. It was and remains a well-developed and extensive system. Unlike the Christian south, northern Nigerian Muslims viewed Western education as a threat to their community and resisted its inroads regarding it an extension of Christian colonialism. Therefore, as Muhammad indicates, Islam is often "subject to continuous attack as unsuited to modern society" by those who advocate a national Western-oriented educational system as the means to national integration.

However, in recent times Nigeria's Muslim political (primarily military) leadership and western-educated Muslim intellectuals, a minority of the Muslim community, have supported a policy of national integration (Nigerianization) through education. Given the strength and extensiveness of the traditional Islamic education system a struggle between traditional and modern elites is inevitable. For the former, such an approach threatens the integrity of their community and way of life as well as their own authority. Whether Islam will prove sufficiently flexible to accommodate a merger of cultural traditions in Nigeria must certainly be a key concern for Nigeria's future.

Lucy E. Creevey's "Religion and Modernization in Senegal" tests the validity of the hypothesis that as Senegal modernizes politically, economically, and socially, religion and religious attitudes should modernize, that is, "emphasize rationality and social concerns and play down the importance of ritual, the notion of punishment or rewards in Heaven and the necessity of obedience to the religious hierarchy."

A distinctive feature of Islamic history in Africa is the roles Sufi brotherhoods have played. Although Sufis are thought of primarily as mystics, in Africa *marabouts* (Sufi leaders) have often exercised both spiritual and political (including military) rule as in Libya and the Sudan. However, in Senegal the *marabouts* did not confront French colonialism militarily. Rather, they facilitated peasant acceptance of French programs and, as Creevey notes, became "major entrepreneurs reinforcing and expanding their political influence." Since Senegal's population is 80 percent Muslim, it is not surprising that *marabout* political importance increased during the independence movement and postindependence (1960) period.

Creevey analyzes the interaction of Islam and change in the 1970s, during which time two patterns seem to have developed indicating that modernization in Senegal has had differing results. On the one hand, it may not be rendering society more secular but rather spreading a regularization of Islam. Senegalese Islam's heavy reliance on superstition and irregular Islamic praxis seems to be disappearing and giving way to a stricter observance of Islamic belief and practice. Thus Muslim society may be said to be "more religious." On the other hand, the traditional patron-client relationship between the *marabouts* and the people is changing. Although their role in national politics has diminished only slightly, at the local level Muslims are often turning to alternative modern associations and institutions to meet temporal needs formerly satisfied primarily by their *marabouts*. Creevey concludes that the long-term effect may well be the differentiation of religious and secular roles so that *marabouts* will come to be regarded primarily as religious teachers.

As is demonstrated by the chapters in this book, the interaction of the Islamic tradition with modernity is indeed a dynamic and complex phenomenon, manifesting itself in varying ways from one Muslim country to another. Tendencies to treat Islam as a static, monolithic reality and simply project and predict a course of modernization similar to the path traveled by the West have been premature and misleading. Islam, like modern civilization, itself is characterized by diversity. Therefore, those who wish to study and/or understand developments in the Islamic world will need to avoid underestimating the vitality of Islam and, at the same time, to realize that the unity of Islam manifests itself in different countries and situations in diverse ways. Thus while some comparisons may be useful, the role(s) of Islam in sociopolitical change must be studied primarily on a country-by-country basis if we are to avoid replacing one outworn set of presuppositions and catch phrases with another.

ISLAM and DEVELOPMENT

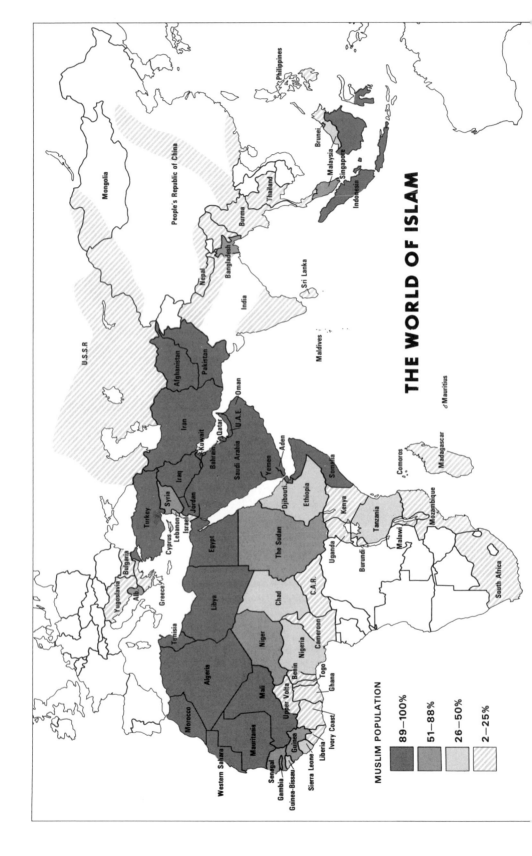

THE WORLD OF ISLAM

MUSLIM POPULATION

- 89–100%
- 51–88%
- 26–50%
- 2–25%

Islam and Political Development

Michael C. Hudson

$\mathcal{T}$O MANY MUSLIMS POLITICAL DEVELOPMENT is unthinkable without Islam; to many Western social scientists Islam, like religion in general, is at best an impediment to political development. This chapter is an attempt (1) to clarify the conceptual misunderstandings that contribute to these conflicting perceptions, (2) to discuss how modernization has affected the Islamic element in Middle Eastern politics, and (3) to analyze the changing functions of Islam in contemporary political behavior in this region.

THE PROBLEM OF DEFINITIONS

When some Muslim leaders vehemently reject Western political practices and some Western observers dismiss Islam as a primitive, even barbaric, influence in politics, they are in part expressing different values; but the intensity of the conflict is also due in some degree to mutual ignorance and the effects of pervasive negative cultural stereotyping on each side. Not only is there a long and dishonorable bias against Islam in Western popular culture,[1] but some Orientalist scholars have created a mythology about the "nature" of the Islamic mind and culture that predisposes the uncritical student against the possibility that Islam and progress (or development) are compatible.[2] Fortunately, the work of insightful scholars such as Maxime Rodinson has challenged the conventional wisdom that Islam is an impediment to the growth of modern capitalist and socialist economies.[3] But conventional attitudes in the West still view Islam as a negative social and political force.

On the other hand, one need only read Ayatollah Rouhollah Khomeini's denunciations of Western secularism, corruption, imperialism, and institutionalized sin to conclude that powerful Muslim leaders may also be victimized by biased perceptions and judgments.[4] Obviously it is important for Muslims and non-Muslims to liberate themselves from these distortions if fruitful dialogue is to take place, especially since semantic confusions and real differences may still exist. "Political development" from an Islamic point of view is different in many important ways from the "political development" envisaged by Western, non-Muslim writers. It is evident, therefore, that any useful discussion of Islam and political development must identify conceptual differences at the outset and then settle upon clear definitions.

Western Perspectives on Islam

Western social scientists are the product of a nineteenth-century positivist, relativist, and empiricist tradition whose philosophical horizon is narrower than that of the classical and medieval periods. In the latter periods the search for the "good society," the just social order, and the implementation of natural and divine law were fundamental preoccupations. Materialism, secularism and, more recently, behaviorism have relegated the ethical, normative issues to a lower order of priority in favor of the search for trends and even laws of behavior. But the Islamic intellectual tradition has not undergone such a metamorphosis, or at least not so completely. This difference in perspectives helps explain the communication problem that Muslim and non-Muslim observers face in discussing the development question.

Despite their rejection of normative concerns, Western development scholars, Marxist and non-Marxist, propose general development process models that lead, curiously enough, to the "good society" in one form or another. In the Marxist model the dialectic of economic forces and relations develops into a classless—ultimately stateless—society in which exploitation and waste are nonexistent. Also nonexistent are any of the atavistic religious myths that, in the Marxist interpretation, have been generated to legitimize previous existing inequalities. In the non-Marxist models formulated since World War II by American students of comparative politics, political development is indicated by structural differentiation and cultural secularization.[5] The state and other political structures become more complex, governmental capabilities increase, national identity and loyalty become stronger, organized political participation increases, and the distribution functions of the state improve. A theocracy, or even a polity in which religious ideology or actors play a significant role, would seem to be excluded by definition from the category of developed or developing political systems. Many Western development theorists therefore view the persistence or revival of religion in politics as regressive (or "negative development" in the curious phraseology of Almond and Powell), which occurs when there is "a decline in the magnitude or a significant change in the flow of inputs" into the political system.[6] To put the matter crudely, by Western standards political development is inversely related to religion in politics because secularism is a fundamental criterion of political development.

Islamic Perspectives on Political Development

If the Western political development paradigm requires evaluation on empirical grounds (notwithstanding the normative shadows cast by certain development criteria), the Islamic political development paradigm is an unapologetic normative statement. Muslim political theory employs today the same prescriptive mode of discourse that dominated Western political theory until modern times.

The ideal (developed) Islamic polity is first and foremost a community of believers in the Word. Members of this *umma* are self-conscious of their membership and that of their fellow believers. Reciprocity is enjoined; each member understands his responsibilities to the community and to God. "God commands justice, the doing of good, and liberality to kith and kin, and He forbids all shameful deeds, and injustice and rebellion: He instructs you that ye may receive admonition."[7] Each member can expect justice at the hands of the community. The individual ethical behavior prescribed in the Quran applies to the entire community, and it is the responsibility of the state, as organizer of the community, to promote and facilitate such behavior.

The politically developed Islamic society is a lawful society. Rulers and ruled alike are governed by the *sharia,* as interpreted and applied by the learned scholars of Islam, the *ulama,* and the legists, the *fuqaha.* As a religion of worldly as well as divine concerns, Islam is preoccupied with the regulation of man's conduct in accordance with the principles of justice and equality transmitted by the Prophet. Ideally, the political leader of the community is also the spiritual leader, the *khalifa* (caliph) or *imam;* and his legitimacy is conferred by the *baya* (confirmation oath) of the leading members of the community. Although Islamic doctrine is not entirely clear about the structure of communal leadership (and long before the caliphate was abolished in 1924 that office has ceased to have political force), it is clear that whatever the form of leadership – divinely inspired or worldly – it should be guided and limited by the Word and Law of God. The Quran also prescribes consultation as the means of reaching decisions. In making community policy, the faithful are enjoined to consult with one another.[8] Those engaging in the consultation process are understood to be the spiritual leadership that represents the community. This body, known as the *ahl al-aqd wa-l-hal,* is composed of *ulama* who represent the community and perform a limited legislative function. Through this consultation process, *al-shura,* a correct communal consensus, *ijma,* emerges over the application of divine injunctions to particular practical issues.[9]

Not only is the Islamic community "justly balanced," but it also ideally is imbued with a moral mission and an activist posture.[10] The Quran states: "Thus we have made of you an *umma* justly balanced, that ye might be witnesses over the nations." Another passage exhorts Muslims to work actively to improve their condition: "Verily never will God change the condition of a people until they change it themselves."[11] This dispels the Orientalist myth of fatalism as an Islamic trait. In political affairs the Word is clear: build, develop the community to carry out its divine role in the world.

These Quranic principles are elaborated by the great Islamic political philosophers. To suppose that the Islamic intellectual tradition has not helped elucidate the great issues of political theory – the relation between divine and practical law, reason and rationality, the virtuous society, the moral basis of the state, the nature of sovereignty and right rule, justice and responsibility, the possibility of social and political evolution – is to forget Al-Farabi, Al-Ghazzali, Averroes, Al-Mawardi, Ibn Khaldun, and other great thinkers.[12] Furthermore, to consider Islam static and rigid as a political phenomenon (and hence incapable of adapting to modern socioeconomic and political conditions) is to assign too much weight to the "closing of the gate of *ijtihad*" (individual interpretation of Islamic law) by the religious scholars of the third Islamic century and to neglect the substantial additions and innovations in law and sociopolitical thought from the end of the eighteenth century to the present. As Constantine Zurayk has argued, the greatest challenge to Islam in all its history has been that posed by the West, culturally and politically, over the past two centuries.[13] The reformers of the early twentieth century – Al-Afghani, Abduh, Rida, and others – constitute evidence of a vitality and liberalism in Islamic political thought even as the *umma* was succumbing to Western domination. In summing up this trend as crystallized in the thinking of the Moroccan nationalist Alal Al-Fasi, Albert Hourani writes: "Islam exalts reason and freedom, encourages progress, and rejects all intermediaries between man and God. It should be the basis of a truly national education, and of a modern legal system. . . . Islam could also be the basis of economic life; for there is a specifically Islamic teaching about the use of property, and if accepted it will ensure social justice and liberate men from 'economic servitude.'"[14] Despite the pessimism expressed by some scholars that there has been a dearth of creative Islamic political thought since the time of Abduh,[15] it is surely premature to conclude that Islamic philosophers cannot once again devise programs relevant to the present social conditions of the Islamic world that will promote Islamic development goals. There are sufficient bases both in original and reformed Islam for an accommodation to today's widespread impulses toward meaningful popular participation. The consultative tradition in Islam and the recognition of the need for man-made law even in a society obedient to God can be supportive of, rather than be incompatible with, principles of popular, representative government.

In terms of its theological and philosophical principles, then, Islam cannot fairly be considered intrinsically "primitive" or anachronistic —certainly no more so than the classical Judeo-Christian political philosophies with which Islam had such fruitful interaction. It is far from self-evident that a polity informed by Islamic religious principles is incompatible with contemporary socioeconomic circumstances. The question to be asked is not the crude, falsely dichotomous "Is Islam compatible with political development?" but rather "How much and what kinds of Islam are compatible with (or necessary for) political development in the Muslim world?" One can envisage a range of roles for Islam in the modern political system, from fundamentalist theocratic models (such as those described in Ayatollah Khomeini's *Islamic Government*[16]) to consensual, integrative, and normative advisory functions (such as President Sadat envisages).

Islamic Development versus Western Development

On the normative level even a cursory glance reveals that Islamic political development and Western political development have some characteristics in common but others that are in conflict. The problem is complicated by the fact that there is a variety of normative positions on each side owing to the richness of the respective traditions. Differences are easier to see than similarities, especially when fundamentalist Islamic doctrines are juxtaposed against uncompromising secular Western positions. Encounters of this kind are often heated and unproductive; they can degenerate into an exchange of accusations, with the Western modernists asserting that Islam is antidemocratic, that it encourages the tyranny of a priesthood, suppresses the rights of women, and discourages scientific inquiry, among other things. Islamic fundamentalists retort that so-called "modern" practices are corrupt and unjust: secular political systems, they say, are devoid of principles and subject to the manipulation of narrow, often debased, private interests; women in Western society are vulnerable to its dehumanizing and corrupt effects instead of enjoying protection; the West uses science and technology for exploitative, dangerous, and even frivolous purposes. Ayatollah Khomeini, to take a recent prominent example, condemns the "satanic" aspects of Western society and politics, especially its imperialistic foreign policy. He finds serious faults with the administration of justice in the West and accuses it of waging a campaign to weaken Islam by teaching the separation of church and state.[17] Some of the hostility between these extremes is due simply to applying one's own ideals to the perceived realities of the other side. Western modernists hold up the model of a pluralist system legitimized by popular representation under a rule of man-made law with a substantial degree of individual freedom; they see none of these ideals realized in Muslim societies and conclude that Islam is at fault. They do not examine as closely as they should whether their own societies meet their own ideals. By the same token, a strict Islamic ideal society must be that in which people and their rulers observe the law of God; but they do not have to look abroad to Europe or North America (although they do) for "grim realities" against which to apply these standards, for in their own societies they can see the consequences of secular modernity, "exported" by Western colonialism. Some of these consequences — such as the disruptions caused by industrialization and urban growth, the uncontrolled exploitation, the collapse of moral standards — might indeed appear "satanic." Neither side in such debates appears to be properly aware of positive elements on the other side. Militant American feminists who attempt to "liberate" Iranian women are probably ignorant of the positive historical contributions of Islam in this area and surely do not comprehend the complexity of Iran's postrevolution situation, while the stern Muslim critics of Western decadence appear to ignore the extent to which the rule of law, justice, and civic consciousness have contributed to a "good society" in the industrialized countries by Islamic philosophical, if not religious, standards.

In spite of these perceptual weaknesses on each side, it is still simplistic to conclude that there really are no significant normative differences between the two traditions. The fact is that the politically developed Islamic society is God centered whereas the politically developed Western society is man centered. No matter how liberal or materially successful either may be, no matter how tolerant each becomes of the other, there are no grounds for predicting a unilinear trend toward a universal condition of political development on the normative level. Different societies and cultures have different ideals.

THE EFFECTS OF MODERNIZATION ON ISLAM

Turning from the normative to the empirical, it is necessary to discuss both Islam and political development in operational, measurable terms rather than as vague essences. Accordingly, let us speak of Islam in its two visible political manifestations: as an identifiable ideology and as specific actors and groups whose influence and power are derived from their claim to Islamic ideological legitimacy. As for political development as an objective process, we cannot simply reject the term because of our skepticism, expressed above, about its ethnocentric normative overtones and its stipulation of secularization as a component or consequence. It is too firmly embedded in the paradigm through which the Third World is understood to be abandoned overnight. But it can be placed "on probation." Since we are inquiring whether a re-emphasis on Islam may actually accompany other indicators of "development," let us introduce an alternative concept that excludes the requirement of secularization. We shall speak instead of social mobilization, by which we shall mean the interrelated trends toward the growth and increasing complexity of social structures and values.[18] What then are the interrelationships between specific Islamic ideologies and structures in a Muslim world in which population growth, urbanization, media exposure, education, industrialization, the mechanization of agriculture, highly unevenly distributed new wealth, and related trends are simultaneously strengthening and challenging the existing political systems?

Secularization Re-examined

As we have seen, the conventional Western developmental paradigm, Marxist and non-Marxist, depicts a trend toward secularization. While the presence of religion in the poor, agricultural, undifferentiated societies that make up the Third World is hard to overlook, social scientists have generally accepted for empirical analysis the model that predicts the gradual transformation or even disappearance of religion as a pervasive system of symbols and values. For example, Donald E. Smith, taking the case of Islam, presents a schema according to which it is moving from a "traditional" character through "modernist Islam," "Islamic socialism," "socialism," to a "secular humanism-pragmatism" that is compatible with the needs of modernizing societies.[19] Other writers too have discerned a basic erosion of Islam as a value system and as a political actor in the emerging national states.[20]

One of the most cogent and sophisticated variations on this paradigm is Manfred Halpern's 1963 study, *The Politics of Social Change in the Middle East and North Africa.* While Halpern discerns a major transformation under way in which religion, like traditionalism in general, is disintegrating under the impact of modernizing attitudes and the "new middle class," he also observes that the religious factor may not disappear altogether. Halpern feels that the liberal reformist movement in early twentieth century Islam failed and that the established Islamic actors, especially the *ulama,* have been swept aside into essentially marginal positions by the secular modernist trends in thought, law, technology, and bureaucracy.[21] But he dwells at some length, and rightly so, on the populist, fundamentalist Islamic opposition movements, particularly the Egyptian Muslim Brotherhood, that have arisen as one of a number of responses in "the range of political choices" open to the modernizing Middle Eastern polities. Halpern labels such movements as "neo-Islamic totalitarianism" and describes them as essentially fascist organizations inasmuch as they "concentrate on mobilizing passion and violence to enlarge the power of their charismatic leader and the solidarity of the movement."[22] These millenarian movements, in his view, are one of several backward-looking manifestations of the social and psychological frustrations facing the modernizing Middle East. Halpern notes that their influence (as of the early 1960s) had declined because the reformist nationalist movements of the 1950s had succeeded in channeling popular discontent, and he warns: "The potential following for such movements, however, continues to grow as nationalist reformers speed the process of modernization and thus inescapably incite the political consciousness for ever larger numbers of tradition-bound men by involving them in untraditional and unresolved problems."[23] Perspicacious — indeed, almost prophetic — as this observation is, it still treats such movements as throwbacks or deviations from the general trend toward modern, "moderate," political development, rather like one views environmental pollution as a potentially dangerous byproduct of modern industrialized societies.

The tendency of writers on Islam and modernization, then, has been to emphasize (1) the inroads which secular, rationalistic ideas have made into Muslim societies, displacing religious orientations, as the result largely of the impact of the West; (2) the decline of influence of the Islamic actors — the religious and legal elites — in the political process, in the face of the rising military officers, technocrats, businessmen, and intellectuals; (3) the failure of liberal Islamic reformers to accommodate Islam with the ideas of modernization; and (4) the atavistic nature of popular, fundamentalist Islamic political movements.

Certainly there is truth in these characterizations. But, given that the scholarly community (Orientalists and social scientists) has been surprised by Islamic revivalism, they now must be re-examined with a more skeptical eye. Nobody familiar with the last two centuries of Middle East history would deny that Western values and technology made an imprint on Muslim elites. But only cursory attention has been devoted to how the other 90 percent of the population was affected. In 1839 or even 1920 it may have been irrelevant to study the great mass of society, but since then the rapid induction of the masses into the ranks of the politically mobilized or mobilizable (owing to greater physical mobility and mass communications) requires one to ask whether they have been as secularized as were the elites, with their longer and more complete immersion in Western ways. There is no evidence that the Islamic faith of most people has been deeply shaken or that Islam does not continue to inspire political legitimacy. Some Muslim intellectuals might reject Islam after studying in Europe or America, but it is less clear that a farmer who recently migrated to a Cairo working-class neighborhood would also break with his Islamic upbringing.

If people in general have not become secularized because of modernization as completely as had been assumed, then the greatest setback to Islam has been the curtailment of the political influence of the Muslim religious-legal establishment. While the political role of this elite since the Middle Ages may have been exaggerated, the termination of the caliphate, the establishment of territorial states, and the encroachment of European positive law has even further reduced the political status of the clerical establishment. Even Pakistan and Saudi Arabia, where the role of the *ahl al-aqd wa-l-hal* has retained its formal preeminence, the real influence of the *ulama* and *fuqaha* has been secondary to that of the prince. Political parties, Western-style constitutions, military juntas, bourgeois lobbies, technocratic bureaucracies and trade union federations have largely displaced the Muslim *qua* Muslim actors.

But to affirm that the Islamic establishment has been reduced in influence does not mean that contemporary political systems have been de-Islamicized. Virtually none of the new actors in Middle Eastern political systems are anti-Islamic or even avowedly secular. Apart from the singular but unsuccessful Ataturk experiment and that of the Shah of Iran (also unsuccessful) the cases are few: the indigenous communist parties of the region, the Syrian Social Nationalist Party in the Fertile Crescent and a few other minor groups. The most successful new leaders, regimes, and movements have declared their support for Islam, even if Islam is not their principal legitimacy resource. These newcomers include the remaining modernizing monarchies and the Nasserite and Bathist nationalist movements. The reports of an Islamic resurgence thus have been somewhat exaggerated.

The Islamic reform movement of the early twentieth century, mentioned above, has been judged by most historians as a good try but ultimately a failure. Yet some of what Muhammad Abduh and his followers preached has been achieved. To be sure, Abduh would be dismayed at the dictatorial character of most of the regimes in the Muslim world today. But he might be pleased that institutional Islam today is not completely monopolized by traditionalists, that *ijtihad* and accommodation with the realities of modern society take place, and that Islam is probably better understood among the masses than it was among Egyptians in his time. According to Hourani, Abduh's Islam transformed *maslaha* into utility, *shura* into parliamentary democracy, and *ijma* into public opinion. "Without intending it, Abduh was perhaps opening the door to the flooding of Islamic doctrine and law by all the innovations of the modern world. He had intended to build a wall against secularism, he had in fact provided an easy bridge by which it could capture one position after another."[24] Certainly a conservative Muslim might conclude that Islamic reform succeeded all too well. Today the Ayatollah Khomeini regards the loss of control by the *ulama* and *fuqaha* as a calamity. But when one observes the obvious vitality of Islamic observance, the attention to Islam in the school curricula, the strengthened "voice" which modern technology has provided Islam, and the *modus vivendi* between Islamic scholars and the institutions of higher education, science, and technology one is tempted to conclude that reports of the demise of Islamic reform are premature.

The Roots of Islamic Political Fundamentalism

What, then of "neo-Islamic totalitarianism" — the populist, fundamentalist movements that Halpern identifies as an atavistic byproduct of the modernization process? It is the proliferation of such groups since the early 1970s that has led political observers to perceive an "Islamic resurgence."

First, it is important to describe these movements carefully. To characterize the Muslim Brotherhoods of Egypt and the Fertile Crescent, the Iranian revolutionary regime, and a number of smaller Muslim political organizations as "fascist" or "totalitarian" is tempting politically but questionable from an academic standpoint. The Egyptian Muslim Brothers, for example, were not nationalist fanatics glorifying race or nation above all else in the manner of a Mussolini or Hitler; and they specifically rejected the idea that the leader *(imam)* must be worshipped or given absolute authority. Nor did the movement call for a retreat to the past, for while wishing to reemphasize the Quran and the Sunna (carefully edited) they rejected the accumulated legal tradition of *fiqh* and called for the opening of *ijtihad*.[25] Similarly, many Western analysts dismiss the Islamic revolution in Iran as medieval, despotic, irrational and chaotic. Yet the remarkable history of this revolution and its leader deserves more dispassionate analysis. How is it that Islam, pressed into the service of a genuine popular uprising, could help topple the archetype of a wealthy, modernizing dictatorship, buttressed with the most advanced technologies of control? The ongoing attempt to establish an Islamic republic with a constitution, parliament, and popular elections under the tutelage of an Islamic arbiter cannot be dismissed as simply an irrational anachronism, a deviation from the trail to modernization and enlightenment so intrepidly blazed by the deposed Shah. To be sure, these movements display genuine militancy, uncompromising rejection of what they call the corrupt sociopolitical order, and a certainty of the rightness of their position, but as much can be said of progressive as well as reactionary movements. Without stricter criteria or better evidence, one cannot label the Islamic movements as any less "reasonable" or more "passionate" than other political forces.

A second issue to consider is whether the conventional explanation for this phenomenon — namely, that it is the result of the tensions and dislocations of the modernization process — is sufficient. There is merit to this argument insofar as it corrects the more naive political development thesis mentioned above; for it proposes that modernization may intensify rather than dilute primordial identifications and worldviews. But where exactly do these tensions and dislocations occur, and what evidence is there that they generate enough social or psychological frustration to trigger political action? It is not obvious, upon reflection, that the processes of modernization generate such amounts of aggregate frustration. As

Daniel Lerner reported in his landmark study of Middle Eastern modernization: "a very powerful finding of our study is that the Middle Easterners who are modernizing consider themselves happier than those who remain within traditional lifeways."[26] Modernization, then, may not be the primary cause of these fundamentalist eruptions; one should also consider whether specific political issues and conditions may not be the main generators of "neo-Islamic totalitarian" movements.

The political arena must next be analyzed according to its internal and external dimensions. On the internal level one should look beyond "normal" politics, for such is not sufficient to generate these militant movements. In most Middle Eastern states there is a more profound problem — insufficient legitimacy.[27] The basic rightness of leaders, regimes, and political systems is not widely and deeply accepted. Regimes, fearful of the instability which illegitimacy can generate, compound their problem by denying or restricting political participation. At this point the social mobilization factor enters the equation. Among its several effects is the dissemination of democratic norms — norms which, as observed above, can be perceived as compatible with Islamic ideas of equality and consultation. But leaders and regimes, while attempting to build a satisfactory legitimacy formula — which almost invariably includes an Islamic element — in practice tend to force opposition movements into structural and ideological militancy. In a self-confirming prophecy, regimes, by their repressive behavior, actually magnify the depth and breadth of the opposition, forcing it even farther from "normal" political activity (such as would befit a "loyal opposition" in a strongly legitimized political system) and into greater reliance on quasi-military organization, mass mobilization capabilities, clandestinity, and ideological absolutism. Since opposition movements as well as incumbents in weakly institutionalized modernizing societies must work to acquire their own legitimacy, they too search for symbols that will help mobilize support. Islam, as we are now discovering, can be quite as effective in legitimizing an opposition movement as it has been historically in legitimizing incumbent regimes.

The external political environment also plays an important part in generating Islamic-colored political activity. What is too often minimized in the conventional "response to the crisis of modernization" explanations is the central importance of foreign imperialism as a stimulus to these movements. The Muslim Brotherhood mobilized hundreds of thousands of Egyptians in response to the intrusion of Britain in Egypt and of Britain and the Zionist movement in Palestine. The Iranian revolution derived much of its extraordinary energy from its stand against Western encroachment manifested in the intimate relationship between the United States government, the oil companies, and the Shah. Certainly along with the political struggle there has been a rejection of many of the social and cultural symbols of the foreigner on the part of various Islamic movements. But it is important to understand this as part of the political struggle between the states of the Islamic world and the industrialized powers seeking influence in the Islamic *umma*. To speak of a generalized Islamic resurgence against the West is to oversimplify the issue. What there is is an ongoing series of political conflicts in which Islam as an ideology of integration and solidarity is being used to fortify the position of those leaders, regimes, and opposition movements that are resisting what they see as continuing encroachment by the stronger powers outside. To try to identify some peculiarly Islamic trait as the cause of the various conflicts between the West and the Islamic world is to miss the point that these conflicts are political, not religious, and that they do not differ fundamentally from the conflicts between the West and the Third World in general. In the Middle East Islam is one of a number of solidarity myths, such as nationalism, that are invoked in the struggles with the outsiders.

THE POLITICAL FUNCTIONS OF ISLAM TODAY

After this expressed skepticism about the conventional analysis of Islam and modernization, it remains to specify what roles Islam is playing in the politics of Muslim societies in the 1980s. In order to do so, it is worth recalling again the importance of clear definitions. For reasons discussed above we have provisionally quarantined the contaminated concept of political development and prefer to speak of the loads and capabilities of political systems in socially mobilizing societies, and how political actors (both incumbents and oppositions) seek to develop effective legitimacy formulae to maintain or achieve power and stability. We have already dwelt on the importance of defining Islam clearly for, as Suad Joseph has noted, the term has been used by scholars in a variety of ways — not just as Islamic religion but as Islamic socialism, Islamic society, "the venture of Islam," "the challenge to Islam," scholarly Islam and popular Islam, universal Islam and sectarian Islam, and most recently "Islamic resurgence."[28] For present purposes it is sufficient to focus upon Islam in two observable political manifestations: first as *actors and organizations* in the political process whose influence is derived predominantly from their Islamic vocation, and whose formal purpose is to implement Muslim religious, legal and political precepts. Second, Islam is considered as *political ideology,* those symbols and values relevant to public affairs that carry weight owing to their origin in or association with Islamic theology and philosophy. What is the significance of Islamic actors and ideology in the years ahead for regimes and oppositions in the Muslim world seeking to maximize their legitimacy and hence their power?

Islam as Actors and Organizations

The manifest decline of the Islamic establishment — the caliphate, the *ulama, fuqaha,* and *shaykhs* — in the twentieth century has gone hand in hand with the diminution of the effective scope of the *sharia.*[29] The Islamic reformers of the *salafiyya* movement in the early twentieth century may have made a convincing case for the compatibility of Islam with the modernizing societies of the Middle East, but they did not succeed in reversing the slide toward marginality of the orthodox Muslim establishment. The determined secularism of Kemal Ataturk was not emulated elsewhere, nor however was there any general trend toward the reassertion of Islamic leadership. Islamic political figures and organizations were by no means absent from the scene in the wake of the collapse of the Ottoman Islamic empire — the successes of Ibn Saud and the significant but unsuccessful efforts of Islamic-nationalist forces in Libya and Algeria come to mind — but the tide was running in favor of leaders and parties in which the Islamic component was relegated to secondary status. By the 1950s the modern state system of the Middle East was firmly established. As Hisham Sharabi wrote in 1966, "With the exception of Turkey, Islam has not been *officially* dethroned or its institutional structures openly abolished: in the contemporary Arab world (except for the states and principalities of Arabia) Islam has simply been bypassed."[30]

How then does one account for the apparent political revival of Islam since the early 1970s? Islam as a political ideology, as we shall argue below, does enjoy renewed importance, but in terms of Islamic actors and organizations there has been little revival, even in the conservative traditional states of Arabia. Kings and presidents continue to monopolize the growing capabilities of the state, while the professional Islamic establishment has fallen firmly under their control. The single and obviously important exception to this situation is Iran, where the existence of historically independent Shiite *mullahs,* with strong local followings, has provided a unique organizational substructure for a successful revolution.

Islam as Ideology

Islam, however, is much more than the historical "religious institution" in terms of its political significance. It is a salient political ideology. As such it performs an integrative function in the state political systems of the Middle East. It also has the potential to play a disintegrative role should it adopt an intolerant attitude toward minority groups. Incumbent regimes are now striving to utilize Islamic symbolism to enhance their fragile legitimacy. Most significantly, Islam is becoming an important tool in the hands of opposition movements, whose concerns are not basically religious.

If a polity integrated in terms of basic identity and values is more likely to display stability, economic growth, and effective policies, then it is important to ask to what extent Islam as an ideology contributes to integration in the Muslim states. While the Islamic impact varies from country to country, it would not be an exaggeration to evaluate it as very significant in general. Most state constitutions feature Islam as the basis of the society or as the national religion. Both incumbent leaders and opposition politicians constantly invoke Islamic symbols in daily political discourse. Official support for Islamic establishments — teachers, mosques, educational programs, religious endowments — is considerable and apparently growing, particularly in the oil-exporting states. Rural people in the Middle East are undoubtedly more conscious of and educated about their faith than ever before, owing to the modernization of the country-side. The very instruments of Western technology which some scholars thought would hasten the decline of Islamic consciousness have surely strengthened it. An important consequence is a stronger sense of community; and, except for a few militants who see existing states as inherent obstacles to the achievement of the universal Islamic *umma,* this heightened awareness tacitly accepts existing state jurisdictions. Many Muslims may hold a diffuse pan-Islamic worldview, but there is no effort to erase existing sovereignties in favor of a revived caliphate. So Islam is performing a solidarity function: it is strengthening national identities and overshadowing parochial class, regional, and ethno-sectarian cleavages in most Muslim countries.

If enhanced Islamic consciousness strengthens consensus in the political community (generating acceptance of "the rules of the game," as American political scientists used to say) it may also be creating strains with respect to minority sects and ethnic groups. The ruinous civil war in Lebanon was not a religious war, nor were the Muslims more aggressive and intolerant than the Christians, but it demonstrated that a calamitous political and social situation could trigger brutal sectarian hostilities. Certain minorities, notably the Bahais and Jews, have felt threatened by the Iranian Islamic revolution. Sunni versus Alawite sectarianism has been aroused by the uneasy political conditions in Syria. Even some Muslim elements in Egypt, despite that country's record of good interfaith relations, have created fear and uncertainty within the large Coptic Christian minority. Viewed in its historical context, Islamic society has been relatively tolerant of minorities, doctrinally assigning "people of the Book" (Jews and Christians) to protected but unequal *dhimmi* status. A half century of liberalism has largely wiped out the discriminatory aspects of this status, except in the traditional desert kingdoms. If fundamentalist Islamic ideological currents should propel regimes or oppositions back toward inequality or intolerance, then the cohesiveness of the political communities would be weakened.

How Incumbents Use Islamic Ideology

To what extent can incumbents capitalize on Islamic ideology? Incumbents have the advantages of the media and educational arms of the state, and they control through subsidies the religious establishment itself. But they cannot automatically monopolize this particular form of ideological legitimacy because Islam as a belief system far transcends its formal organizational manifestations. Opposition movements can stake out their own claims to Islamic legitimacy. Just as incumbent and opposition politicians in the past have tried to outbid one another on similar powerful issues like pan-Arabism and Palestine, so today there is a struggle between established leaders and opposition groups, and among various opposition groups, to represent the purest, truest — and often the most extreme — form of Islam. In polities with profound political problems, domestic and foreign, the tendency toward ideological extremism is exacerbated. Such outbidding increases tension within the tacit coalition of social elements that incumbents need for their legitimacy: the religious and relatively secularized elements, the majority and the minority communities, and the different Islamic subcommunities. So the Islamic "card" has its limitations for incumbents.

Nevertheless, established regimes today are emphasizing their fidelity to Islam. While systematic studies are lacking, an increase and intensification of Islamic symbols has been widely observed throughout the Middle East by competent academics and journalists. Virtually all incumbent regimes are reemphasizing their Islamic legitimacy, even though Islam has always been a part of their legitimacy formulae. Perhaps the most notable case is Pakistan, the first of the post–World War II "new states" to establish itself completely upon an Islamic foundation. Pakistan's subsequent turbulent political history appeared to demonstrate that Islamic legitimacy is not easy for an incumbent regime to maintain, nor is it in itself sufficient to ensure stability. Yet today the shaky military dictatorship of Zia al-Haq has little else except Islam to cling to as a means of legitimizing itself. Despite its conspicuous embrace of Islamic fundamentalism, the case of the present regime in Pakistan suggests that incumbents cannot rely on their self-proclaimed Islamic rectitude alone to achieve legitimacy and stability. Another prominent example today is, of course, revolutionary Iran, which has styled itself as the standard bearer of revived Islamic government. The most prominent examples in the Arab world are Algeria, Libya, and Saudi Arabia. Under the late Houari Boumedienne, a devout Muslim trained in the traditional *madrasa* (religious school), Algeria's revolutionary government stressed the Islamic aspect of Algerian identity and adopted policies to strengthen religious awareness. The Libyan revolutionaries led by Muammar Al-Qadhafi ventured forth in a number of ideological directions during their first decade of rule but none was more important than the insistence on rededication to Islam in its purest form. The very essence of the Saudi Arabian political system, the Saudi leadership insists, is Islam; heirs to the Wahhabite fundamentalist denomination, the royal family today rules in principle according to the Quran and the *sharia,* enforces a particularly strict doctrine of social behavior, and relies heavily on its own claims to Islamic rectitude for its political legitimacy. To opponents who complain of a lack of freedom and democracy, the reply is that the Saudi system, through its strong adherence to Islamic principles, actually provides both — without the flaws and corruption of Western-style secular representative government. Islamic ideology is prominent in these governments, but it is also present in most other Middle Eastern states. Egypt under Anwar Al-Sadat asserts its preeminence as the seat of Islamic scholarship, and Sadat has invoked Islamic authority in defying what he terms the false Islam of Ayatollah Khomeini in Iran. In the rival Bathist regimes in Syria and Iraq, each concerned about the opposition attempts to mobilize with religious symbols, the governments go out of their way to refute allegations that they are hostile to Islam. Subjected to attacks on religious grounds from Iran, the small Arab shaykhdoms of the Gulf have tightened their restrictions on alcohol and unseemly social behavior, in order to enhance their Islamic credentials. If there is anything new in the instrumental use of Islam as a legitimizing political ideology by incumbent regimes it is a difference of degree rather than kind.

How Oppositions Use Islamic Ideology

A significant change, however, is the extent to which Islamic ideology has become a tool of opposition movements. Given the fact that there has been little development of institutionalized procedures for political change — no "loyal opposition," no "normal" succession process — the political environment in which the opposition must function is hostile. The opposition's problems in the 1960s and 1970s have been exacerbated by the growing technological capacity of the central government to control its population. Furthermore, in the Arab world one of the most salient ideological rallying cries — Arabism — has been somewhat monopolized by the nationalist "revolutionary" regimes that came to power during the 1950s and 1960s in the more socially mobilized countries — Egypt, Syria, Iraq, Algeria, and Libya; and even several of the traditional monarchies once regarded as reactionary, such as Saudi Arabia, Jordan, and the Gulf shaykhdoms, have registered some nationalist legitimacy by virtue of their stands against Israel and (excepting Jordan) their limited use of the oil weapon. Under these circumstances Islam bulks large as a potential ideological weapon for opposition movements to use to undercut established regimes. Because Islam is a major aspect of individual and social identity, because it is so pervasive, because its salience has been enhanced through social mobilization, and because — by virtue of its high ideals and relative lack of structural hierarchy — it does not lend itself to long-term monopoly by incumbent regimes, it appears to be increasingly effective as a destabilizing instrument. The conventional analysis of "resurgent Islam," as we have noted, sees people turning to religion because of the turmoil and dislocations of modernization. Our alternative hypothesis suggests that there are persistent political conflicts in Middle Eastern political systems: they revolve around the fundamental questions "Who shall govern?" "How are legitimate rulers to be selected?" "Who shall enjoy, and decide who shall enjoy society's resources and wealth?" "How shall the community's relations with the outside, often hostile, countries of the world be conducted?" Opposition movements with little hope of achieving power without mobilizing popular pressure against the regime look therefore to Islamic ideology as an instrument rather than as an end in itself for settling these basic political problems.

Turkey, as noted above, is the only state in the Islamic world to have directly and vigorously rejected Islamic institutions in the conduct of political and social affairs. Sixty years after the Ataturk reforms it has become commonplace to note that there has been an important revival of Islamic observance in Turkey. It is also distressingly evident that Turkey today is experiencing serious economic and political difficulties. As living and working conditions for Turks deteriorate, rightist and leftist extremism takes on a violent character. But the specifically Islamic content of the opposition in Turkey does not appear to be very high. The National Salvation Party, the main expression of Islam in Turkish politics, remains a minority party; and its share of seats in the 450-man National Assembly actually declined between 1973 and 1977, from 48 to 24. An outbreak of ostensibly sectarian violence in December 1978, in the town of Kahraman Maras above the Syrian border left more than 100 people dead; but while the fighting pitted Sunni Muslim Turks against Alawite Muslim Turks, the real cause of the disturbance was said to be political. The Turkish case, therefore, appears to support our alternative hypothesis: Islam is used as an instrument to fight political battles that revolve around non-religious issues; and in this case the politicians of religion have not succeeded in fusing Islamic ideology with nationalist legitimacy, as has happened in Iran and could happen in several Arab states.

The Iranian revolution, of course, is the preeminent recent example of a successful Islamic opposition movement. It is also the only example. Furthermore, while there is a clear religious tone to the declarations of the revolutionaries, most observers have identified important nationalist and anti-imperialist grievances as well that are not peculiarly Islamic or even religious. The potent ideological legitimacy formula devised by the Shah's many enemies generated a broad national appeal through its calls for democracy and popular representation, social justice, and an end to the corrupting dependence of the imperial ruling circle on the United States. As such, it fits comfortably into the category of Third World liberationist ideology in general, a category in which religious appeals are often but not always present and important more for political utility than substance. Furthermore, it is possible that the "Islamic" character of the new regime may diminish with time. This is not to deny the importance of Islam as a factor in the Iranian revolution but only to place it in perspective. One important reason for its effectiveness was the existence of viable, independent Islamic actors — the *mullahs* and *mujtahids,* with their local followings and organization, who could give tangible demonstration of the exiled Ayatollah's influence. In the Islamic Middle East, however, such Islamic structural viability is the exception rather than the rule because, as has been mentioned, the state has come to dominate and co-opt the religious establishment in virtually all the Sunni-rite societies.

If the Iranian case is unique in the confluence of the Islamic factor both in its ideological and structural manifestations, this does not mean that Islam is unimportant in those polities in which its impact is mainly ideological and lacking in structural reinforcement. Its increasing salience in this domain makes it a weapon of growing importance for opposition movements whose *raisons d'etre* are not fundamentally religious but, rather, political. Indeed, the very emasculation of the government-dominated Islamic establishment opens the way for opposition movements to bid for Islamic legitimacy.

The initial modern expression of such organized opposition was the Egyptian Muslim Brotherhood in the 1930s and 1940s. But the 1970s have seen the emergence of a far more radical form of Islam in the opposition to "revolutionary" regimes like Egypt, Syria, Iraq, and Libya, and in "traditional" regimes such as Saudi Arabia, Bahrain, Kuwait, and the United Arab Emirates. Popular Islam may also emerge as an opposition factor in Tunisia, Morocco, Jordan, and the Israeli-occupied Palestinian territories. In all these countries the Islamic ideological complaint has four aspects: political, national, social, and moral. The political complaint is over who shall hold power and how he shall be selected. The national complaint is over the regime's lack of militance or sincerity in pursuing all-Arab and Islamic goals, most importantly the liberation of occupied Jerusalem and Palestine. The social complaint is over the maldistribution of wealth and the creation of a small upper class of conspicuous consumers. The moral complaint is over the allegedly corrupt personal deportment of the leaders and ruling elite and their excessive lenience in the enforcement of public morality. It is apparent that the first three complaints are readily compatible with the ideological charges leveled by other significant opposition elements, such as the pan-Arab parties, the partisans of the Palestinians, the Nasserites, various socialist and communist organizations, and local politicians out of power; and that they would generate support within potential or habitual opposition sectors such as the high school and university students and the industrial labor force. If the Islamic opposition groups are distinctive in terms of their moral conservatism and insistence upon wider and more rigorous application of Islamic law, this distinctiveness will not necessarily preclude cooperation in an opposition coalition—at least until the battle has been won.

In Egypt under the rule of Sadat, there has been a recrudescence of public political activity by the Muslim Brotherhood, which had been banned in 1954 after its attempted assassination of Gamal Abdel Nasser.

Nasser and his pan-Arab ideology had not been anti-Islamic in the manner of Ataturk, but they had relegated Islamic concerns to secondary status and were in no sense prepared to allow religious actors and groups to share power. Nasser's persecution of the Brotherhood is best understood in political rather than religious terms. Today, not only is the Brotherhood officially tolerated, it has come to be regarded by a newer stratum of Muslim activists as having virtually sold out to the "establishment," much in the way that Maoist and other New Left movements came to hold traditional Communist parties in contempt.[31] A more radical organization, Takfir wal-Hijra, which in 1977 assassinated a former minister of religious affairs who was critical of Islamic radicalism, is said to have a certain following among Egyptians inside and outside Egypt even though it is banned and over 600 of its adherents are in prison. Other groups such as Al-Jihad, Al-Ittissam, "The Youth of Muhammad," and "The Sons of Muhammad" have also emerged in behalf of Islamic fundamentalism in Egypt. The casette tape recordings of sermons of Shaykh Imam are circulated clandestinely. The attire of female university students on Egyptian (and other Arab) campuses constitutes visible evidence of the new Islamic fundamentalism. In spite of President Sadat's defense (in the name of Islamic compassion) of his giving haven to the exiled Shah of Iran, and in spite of his attacks on the Ayatollah Khomeini's alleged deviation from the true Islam, the Egyptian leader has been the target of hostile demonstrations by fundamentalist students. Perhaps the most important bond between the Islamic right and the pan-Arab nationalist left is disapproval of Sadat's accommodationist policy toward Israel. In Egypt as elsewhere in the region, it is important to note that the struggle is not simply between an Islamic opposition and the regime but between an Islamic opposition and regimes that are supported by (and that support) the Islamic establishment.

In Syria, the Baathist regime of President Hafiz Al-Asad has come under persistent harassment from Muslim organizations based in the bazaar and traditional manufacturing quarters in Aleppo, Hama, and Homs. Here the manifest struggle seems to be between a Sunni majority in opposition to an Alawite (Shiite) ruling group; but in fact the sectarian characteristics are only symbolic of what is basically a partisan struggle for power. Alawite notables are gunned down not because they are Alawites but because they are identified with an entrenched and allegedly corrupt regime. Iraq's Baathist regime, largely Sunni, faces the occasional flareup of anti-regime sentiment in the Shiite holy cities of Najaf and Kerbela; and it must cope with Iranian incitements to Iraqi Shiites to revolt. But again, sectarian hostility is a minor factor; the potentially serious challenge to the Iraqi regime arises from its lack of popular participation, a situation which generates opposition from many quarters, not just Shiite or Islamic. The regime's decision in 1979 to hold parliamentary elections in 1980 — the first in twenty-two years — is indicative of its concern over this problem. Libya has already been mentioned as a regime that has sought systematically to utilize Islam in its legitimacy formula; but in his zeal to do so Colonel Qadhafi has outraged the *ulama* with his own fundamentalist interpretations, and so in a peculiar twist on the typical situation the Libyan orthodox establishment finds itself in opposition to a fundamentalist incumbent.

Each of the countries just mentioned has experienced at least one modernizing or "revolutionary" change of government and (except for Syria) each has overthrown its monarchy. All four (even Libya) have had considerable exposure, positive and negative, to Western political and cultural influence and today rank high on indicators of social mobilization. Despite the growth of their governmental capabilities, owing largely to technological advances, they remain only thinly legitimized ideologically, personally (through their leaders), or structurally. Beset with political, national, social, and moral defects, they are vulnerable to any sudden cascading of problems in these areas. With its potentially intense and pervasive ideological power, an Islamic movement could set in motion a major challenge to these regimes. One cannot safely conclude that these societies (particularly Egypt, Syria, and Iraq) are now immune to the Islamic appeal simply because they have been relatively modernized for quite a long time, because one can no longer assume that social mobilization brings about political secularization, political development theorists to the contrary notwithstanding. To be sure, neither can one assume that there is a silent majority of radical Islamic fundamentalists ready to be ignited, and so the prospects for revolutionary Islamic theocracy are probably not high; but given the fact that Islamic opposition is generally compatible with other kinds of opposition it is possible that it could serve as the catalyst for serious challenges to these regimes.

What of the nature of opposition in the relatively traditional societies of Saudi Arabia, Kuwait, and the other Gulf emirates? Before proceeding, a caveat is in order: in these sparsely settled, oil rich societies we are confronting a highly unusual, if not unique, sociopolitical situation, and since there has been little empirical research it is difficult to speculate intelligently about their political future. But two approaches can be identified. The first holds that there is a conservative political consensus, anchored by Islam, that has survived all the shocks of recent modernization and regional upheavals, and that the existing patrimonial regimes reflect it. This view stresses the traditional legitimacy of the ruling families, which rests both upon Islam and tribal values. It follows that such regimes are not likely to be threatened by any Islamic opposition because of their monopoly of this valuable political commodity. The second approach gives credence to the possibility that there is no longer a cohesive traditional political community in these countries but rather a "beginning of ideology" along a spectrum from Islamic fundamentalism to secular democratic socialism, and it proposes that existing regimes may no longer enjoy the reputation of Islamic rectitude in those strata of society for which such a thing is important. From this perspective the existing patrimonial systems may be vulnerable on a variety of grounds, including Islamic ones. This view hypothesizes that because the political culture has become fragmented, complex, and sophisticated — more like the political culture of the more completely modernized eastern Mediterannean societies — the criteria of legitimacy have changed. Traditionally, political opposition was non-ideological, personalistic, and parochial; but tomorrow it may crystallize around the same political, national, social, and moral issues that galvanize opposition movements elsewhere. If this is the case, then a confluence of grievances might bring together a formidable coalition of opposition groups, and Islamic fundamentalism could conceivably provide the initial ideological glue to hold it together.

Which of the two perspectives one adopts decisively affects one's interpretation of unfolding events. For example, the takeover of the Grand Mosque in Mecca in November and December 1979 has been assessed by some observers as an isolated incident, the work of religious fanatics and dissident tribesmen with historical grudges against the ruling Saud dynasty. If, according to the first approach, the Saudi regime were indeed the embodiment of Islam, then the rebels of Mecca could be seen as marginal deviants, and their adventure, although prolonged and bloody, simply an unpredictable flareup, an anachronistic throwback to the conflict between the "religious fanatics" of the Ikhwan against King Abdel-Aziz Ibn Saud in the 1920s. On the other hand, the less sanguine perspective would interpret the events of Mecca as indicative of a serious challenge to the legitimacy of the ruling house. By boldly attacking the regime on its most secure flank with significant impact, the rebels could be seen as demonstrating that there was more widespread and organized disaffection with the moral and religious credentials of the regime than anybody had suspected; and to the extent that the rebels included more than religious or tribal fanatics it suggested that the regime's legitimacy on political, national, and social grounds might also be more open to question than had been thought. By the same token, the tension and occasional disturbances reported in several of the Gulf principalities could either be evaluated as the work of malcontents lacking any organic ideological support or else as the initial rumblings that portend a major upheaval.

It appears then that Islamic actors and structures have in general lost independent influence. The *ulama,* the *fuqaha,* and the *shariah,* the schools and the mosques — not to mention the defunct institution of the caliphate itself — have given way to other actors and structures. This decline of orthodox Islamic organizations, however, cannot be taken as a sign of the retreat of Islam in general, because Islam considered as political ideology, and as a resource for the legitimation of regimes and opposition parties for which legitimacy is a scarce commodity, appears to be playing an increasingly important role. Islam as political ideology is becoming an increasingly useful instrument for opposition movements because of its considerable compatibility with other opposition ideologies, and also because of its enhanced ability to mobilize large numbers of people.

Islam and Modern Economic Change

John Thomas Cummings, Hossein Askari, and Ahmad Mustafa

$\mathcal{T}$HE MIDDLE EAST HAS BEEN, at various times in its history, one of the commercial centers of the known world; frequently it has been *the* major commercial center. With the birth of the prophet Muhammad in the sixth century of the Christian era and the introduction of Islam in the seventh century, the region embarked on prolonged growth along the path of economic, social, and cultural expansion. However, with the onset of the industrial revolution in Europe and later in the new world, the Middle East appeared to lag behind. This divergence in economic performance has prompted many observers to question the compatibility of Islam with the process of economic development.[1]

In more recent history, since the revenues of the oil-exporting countries of the Middle East began to increase in the 1950s, and more dramatically since 1973, casual observers saw little conflict between Islam and contemporary capitalism because of the rapid penetration of western influence into the area. However, in the aftermath of the revolution in Iran during late 1978 and early 1979 and in the face of potential eruptions in Turkey, Pakistan, and elsewhere, the question of the compatibility of Islam and modern capitalism has evoked much interest.

On the other hand, the interface of Islam with the other major western model of economic change, Marxist socialism, has been much more limited.[2] The possibility of a symbiotic relationship between Islam and Marxism has tended to be dismissed on religious grounds; that is, the basic contradiction between theism and atheism has headed off much discussion of how these philosophies might react on more purely secular (that is, economic) grounds.

In this paper we will first examine Islamic thinking relative to cer-

tain critical aspects of the workings of an economy—taxation, interest
and banking, rent, inheritance, private ownership, and income distribution. These doctrines will then be examined and related to Western economic thinking.

Although we have indicated above that the confrontation of Islam with Western economic thought must be considered in the context of
both major Western offshoots of modern economic thought — capitalism
and Marxism — the bulk of our consideration below discusses the interplay
of Islam with capitalism. The justification, given our limited space, is
simple: this has been Islam's dominant historical encounter through 1980.

In the final section, the interpretation of these doctrines is related
to the current economic and social change occuring in the Middle East.

ISLAM AND TAXATION

Islam, unlike other major religions, has given its followers a detailed prescription for an economic system. This is provided through the Quran,
the *Sunnah* (the example of the prophet Muhammad, i.e., his personal
acts or sayings, or those of others approved by the prophet), the *Ijma* (the
consensus of the Muslim *mujtahids* — religious scholars), and the *Qiyas*
(personal opinions based on analogy and on religious doctrines). Specifically, questions of taxation, government expenditure, inheritance, private ownership, social and economic welfare (distribution of income,
poverty, etc.), interest, land tenure, natural resources, wage rates, as well
as other factors, have received attention, and are thus an integral component of Islam.[3]

In Islam there are two tax structures: one for Muslims, which derives directly from the sources mentioned above, and the other for non-
Muslims.[4]

The principal tax[5] on Muslims is *zakat*. Although the term has
been used in many different ways,[6] there are three major situations where
zakat is applicable — relative to the ownership of animals, of gold, silver
and articles of trade, and of the produce of the land.[7] While in theory
zakat is linked to all assets which produce an economic return, in practice
it has been applied to commercial and agricultural capital. In short, *zakat*
is a rather generalized wealth tax.

As Islam's traditions have evolved, *zakat* has been accorded the
central status of being one of the five pillars of Islam. The rendering of
zakat to poor Muslims is a divinely revealed requirement for those who

wish to believe eternal salvation[8] along with the following obligations: (1) *shahada,* the profession of faith in the One God and in His prophet, Muhammad; (2) *salat,* regular daily prayer; (3) *sawm,* prescribed fasting during the holy month of *Ramadhan* (when the Quran was revealed); and (4) *hajj,* the making of the pilgrimage to the holy places associated with the prophet Muhammad (Mecca and Medina). These rank with the Old Testament Decalogue and New Testament Beatitudes in religious significance.

In large part, the meanings attributed to the word *zakat* itself indicate the problems of considering it merely as a tax, merely as a conventional source of government revenue. Its obligations are founded in Quranic injunctions, such as those praising those who "expend of that We have provided them, secretly and in public, and who avert evil with good — theirs shall be the ultimate abode,"[9] and "those in whose wealth is a right known for the beggar and the outcast."[10] Obviously, in theory, *zakat* is to be *given* willingly, not to be paid begrudgingly, if the divine law is to be fulfilled. Its obligations are to the community as a whole. They are to be made specifically and directly to the community's less fortunate members, not to an impersonalized government nor to its revenue-collecting agencies.

The etymological derivation of this important word has been traced to verbs that in English translate most closely as "to be pure" or "to be pious."[11] *Zakat* also signifies virtue in general, as well as — in the Quran — giving and the pious gift.[12] Thus *zakat* is seen as an act of purification for one's sins, a means of reducing selfishness and expiation of blame for past selfishness, thus leading to self-improvement.[13] Others have emphasized its link to the verbs "to grow" and "to increase,"[14] and have interpreted the giving of *zakat* as leading to a significant increase of blessings — of material property in this world and of spiritual merit for the next.

Whatever interpretation is adopted, *zakat* is primarily a voluntary act of piety, and a far cry from what most modern-day taxpayers experience when confronted with increased income levies or complicated regulations. The act of giving to the poor and needy in the form of *zakat* is clearly to guarantee the poor, the orphaned, the elderly, and the like the necessities of life. It is in a sense intended as a system of social insurance and security for all of those who become destitute in Islamic society, and is supported by a tax on net wealth rather than on income. God might will that even the most fortunate will be destitute tomorrow; thus, those that give today may receive tomorrow!

Muslim-held assets subject to *zakat* were not spelled out specifically in the Quran. Therefore, they have been much discussed by various scholars of Islamic law. It is generally recognized that only wealth above a certain minimum level and held for 12 months or longer[15] obligates its owner to pay *zakat*. In addition, a large number of items are exempted.[16]

The manner by which *zakat* is to be collected has also been a subject of some dispute among legal scholars, with the principal point of agreement being what constitutes *apparent* property (on which *zakat* is generally collected by representatives of the state or community) as opposed to *non-apparent* property (on which it is disbursed directly by the owners).[17] Others have argued that, to ensure proper distribution among the needy, the state should oversee all *zakat*, with the right to collect it by force when Muslims ignore their obligations, or when the needs of one area in *dar al-Islam* (the territory of Islam) exceeds the ability of that part to collect enough *zakat* from its residents.

The Quran is specific as to those who are eligible to receive the alms distributed under *zakat* provisions. "The free will offerings are for the poor and needy, those who work to collect them, those whose hearts are brought together, the ransoming of slaves, debtors, in God's way, and the traveller; so God ordains."[18] In short, in the time of the prophet Muhammad, virtually all of those who might experience need had a valid claim on the beneficence of the entire Islamic community.

The state was also authorized to collect additional taxes if *zakat* was not sufficient for meeting the needs of those with a claim to assistance. For example, the state could impose other forms of taxation for particular needs and programs. On the one hand, *zakat* was not intended to be used by the state for purposes and recipients other than those stated above, but on the other hand, it was specifically recognized that the legitimate claims for community revenues were not limited to *zakat*. Let us consider specific levies.

Zakat due from those who owned flocks varied according to what animals were involved. For example, the Hanafi lawyers decreed a rate of about 2.5 percent (above a minimum herd size). For camels, no tax was due on the first five animals, but above this, specific levies were spelled out in terms of animals of different values; for example, in ascending order, goats, young she-camels, and mature she-camels.[19] For sheep and goats (*ghanam*), Hanafi, Shafi, and Maliki lawyers alike agreed there was no levy due on herds with less than 40 head, but above this level, the obligation rose proportionately.[20] Generally, these rates indicate a 2.5 percent tax on capital tax. In most cases, this resulted in a neutral or proportional tax.[21]

While *zakat* due on livestock was defined in specific physical terms, that which was expected on gold, silver, and articles of trade was based on commercial value. Again the rate was proportional, at 2.5 percent with an initial exemption, and in these cases (after the exemption) strict neutrality of taxation was likely.

Zakat was not the only fiscal obligation incumbent on Muslims. Some taxes that were employed by secular authorities (the khalifate) during the centuries following the Prophet's death were not agreed upon by all religious authorities at the time of their imposition. Nevertheless, Islam obviously incorporated the principles of flexibility of state authority over fiscal formulation and of individual responsibility to follow the guidelines of secular power.

The tax on land, the *ushr* or tithe, were due when and only when there actually was any output. No minimum exemption was allowed, nor was a year's ownership needed before the obligation fell. Typically, the due depended on the quality of the land (for example, 5 percent on irrigated land, 10 percent on rain-fed land). It was applied to gross output, before deduction of most production-related costs; however, it was obviously denominated in terms that recognized some production costs.

The obligations of *zakat*, as mentioned above, fell only upon Muslims. They were the dues, imposed by God on individual believers, toward the rest of the community. However, *dar al-Islam* expanded rapidly in the century after the prophet's death. Large populations of non-Muslims were conquered and incorporated into the khalifal empire. Contrary to popular modern belief, conversion by force was forbidden. The faithful soon became a minority within their expanding conquests. The need for secular taxes rapidly became more apparent.

Muslims, under the provisions of *zakat*, were obligated toward their fellow believers. As believers, they were also required to strive for the expansion and protection of *dar al-Islam,* undertaking military service if necessary. On the other hand, Christian, Jewish, and Zoroastrian subjects of the Muslim khalifate fell under neither obligation. Yet as citizens of a dynamic state, they could hardly be excused or expect to be excused from all fiscal responsibilities.

One tax that hit all citizens regardless of religion was the *kharaj* — literally, the revenue derived from a piece of land. Over the long history of Islam, no universally accepted definition of *kharaj* land has emerged. All commentators agree on its neutral nature; that is, the payment of *kharaj* depends, not upon the religious beliefs of the taxpayers (or upon other such personal categories), but upon the status of the land on which the tax is due.

Unlike *zakat, kharaj* is a form of taxation that can be changed by the Islamic state since it is not ordained in the Quran. Rather, its provisions are based on *ijma*—the consensus found in the teachings of the religious scholars. As circumstances change, so may *ijma*. The flexibility regarding *kharaj* finds expression in the detail expounded by the legal commentators.[22]

The *kharaj* tax can be divided into two parts—fixed and proportional. Fixed *kharaj* rates were collected from all land suitable for cultivation, and were assessed in kind—so much per unit of land or per tree. The rates for several crops were decreed by the second khalif Umar and were considered thereafter to be immutable. For those cases not so covered, rates were set according to the tax-bearing capacity of the land—which depended upon the quality of the land, the crops grown on it, and the method of watering it. Rates varied from 20 to 50 percent of the output that might be expected from the land. Whereas many scholars argued fixed *kharaj* was due regardless of actual output, proportional *kharaj* was a percentage of what was actually produced.[23]

The *jizyah,* or poll tax, was imposed only on non-Muslims. Its origin is Quranic: "Fight those who believe not in God and the Last Day and [who] do not forbid what God and His Messenger have forbidden—such men as practise not the religion of truth, being of those who have been given the Book—until they pay the tribute out of hand and have been humbled."[24] In a sense, this tax was placed on non-Muslims for their disbelief and/or as a payment for sparing their lives, since it then guaranteed their security. On the other hand, it can also be seen as a levy due in place of military service, to which all Muslim males were at least theoretically liable. Non-Muslims were *ipso facto* exempt, and thus were subject to help pay for the state's upkeep and defense. Women and children, who of course could not fight, were exempt from *jizyah.*[25]

The amount of the jizyah was variously decreed. In some cases, it was fixed by treaty with a tribe as it acceded to Muslim rule, with either a lump sum payment or a regular per capita levy (or both) imposed. Alternatively, the *jizyah* was imposed by Muslim leaders on those who were conquered by force of arms. The tax was somewhat progressive at first glance, recognizing that, as Muslims had varying military obligations depending upon relative wealth (the poor were private soldiers, but the rich were required to outfit themselves as horsemen), so should non-Muslims be assessed *jizyah* in proportion to their ability to pay. Again as with *kharaj, jizyah* was not explicitly spelled out in the Quran. Thus, the rates were based on *ijma*—in particular, on precedents established during the khalifates of Umar, Uthman and Ali (the second, third, and fourth deputies of the prophet). The annual rate for the rich was 48 dirhams; 24 dirhams were due from the middle class, and 12 dirhams from the poor.[26]

Still another source of revenue was the tax on mines.[27] Basic disagreement on the type of levies on such property was present among the various schools of law. The Shafi school included such wealth within the provisions of *zakat,* while the Hanafi did not.[28] According to the latter, no matter who owned the mine, one fifth of the deposit was due as tax to the state. However, only certain types of mineral deposits were subject to any taxation. For example, ores which could be refined into pure metals (gold, silver, lead, etc.) were taxable; other deposits (coal, water, etc.) were not.[29]

This discussion of taxation has been, of necessity, brief; as a consequence, most of the circumstances in which Islamic law has been applied have been neglected. To appreciate fully the implementation and the resulting impact of such taxes, one must interpret them as an integral component of Islam. As we have indicated above, the basic Islamic levy, *zakat,* is far more an obligation imposed by God on the faithful for the general welfare of the community than a tax promoted by the state for the sake of collecting the revenues needed for its own purposes. The levies imposed in this way on Muslims, and in a general fashion the more secular taxes on Muslims and non-Muslims alike, are rooted in a theologically derived premise that those who have received from God ample material blessings are obliged to share, in concrete fashion, with those who are less well off. One contemporary Muslim scholar, in commenting on Islamic economic doctrines, has made the following points in commenting on what is the most central aspect of Muslim belief — *tawhid,* one-ness or unity:

Tawhid is a coin with two faces: one implies that Allah is the creator, and the other that men are equal partners or that each man is brother to other men. As far as economics is concerned, this means *equality and cooperation.* Thus, divinity in a Muslim society is only for Allah. This means, in economic terms, that natural resources in the universe, such as land, capital, general circumstances such as shortages for reasons of war or disasters as well as laws of nature, *all these belong to the whole of society,* and *all its members have equal shares and right of access to them.* No man has the right of claiming a *bigger* share since he does not create or generate power independently. . . .

If a man is not going to use certain resources over which he has priority, he should *give it up to another member of society* and should not claim ultimate individual ownership over the income produced by that resource. He should know that he is not the creator. He should give to the weaker members of society *the extra income* which is due to the productivity of those natural resources that are used by him *beyond his equal share.* . . .

> Differences in income (in Islamic society) could not be very big and they are limited by *differences in human capacity for work and not by individual claims on natural resources.* Income related to these resources is a collective claim and its fruits should be divided equally. Private ownership here is only a matter of priority.[30]

In short, we have presented above only a brief outline of the Islamic system of taxation and in all likelihood, not very much of its spirit or of the ways that in actuality it was implemented in Islamic societies. However, at least for the case of *zakat,* the above does present a sketch of what each Muslim must do personally, beyond the immediate needs of the state for operating revenues, to support society and to meet his or her obligations toward the community.

ISLAM AND INTEREST (USURY)

While other religions have looked somewhat unfavorably upon money-lending where interest is paid, Islam traditionally has quite forthrightly forbidden it. This attitude toward the taking of interest *(riba)* is derived from the Quran: "Those who devour usury shall not rise again, except as he rises whom Satan of the touch prostrates; that is because they say, 'trafficking is like usury.' God has permitted trafficking and forbidden usury. . . . God blots out usury, but freewill offerings he augments with interest."[31] Nevertheless, the Quranic ban on *riba* has still allowed for some differences among Muslims as to precisely what was outlawed — the taking of interest or loans that lead to economic exploitation.

The reasons for prohibition of *riba* in Islam are quite clear. First, interest and/or usury increases the tendency to direct wealth into the control of a few; in the process it tends to dehumanize man's concern for his fellow man. Second, Islam does not allow gain from economic activity unless it is also subject to a loss; the legal guarantee of at least nominal interest would be viewed as a sure gain. Third, in Islam wealth should be accumulated through personal activity and hard work, as opposed to the selfish motive of getting the highest possible interest.[32]

Strictly orthodox interpretations of Islamic law indicate that interest and methods which have the same effect, such as ill-disguised "service" charges, are outlawed. Thus, the banking system, as it exists in capitalist countries, should be impossible in any country that adheres closely to Islamic law.

However, the prohibition of interest need not preclude the useful role played in a dynamic economy by a banking system. In an Islamic society banking could, in our view, still have the same basic role and function as in a Western society—a sink for savings and a source for investment.

The form would of course have to be different. As in the West, money would be deposited at a bank either in a demand deposit (checking) or time deposit (savings) account. Service charges could be levied on demand deposits, but no return would be given on such an account if the security of the original deposit was guaranteed. On savings deposits, there would be no contracted positive or negative return. The bank would, as in a capitalist society, decide as an individual institution (possibly under official guidelines) on its desired level of reserves in relation to both savings and demand deposits by evaluating potential investments. However, as opposed to capitalist bank practice, it would not loan its funds to its clients but would instead become a partner with the clients in business ventures. In this way, if the venture prospered, the bank's savings depositors (who had thus taken risks) would be rewarded with a share of profit—but there would be no guarantee of this outcome.

Banks constituted in this manner have been operating for some time in several Muslim countries, most notably in Saudi Arabia and Libya. One bank with international implications is the Islamic Development Bank (IDB), founded in 1973 and now with 34 member countries. By early 1978, about $215 million had been pledged to some 32 projects in 19 countries. Some loans are to be repaid without interest but others involve the IDB as an equity partner in industrial projects.[33]

At least in theory the prohibition of interest need not lead to a reduced level of savings and investment. Certainly a banking system based on equity ownership rather than interest would use somewhat different operating techniques. It would, for example, probably be somewhat more conservative in its "loan" evaluations and might maintain somewhat higher reserves than Western capitalist banks.

Basic questions about interest in Islam remain to be settled, especially in terms of whether it is the very concept of interest or of its possible use as a means of economic exploitation that is the true target of Quranic injunctions. For example, when governments (or their affiliated banking institutions) borrow from their citizens under conditions that include some payment of interest, can any element of exploitation be present? Rather, in societies where a degree of inflation seems inevitably present, might not interest rates in line with inflation (the existence of which is largely a government responsibility) merely be seen as maintaining, rather than increasing, the value of capital?[34] Furthermore, whether the borrower is a private individual, a corporation, or a foreign government, the possibility of a loan default is present. Thus, the lender is at some risk. In this way, a banking system could evolve that was based on laws that increased the lenders' risks, for example, one that gave claims against a bankrupt corporation similar to those of equity owners, rather than preferences at the head of the queue of creditors. Though this is a considerable change relative to established Western capitalist banking practice, such a system could still provide a conduit between those with surplus capital and those in promising investment situations. In particular, in economic terms, it takes on the role played by interest in the West — as the price or allocative mechanism for a scarce input (capital) to the production process; the lack of such a mechanism almost inevitably leads to a squandering of the input in question.

ISLAM AND RENT

From the discussion of *riba* above, it can be seen that there are some similarities in the Islamic teachings on rent and on interest. To receive rent on virgin land or resources is prohibited. However, if the owner has improved the land or resources, through labor and/or capital investment, rent can be levied in proportion with the improvements that have been made.

Rent on land must be paid in money according to pre-arranged terms, and sharecropping, according to most interpreters, was forbidden. As one scholar has maintained, in stressing the analogy between sharecropping and the charging of interest: "Sharecropping in such a case would mean *riba* since it is likely that one of the parties will get more or less than he should. Islam has no intention of committing *riba* or injustice toward anyone, worker or owner."[35] In other words, one of the parties would receive a share not in proportion to the risk involved. Using similar arguments, the wages of agricultural workers were interpreted as having to be paid in cash according to specific terms arranged in advance, and not linked to a share in output.

As we have seen above, Muslim land and resource owners incur financial obligations to the larger community based on their wealth. According to Shafi interpretations, *zukat* was due on both agricultural output and mineral produce. Other schools treated the former as subject to the tithe *(ushr)*, in a different category from *zakat*. In any case, landowners and farmers owed some share of their economic return to the community.

ISLAM AND INHERITANCE

Islamic inheritance laws are aimed at achieving a wide distribution of wealth amongst the close relatives of the deceased; at the same time the laws are geared to avoid hoarding and individualistic discrimination and squabbling within the family unit. In essence, the fabric of the family and society are put ahead of the emotional whims of the deceased.[36]

This body of law can be summarized:

1. The deceased has the right to transfer one-third of his or her property as desired.

2. Women are entitled to share in inheritance along with men.

3. The share of women, except in a few cases, is half of that of male heirs in the same category.

4. The inheritors include the members of the inner family—the children, parents, and spouse—but other relatives find a place in the share of distribution.

5. The State inherits the estate of a person without a legal heir and pays the just debts of those who die in poverty.

6. The general principal of distribution is dispersal of wealth from one to many, rather than its channeling from many to one.[37]

Inheritance laws, although complications obviously made them an important subject for lawyers in the specifics of their interpretation, are nevertheless firmly rooted in detailed Quranic guidelines.[38] Those who cheat the helpless of their just dues or who themselves are not generous out of their own inheritances are strongly condemned: "Those who devour the property of orphans unjustly, devour fire in their bellies, and shall assuredly roast in a Blaze."[39]

In short, Quranic injunctions had the effect of reducing if not eliminating intra-familial strife over the estate of the deceased. Under the law, little was left to chance. On the one hand, the deceased could not disinherit a legitimate heir. On the other hand, the rights of weaker heirs were protected and based on their relationships to the deceased, not on their ability to command the services of probate lawyers for prolonged litigation.

One specific point needs further comment in light of contemporary attitudes. The apparent discrimination against women—daughters inherit half the shares of sons, for example—is deceptive. In fact, in the context of the times when the Quran was revealed, this provision represented a considerable advancement for women's rights. Firstly, it guaranteed a share to a daughter, for example, even though she had left her father's household to join that of her husband. Secondly, other provisions of Islamic law made such inheritances the personal property of Muslim women. Their husbands and brothers had no claim over such property, though wives and sisters had a claim for legitimate support needs on the property of their male relatives. Thus, for nearly fourteen centuries Muslim women have had independent property rights that have been denied to women in most Christian countries until very recently.

ISLAM AND PRIVATE OWNERSHIP

To appreciate Islamic doctrines on private ownership, it may be useful to begin with a brief summary of general Muslim economic principles: (1) God created the world with natural abundance for people to enjoy and change; (2) they are, therefore, the owners of all such fruits in the world that result from their endeavors provided they commit no injustice or wrongdoing; (3) they must, however, pay attention to the short- and long-run needs of society at large. As a part of this, the basic needs of the destitute must be met since they also have a claim on the abundance of society at large.

Nearly all interpretations of Islamic economic thinking arrive at the conclusion that the Quran undoubtedly embraces the right of private ownership.[40] However, private ownership is different from absolute ownership — this is God's alone. Legal ownership is the right of priority, of enjoyment and transfer of such property. Specifically, no man can claim virgin resources if he does not use them productively. Thus, in so far as such a resource exists and is not being used, then another Muslim can claim it for himself or herself free of charge; this is encouraged to prohibit unproductive hoarding and to increase economic opportunity for all. In the case where an individual has made improvements on virgin resources, the only price that can be charged must be equivalent to such improvements; to charge a higher price would be illegal, since the owner would be getting paid for the asset's creation, the due for which is God's alone.

But while Islam encourages private ownership in this sense, it is clear that such rights are not totally unconditional. First, the prophet Muhammad mentioned many individual needs and added that any excess of these overall requirements was not permissible. Second, if *zakat* falls short of social needs, then the state is authorized to impose additional taxes, since the poor have additional claims (other than *zakat*) on the wealth of the rich. Third, general redistribution could be applied to productive assets (i.e., on priority of use) and to consumption of (or the right to consume) the output of society. Both forms of redistribution are desirable whenever it is necessary to restore the sense of community, the balance of distribution of resources, social justice, and the freedom of individuals.[41]

ISLAM AND INCOME DISTRIBUTION

We have already discussed this problem in several of the earlier sections. At this point, we need only summarize some of the points made earlier.

The Quran makes it clear that God has created the material things of this world in abundance and that He intends that they be shared, in equitable fashion, by all men and women. Not that every Muslim should receive an equal share of society's produce; rather that all have a claim on enough to survive with a decent standard. The faithful are reminded that others will ask them what is a person's obligation to the poor; the answer is clear:

> O believers, expend of the good things you have earned, and of what We have produced for you from the earth; and intend not the corrupt of it for your expending, for you would never take it yourselves. . . . God promises you His pardon and His bounty. . . . And whatever expenditure you expend, and whatever vow you vow, surely God knows it. . . . And whatever good you expend shall be repaid to you in full. . . . Those who expend their wealth night and day, secretly and in public, their wage awaits them with their Lord, and no fear shall be on them; neither shall they sorrow.[42]

Obviously, what is an individual's from God is not his or hers alone; all Muslims will be judged on their stewardship of what they have earned or otherwise received — on how they have in turn treated those who are less economically fortunate.

No burden of judgment is placed on those who have a demand on the better off in Muslim society: "The freewill offerings are for the poor and needy . . . [for] the ransoming of slaves, debtors, in God's way and the traveller; so God ordains, God is All-knowing, All-wise."[43] That is, God knows who is worthy, and He has made His commandments clear to the Muslim community. We have seen above, in the sections on *zakat,* inheritance, and interest, several groups in society specifically singled out as deserving of protection — widows, orphans, travellers, etc. But, despite the detail that is provided in the Quran, it is clear that God intends that Muslims be generous and that they must honor the *spirit* in which specific injunctions are offered.

And what is this spirit, we may ask. The benefit of doubt, on the day of judgement, clearly favors an assumption of the worthiness of the recipient of the faithful Muslim's boon. Merit accrues to the giver, even if the recipient hid behind a cloak of deception.

It is, again, God's abundance in His creation that is the key element. The prophets before Muhammad had preached God's generosity. Moses had told the Jews that there would be more than enough for an entire generation to survive in the bleakest of wildernesses. He was not believed, and yet in Sinai, his prophecy was proven. Jesus also preached on God's generosity; even though he fed the poor, his word was doubted. Because of this rejection of God's word that the poor must and will be provided for, He sends another, Muhammad, the last or the seal of the prophets, with the final message in this regard: the fruits of creation are for all men and women. The circumstances of human life in this world may result in a few receiving far more than they need, and many much less than is necessary for even the barest level of human existence.[44]

But God will not be mocked. From the primeval time of Adam, He has sent more than two dozen prophets. With the revelation of the Quran through His last messenger, Muhammad, humankind must learn once and for all. He has decreed equality for all men and women in their rights to survive in a fashion that will allow them to come to know His will and to acknowledge His omnipotence. In the last analysis, the hardhearted will show their greed despite this final warning: "Hast thou seen him who cries lies to the doom? That is, he who repulses the orphan, and urges not the feeding of the needy. So woe to those that pray and are heedless of their prayers, to those that make display, and refuse charity."[45]

THE COMPATIBILITY OF ISLAM AND
CONTEMPORARY WESTERN ECONOMICS

One modern Marxist scholar, asking why capitalism should have triumphed in Christian Europe but not in the Muslim countries, has concluded that there is no essential incompatibility between Islamic economic doctrines and either capitalism or economic development. Attacking myths that he says are prevalent among Muslims and non-Muslims about Islam and its history, Rodinson has pointed out: "There are religions whose sacred texts discourage economic activity in general, counselling their followers to rely on God to provide them with their daily bread, or, more particularly, looking askance at any striving for profit. This is certainly not the case with the Koran, which looks with favour upon commercial activity, confining itself to condemning fraudulent practices and requiring abstention from trade during certain religious festivals."[46] He quotes the Quranic injunction to "forget not thy portion of this world"[47] and stresses that the Quran is clear in emphasizing that Muslims should remain of this world.

This is true even to the point of carrying on trade during the most sacred of religious activities, the *Hajj* or pilgrimage to Mecca. Even then, the faithful are assured, there "is no fault in you, that you should seek bounty from your Lord,"[48] that is, seek an honest profit.

After leaving business aside for the noonday congregational prayers, Muslims are not enjoined by God to retire for further prayer or meditation, but to return to their secular affairs: "When the prayer is finished, scatter in the land and seek God's bounty, and remember God frequently; haply you will prosper."[49] While the great religious precursors of western capitalism would have been comfortable with the Quranic identification of God's bounty with material profit and with the idea that God returns His blessings in the form of economic favor for the faithful, no John Calvin or Cotton Mather would have *ever* urged their prosperous burger congregations to go right back to business after Sunday services![50]

Rodinson quotes another modern commentator on Islam[51] to the effect that the *Sunnah,* which report the non-scriptural utterances of the prophet Muhammad, show him praising merchants, certainly not in Islam a parasitic class. Rather, they are people who should enrich themselves so as to be able to help those least fortunate members of the community. Of course, as we have indicated above, this is what would happen in an ideal community of believers, where the rich tender *zakat* to those in need and where no workers or peasants are cheated by the powerful of what they need to support their families.

However, lest we think that the prophet was merely an idealist, Rodinson emphasizes the teachings that those who engaged in commerce were in need of well-defined guidelines which the state was empowered to enforce in the name of the general welfare. He stresses the prominence of laws found in the *Sunnah* which, as mentioned earlier, are not always strictly Quranic in origin.[52] Rodinson might also have quoted some of the Quran's injunctions on practical business matters, for example, those against giving short measure; such cheaters have no doubt as to their fate: "Woe unto the stinters, who, when they measure against the people, take full measure, but, when they measure for them or weigh for them, do skimp. Do those not think that they shall be raised up unto a mighty day, a day when mankind shall stand before the Lord of all Being."[53] The command to "fill up the measure and balance with justice" is repeated throughout the Quran,[54] surely indicating a basic concern with what was probably one of the most committed economic sins[55] in the Arabia of the prophet's time.

Other all too common transgressions of an economic nature did not escape notice in the Quran. For example, the powerful and wealthy must never "proffer it [money] to the judges, that [they] may sinfully consume a portion of other men's goods."[56] Lest contracts or mortgages be later interpreted against one of the parties, most likely the poorer and less influential one, both parties are required by the Quran to define the terms in advance, in writing, and in the presence of witnesses, no matter how small the transaction.[57] Even when the business deal seems relatively uncomplicated, involving transactions where both goods and money change hands immediately, witnesses are strongly advised.[58] In either case, the parties are then enjoined to leave the witnesses alone: "And let not either writer or witness be pressed; or if you do, that is ungodliness in you."[59]

In general, our agreement lies with Rodinson's conclusions. We would add that, while Islam may embrace the basic pursuits of capitalism (profit through business activity, financial returns on investments involving risk, and basic rights for private property), there are critical and important differences between Islamic teaching and modern capitalist practice.[60]

First of all, in Islam, capitalist (or proto-capitalist) practices are acceptable only to the extent that they conform to overall social goals. For instance, if a large segment of society is without the basic needs of shelter, clothing, food, and adequate economic opportunity, then societal needs would, in our view of Islam, obviously take priority over the economic desires of the already wealthy. The form of capitalism that may be deduced as compatible with Islam is one that has clearly defined minimums (for the poor) and maximums (for the rich), as long as there are segments of society that are without basic requirements. Furthermore, Islamic principles direct the state to take all necessary actions to correct any imbalances. Thus, capitalism is endorsed only as long as it is harmonious with and strengthens the social fabric.

Secondly, Islam has within it a practical set of laws that have been derived, over 14 centuries, from Quranic statements and other orthodox sources of divine guidance to man, such as the *hadith,* the sayings attributed in the *Sunnah* to the prophet. These laws, as we have seen, refer to *specific* problems that existed at the time of the revelation of the Quran and, to one degree or another, since then — for example, inequitable income distribution, exploitation of the economically helpless (such as those who must borrow, or the widows and orphans), or to likely situations where cheating may occur in common economic transactions.

Thirdly, Islamic law clearly defines the concept that there are limits on man's claim to natural resouces — absolute ownership, by the principle of *tawhid,* is limited to God. While private ownership is also clearly recognized, it carries with it a social and religious responsibility. Resources of all types, whether they be agricultural land, agriculturally related (like water), or subterranean mineral deposits are referred to in the Quran and/or in the other traditional sources in terms of specific economic concepts, as we have seen. The prices that can justly be charged for production inputs and the taxes (or other forms of levies) dues on wealth or output are two such areas.

For instance, *zakat* (or *ushr,* according to some legal schools of thought) taxes due on the produce of rainfed land were considered to be higher than those from irrigated land. Rain was God's bounty; from what was freely offered by God, a higher return to the poor was demanded. Irrigation implied the farmer (or landlord) had invested labor and capital to husband and to distribute the available water; thus, less was due society from the produce of such land, so that proper returns could be realized for these improvements to the land's natural capacity to produce. In an analogous case, the claimant to virgin land who did nothing to improve it over a prescribed period of time, was obliged (at least theoretically) to surrender it to another claimant free of charge (which, if the land was truly unimproved, was how the first claimant also should have received the land).[61]

Islam then can be seen as compatible with many of the basic principles of western capitalism, especially those which uphold private ownership and the moral validity of profit. The common points it shares with Marxist socialism are for the most part limited to attitudes about the past and present abuses of capitalism that have outraged many adherents of socialism, especially relative to income distribution.[62]

Any socialist system which in effect denies the right to private ownership of productive property must be to some extent in conflict with Islam. Since the Quran and *Sunnah* provide many warnings that absolute ownership is God's alone, and that private property as a human institution has several limitations imposed on its direct use and on the use of the income that derives from it, this conflict should be traced to the socialist rather than the Islamic side. In this regard, it is the Marxist absolute prohibition of certain broad categories of ownership that sets the stage for the problem. Islam, on the other hand, urges moderation and social responsibility within the framework of generally private ownership, while it contains within its traditions many instances where communal ownership may be preferred.[63]

Marx, in direct lineage with Aquinas and Aristotle, enshrined the labor theory of value in his economic philosophy. Thus, Marxist socialism must explain all commodities in terms of the labor necessary to produce them, whereas capitalism relies on the relative scarcities of all the productive inputs (for example, labor, capital, raw materials, and entrepreneurial risk) used to bring the goods to market in order to come up with its explanation of value.

The importance of human labor is emphasized in Islamic tradition; for example, we have the following *hadith*s: "the best income is that earned honestly by the hard-working laborer," and the reply of the prophet when he was asked what kind of earnings were pure and unblemished, "to labour with one's own hands," and that "no one ate better food than the person who labored with his own hands."[64] However, the strongest contrasts are drawn with those who do not work — especially beggars — and not with those whose toil is non-manual.[65]

From its beginnings, Islam has had among its most honored members many who earned their bread in non-manual ways. The prophet himself was a merchant, a trader who knew very well the caravan routes of Arabia and market towns from Syria to Yemen. Most merchants of that day were probably not much more prosperous than the typical artisan or small farmer, and Muhammad treated this group to which he belonged as no more or no less than these others. It was the richer elements of society, however they earned their bread, that were cautioned about their economic duties to the *umma,* the community of believers as a whole. As we have seen above, these guidelines were given to all Muslims so that they might gain salvation. All men and women had obligations to anyone in the community who was less fortunate than they.

If rich Muslims are faithful in fulfilling *zakat* obligations, if they are scrupulous in their dealings with the poor, if they seek only an honest profit and forsake *riba,* if they provide honest work for others at fair wages, they too will enter Paradise. If poor Muslins, on the other hand, never spare a penny for alms, or cheat each other, or take interest on petty loans, they will surely be damned.

Another way to consider this interface between Marxism and Islam is in terms of profit (that is, the return on risk capital), which is at least theoretically anathema to the former. We have seen above that Islamic law has made many distinctions between profit and *riba,* the taking of interest or earning of an economic return when no risk is involved.[66] The mercantile traditions of Islam have given its society an appreciation for the role of risk. Thus, if physical labor (and its earnings) received special recognition from the prophet, this did not mean that entrepreneurial functions were to be considered as unimportant and as undeserving of a reasonable economic return.

Governing the relations between entrepreneurs and manual workers are traditional guidelines similar to the more general ones we have already indicated for those who have greater economic, social, and political power in their dealings with the weaker members of the *umma.* Many *hadith* treat in one fashion or another of the relationship between employer and employee: "The owners who mete out evil treatment toward their servants shall find the gateway of Paradise shut to their faces."[67] "If your servants miscarry your orders or are guilty of grievous wrong seventy times each day, you should forgive them for an equivalent number, for they are your brothers."[68] "What you wear, give your servants to wear; feed them the food you eat."[69] Thus, Islam has from its origins preached the equality before God of employer and employee and warned the former that they exalt themselves before others at the risk of future punishment.

One contemporary Muslim scholar, Hakim Mohammed Said, has argued that Islam tends to differentiate between two categories of legal proscription: some crimes (and some types of punishment) are only between God and the individual, while others take definite social form. He then argues that this dual categorization applies to the entrepreneur-worker relationship. On the one hand, there are many warnings about the abuses of concentrated wealth, as we have seen above; about these the individual rich man or woman is warned they will face strict justice before the bar on the Day of Judgment. On the other hand, the Quran, the *Sunnah,* and the rest of the weight of Islamic law put forth an entire body of fairly specific legislation dealing with the relationships between the economically more and less well off, including employers and employees. The latter includes ethical norms of conduct for both entrepreneurs and workers.[70]

Legal obligations therefore rest on both sides. Neither worker nor employer enjoys any innate moral superiority, though perhaps greater temptations are faced by the richer and more powerful party to the contract. If Islamic tradition sanctifies manual labor by giving it the highest place, it does not give it an exclusive place. Other honest endeavors find room in the hierarchy of ethical activity.

Finally, regarding other points of Marxist economic dogma,[71] there is no particular Islamic preference for Marxist emphasis on economic planning over market forces for the considerable role of the economy's allocative mechanism. On the one hand, the Quran and the *Sunnah* say nothing about market operations to indicate basically negative attitudes. Marx, on the other hand, betrays (despite his careful attempts to achieve a scientific neutrality) a serious philosophical bias against the market, based on his observations of the injustices prevalent in nineteenth century *laissez faire* capitalism.

In fact, on this question as on few others, contemporary capitalism and Marxism have tended to approach and borrow from one another. Partly because of this, politically neutral less developed societies like those of the Islamic world have since mid-1950s seen little reason not to borrow from both camps on this issue.

The last major characteristic of Marxist socialism cited above — limits on individual income and wealth — is in the twentieth century an issue on which East and West differ only in regard to the degree to which limitations are to be imposed. On this question, most developing countries have tended to follow a middle path, and this approach has been particularly attractive to the Islamic world. Islam has always embraced the *principle* of private ownership, as we have seen, but through its fourteen centuries it has tempered this endorsement with cautions. These have extended to both ownership (or wealth) and income questions. Thus, contemporary Islam can sympathize with both the basic capitalist principle of private ownership of wealth-producing assets and Marxist reactions against the extremes of personal wealth possible under *laissez faire* capitalism.

In concluding this section, we would maintain that the totality of Islamic economic tradition sets the stage for a *via media* — a third way — and that the Quran, the teachings of Muhammad and the body of Islamic law rule out both *laissez faire* capitalism and Marxist socialism. In the contemporary world, the former philosophy is somewhat of a straw man since it is practiced nearly nowhere, while the latter is the official system in countries with more than a third of the human population. Islam actually encounters various modified capitalist models, some of which have borrowed heavily from socialist teaching. If Western countries can evolve economic systems of a hybrid nature, might not Islamic countries do the same?[72]

ISLAM AND RECENT ECONOMIC CHANGE

At the outset we should emphasize that Muslim countries have rarely been governed by strict Islamic economic principles. Probably the only times since the founding of Islam that strict adherence has been followed was under the caliphates of Abu Bakr and Umar. In the twentieth century, only Saudi Arabia and, perhaps, Libya have come even close in adhering to such principles.

Furthermore, we should note that a strict interpretation of Islam in a society cannot be achieved by simple dictate of the State. Much more it must be followed by a vast majority of the Muslims. For instance, *zakat*, as we have indicated above, is very much a *personal* obligation;[73] it is thus very difficult for the State to monitor effectively. In any case (within or without Islam) a wealth tax is much harder to administer than, for example, an income tax.

Two issues related to the general discussion in the last section are whether modern Muslim countries could be governed by Islamic principles, modified only insofar as was widely accepted in religious legal circles, and whether these principles would preclude rapid economic progress. From the beginning of this chapter, at least, nothing has been said to indicate why either question must necessarily be answered negatively. It has been pointed out that the theologians and lawyers of Islam do have to define their basic terms in light of modern reality — for example, as regards the *zakat* obligations of those whose wealth is in strictly modern categories (such as diversified common stock portfolios), or whether government-issued interest-bearing obligations[74] violate the prohibitions on *riba*. Without such resolutions (which might reasonably be expected in view of recent escalations in the interest of Muslim academicians and political leaders in these questions), it is difficult to predict whether the major Islamic nations will hew closer to one or the other of two stereotypic lines. On the one hand was a blind following of the European path (which most Western observers, through early 1979, tended to project for Pahlavi Iran, and even for several of the neighboring Gulf region oil-exporting countries). On the other was an unthinking reactionary backlash (ironically applied easily to the same Iran in the early days of the Pahlavi exile).

However, we have cited considerable evidence that Islam not only does not rule out economic progress, but that it clearly endorses several of the basic factors cited frequently by Western commentators as essential in historic economic transformation — private property, recognition of the profit incentive, a tradition of hard work, a link between economic success and eternal reward. Thus Islam seems unlikely to rule out rapid economic growth or even the construction of a strong system more or less capitalist in essence. On the other hand, Islamic principles cannot readily, if at all, be reconciled with economic "progress" that is contradicted by blatant economic and social injustice in the context of general social welfare.[75]

It is of course very difficult to discuss the case of Iran when the very basis of its historical identity is being questioned. Still, we might try to outline some of its recent economic problems. First of all we might ask whether what economic change that occurred during the 1970s has not been in large part haphazard — without very much rational thinking involved in its genesis. For example, in a country with vast natural gas reserves and still very limited export potential for this resource,[76] how much economic sense did it make to embark on a multi-billion dollar program of nuclear power plant construction[77] — whose sheer magnitude ($10 to 20 billion by 1985) was surpassed only by Pahlavist military appetites?

More general is the problem of Iranian agriculture, which, despite the country's much touted land reform, has apparently come through the so-called "Green Revolution" unscathed — that is, unlike most of its neighbors (with which it shared the potential to make good use of the new cereal strains), it has shown few discernible gains in per acre cereal output over the last twenty years. Yet agriculture continues to be the livelihood of some half of the population, and a recently food self-sufficient country has become rapidly dependent on those few countries that are cereals exporters.[78]

This has occurred in part as a price of the emphasis on industrialization, which proceeded with little regard for the principles of comparative advantage or for designing a rational tariff structure that would protect, temporarily, only those industries that promised eventual competition in efficiency (and prices) with the world at large. Such an industrialization, if it proceeded, could well have become the world's most costly peacetime white elephant.

In addition, three more points with major implications for basic Islamic principles should be made about Iran. Firstly, income distribution is among the worst in the world.[79] Secondly, the vast majority of the population has not received its basic needs for food, shelter, clothing, education and health,[80] to say nothing of equal opportunities for advancement. Thirdly, contrary to Quranic injunctions, speculation and hoarding (and its consequent profits) have often been the rule rather than the exception.

These economic changes are clearly irrational considering any society's most basic foundations. When so few benefits accrue to society in general, the question is: to what does a society like Iran turn? The most obvious answer is to its basic documents, to the sources of its foundations. Though Iran has a much longer history than Islam, only one document falls into this category: the Quran.[81]

The Quran, in most economic cases, is a source of general prescription. It usually lacks most of the details (except perhaps for inheritance matters), and therefore could not directly be used for practical economic management of growth. On the other hand, the Quran clearly ties economic advancement to the broad needs of the Muslim community.

If Muslims, perhaps since the time of the earliest khalifs, have pushed the more uncomfortable Quranic precepts regarding economic change and justice into the background, it is not really surprising that an era of sudden affluence has recalled many Muslims back to the foundations of their faith. From what we have presented above, we argue that it is not some primeval move toward scripture *per se* and *in toto* that is involved, but a rewakening of the spirit of the Quran — one that points toward the economic and social justice clearly prescribed in the Quran.

In this sense, the Quran must be appreciated as a personal, social, and economic document. This fortuitiveness, Muslims hold, was divinely ordained; the Quran foresaw the need for many of the programs and institutions of our complicated modern age. Nonbelievers can only wonder at the aptness of many of its provisions in the current context.

However, Muslims cannot rest content with this appropriateness. They are not easily relieved of their obligation to use their God-given intellects to solve existing problems: "It is He who sent down upon thee the Book, wherein are verses clear that are the Essence of the Book, and others ambiguous. As for those in whose hearts is swerving, they follow the ambiguous part, desiring dissension, and desiring its interpretation. And none knows its interpretation, save only God. . . . And those firmly rooted in knowledge (who say) 'We believe in it; all is from our Lord.'"[82]

What better way for Muslim countries to use some small portion of their current wealth to support research into the problem of reconciling their rich heritage with their current economic prospects? What better way than to encourage "Those firmly rooted in knowledge"?

The Course of Secularization in Modern Egypt

Daniel Crecelius

*S*ECULARIZATION HAS BEEN IDENTIFIED as an integral part of the modernization process, yet the great majority of studies on modernization in the Middle East have concentrated on but two aspects of secularization as it has affected traditional Islamic society. These themes have been the separation of religious institutions from those of the state, or to put it another way, the differentiation of political and religious functions, and the ideological response of the *ulama* (learned men of religion) to the spread of Western ideas and institutions.[1] Studies on Islamic reform have been largely confined to the attempts of a mere handful of religious reformers, such as Jamal al-Din "al-Afghani", Muhammad Abduh, Rashid Rida, and Hassan al-Banna (all, incidentally, associated with Islamic reform in Egypt) to restructure or reinterpret traditional Islamic thought and practice. Emphasis has been on their conceptual systems rather than on the impact of their thought on society. Few studies have in fact dealt with the realities of socioeconomic change on the religious institutions and still fewer have attempted the difficult task of evaluating the secularization of the Islamic polity.[2] This paper traces the course of secularization in modern Egypt, to evaluate its quality as well as its impact, and suggests some reasons for the course that relationships between religion and the state have taken in revolutionary Egypt. Before statements on these topics can be made, however, it is essential to review the relationship between religion and the state in traditional Islam.

TRADITIONAL ISLAM AND THE STATE –
COOPERATION AND DEPENDENCE

The separation of religious and political institutions or functions has been achieved with far less conflict in the Muslim Middle East than it has in the Christian West. But results of that separation have been far more disastrous to the Islamic religious institutions than to the Christian ones. Part of the explanation for this lies in the nature of the traditional relationship between religion and the state in the two religious communities.

Traditional Islam represents a system which Professor Donald E. Smith has classified as organic, one in which religious and political functions are fused.[3] Christianity is characterized in his scheme as a church model, one in which there is a close alliance between two distinct institutions, between government and church. The separation of the two institutions in the church model is not necessarily disastrous for the religious institution since it can exist apart from the state. The same cannot be said of religious institutions in the organic religio-political model.

Islam is a revealed religion, hence the community (the *ummah*) is divinely ordered and guided, Allah's desires being revealed to mankind in the sacred *Quran* and the *sunnah* (traditions) of the Prophet. The sum of Allah's commands and prohibitions, most of which had to be deducted from the *Quran* and the *sunnah* through the devices of consensus *ijma* or analogy *(qiyas),* forms the corpus of the sacred law, the *shariah.* In theory the *shariah* provides guidance for every aspect of the life of both the individual and the community, which of course includes the state. The best Islamic society was that which could live as closely as possible to the ideal society outlined by the regulations and the principles of the *shariah.* The *ulama* who devoted their efforts to the knowledge of and understanding of the *shariah* and other religious sciences interpreted Allah's commands and prohibitions for the community; the ruler, whether caliph or sultan, was charged with insuring the application of the sacred law in the community. In theory the ruler and the state were subject to the law, hence subservient to those who were responsible for interpreting it. The only sovereignty was that of Allah and all legislation received divine sanction when enunciated by the *ulama.*

Despite the fact that religious and political functions might be fused in an organic state, a clear differentiation of function somewhat akin to what we know in the West may yet develop. Already in early Islam such a differentiation between the political and the religious was apparent. It became the function of the *ulama* to preserve, study, interpret and propagate the sacred law and religious principles through their teachings, and it fell upon the state to defend and apply the sacred law, insuring that the community would be the closest approximation possible of the ideal Islamic society.

The organic unity of religion and state was particularly symbolized in the institutions of the *shariah,* education, and the caliphate or sultanate. In reality, the ruler dominated the learned men of religion, who usually gave way to the superior force of the military commanders, for the *ulama* did not attempt to *wield* political power so much as to *manipulate* it, hoping to influence state and society through their teachings and pious conduct. As Gibb and Bowen have written in their classic study:

> The first essential function, then, of the religious institution was to indoctrinate all ranks of society (including the members of the ruling institution) with habits of thought and principles of action and judgement in conformity with its ideals. The second was to raise up and maintain a body of scholars and teachers who would by their learning safeguard the principles upon which the religious institution was founded, and by their manner of life win the respect and affection of the people.[4]

This traditional self-view the *ulama* held of themselves as advisers, not rulers, has characterized the Sunni concept of the relationship between religion and the state to the present. Recognized spheres of influence were ultimately differentiated for each sociopolitical group, but the just ruler was expected to consult the *ulama* on all matters of the law in its broadest aspects. The *ulama* had become the legitimizers of political power, the arbiters of social conduct, even the molders of economic policy.

The unity of religion and the state was maintained no matter how wide the political gap between *ulama* and rulers, and the *ummah* was always divinely guided, no matter how far society might stray from the ideal, as long as the rulers recognized the superiority of the *shariah* and gained the approval of the *ulama* for their actions. The *ulama* thus continued to act as the final arbiters of what was pleasing (legal) or reprehensible (illegal), but were often forced to compromise in the face of the superior power of their rulers. They therefore continued to define the limits to which law and custom could accommodate innovation or deviation from the ideal. As long as the state recognized the theoretical superiority of Allah's law, the *ulama* condescended to stretch the toleration of that law to remarkable limits. The preservation of this traditional "veto" power has remained one of the fundamental demands of contemporary *ulama* in their debate with secularists over the relationship of religion and state in modern Islam.[5]

Islamic scholars often remark on the seeming autonomy of such religious institutions as the corps of *ulama,* the law, education, or the dervish orders. It appears, however, that religious autonomy in traditional Islam was largely a function of the sociopolitical or physical distance of the religious institutions from state power. Autonomy even varied within an institution, depending on the relationship a particular level of any institution maintained with the state. Much of the difference in automony between the dervish orders and the *ulama* is to be explained by the stronger and more frequent relations, both formal and informal, that the *ulama* maintained with the military elites. Likewise, village *ulama* were not subjected to the ideological tests which the higher *ulama* and the state might jointly apply to the *ulama* serving in courts, mosques, or schools in urban centers. The higher *ulama* in particular had far less opportunity to develop political or ideological autonomy than did those of lesser rank because of the very close social, economic, and administrative ties they maintained with the state. In eighteenth and early nineteenth century Cairo, for instance, popular insurrections against unjust governments were more frequently led by *ulama* of the districts or of lesser rank than by the recognized religious leaders who held high positions within the religious hierarchy.[6]

Sunni Islam was totally dependent upon the state in its battle against unbelief. The higher *ulama,* working through institutions supported by the state, strove mightily to defend their interpretations of religious truth from Shiah formulations or the excesses of popular religion. They sought to impose their system of belief upon the *ummah* and the state through the application of the sacred law and the indoctrination of the masses through example and learning. The latter was imparted through a vast system of *kuttab*s (the primary school of the Muslim community) and *madrasah*s (the collegiate mosque). Heresies, superstitions, and unbelief were thus held in check by the law and combatted through the spread of education. The military rulers, too, found the law and education useful means by which to control the polity, especially since Sunni *ulama* preached obedience to the ruler as one of their fundamental political principles.

The educational concern of the *ulama* in traditional Islamic history was generally limited to matters religious. Their virtual monopoly over education and the interpretation of the sacred law should not blind us, however, to the antagonistic political relationship which existed between them and their military rulers. Not only were the *ulama* themselves subservient to the state in terms of political power, but the religious institutions which were the very well-spring of the vast influence they possessed were also dependent upon the state for support and sustenance. The great mosques, the numerous *madrasahs*, even the *takiyahs* (dervish "monasteries") of the community were built and maintained at state expense and had their functions supported through an annual allotment by the state or by the alienation of lands or revenues (once again usually donated by the state or higher officials of the state) in the form of *awqaf*.

The organization of the legal system, too, was considered within the proper domain of the state, though it remained the function of the *ulama* to determine the content of the law. The state therefore organized the judicial hierarchy and appointed judges within the system. The state could likewise choose to enforce or abandon certain prescriptions or interpretations, as it did in the ninth century A.D. when it changed direction on questions posed by the Mutazilites. Likewise, a new regime might attempt to change significant segments of the belief system of the *ummah*. In Egypt, for instance, the victory of the Fatimid forces in A.D. 969 meant the eclipse of Sunni teaching and the imposition of a Shiah interpretation. For this purpose the great mosque school of al-Azhar was originally founded.[7] Shiah Islam in turn gave way to Sunnism when Salah al-Din al-Ayyubi wrested Egypt from the last Fatimid ruler in A.D. 1171 and after a brief period of eclipse al-Azhar became the bastion of Sunnism in the Middle East as a result of the support given to it by the revived Sunni state.

The traditional Islamic state appeared as both the patron and master of the legal and educational institutions of Islam. It was imperative, in a state or society ordained by God, that religion and the law be dominated by the state. Nor did the *ulama* or the dervish orders remain totally outside state control, for it was also necessary for the religious state to force a minimum degree of religious conformity on all levels of society and upon all social institutions. My own research has indicated that in late eighteenth century Egypt even the heads of native religious structures such as the dervish leaders, muftis and the Shaykh al-Azhar could not claim or maintain their positions without the approval of the state. All, moreover, had to submit to the discipline of the ruling Mamluk-Ottoman military elites. Society, moreover, was virtually abandoned by both the state and the higher *ulama* to heterodox beliefs and practices, to superstition and ignorance.

We have dealt at some length with the realities of the political relationship between religion and state, between *ulama* and military-political leaders, in order to emphasize the dependence of religious structures upon the state. Though they may be characterized as having an organic relationship, their relationship was not a balanced one of equals. If this analysis is correct, it will help to explain a phenomenon to which I would like to return at the end of this paper, being a topic seldom dealt with by studies on modernization in Islam. This is the determination by some of the revolutionary Islamic states to forge a new relationship between religion and state, a relationship in which the state is totally dominant over religion, one in which the state, not the *ulama,* assumes the chief responsibility for the reinterpretation of Islamic thought, and in which the state makes every effort to utilize religious symbols and principles to reach the religious masses with the messages of Islamic socialism or revivalism.[8] Religious institutions, having been differentiated from those of the modern state over the course of a century or more, are once more drawn into a close, though completely subservient, relationship with the revolutionary state.

THE FATAL BREAK

The reign of Muhammad Ali Pasha (1805–49) marks the beginning of the actual differentiation of political and religious structures in modern Egypt. His decisions and programs have in fact largely determined the course that secularization has taken over the last century and a half in Egypt.

The first and most abrupt move toward the differentiation of religion and state came in the attacks Muhammad Ali made against the political influence of the *ulama.* Between 1809 and 1813 he deposed those among the higher *ulama* who opposed him, assumed the right of the government to appoint or depose all the leading *shaykhs* who comprised the native religious elite, abolished the *iltizam* system of tax-farming and seized the revenues of the *awqaf khayriyah* (pious foundations alienated in perpetuity) which supported religious institutions and their functions. By stretching his hand over the dervish and guild leadership, over provincial and village heads, and by providing a loose administrative framework for their organization, Muhammad Ali increased the control of government over these semi-autonomous structures to limits unknown before his reign. But above all, he departed from traditional principles of Islamic government by refusing to accept the advice and mediation of the *ulama* in the councils of state. The acts of political terror perpetrated against the *ulama* by Muhammad Ali and his son Ibrahim Pasha generally silenced the *ulama* in the highest councils, but they did not keep them from privately opposing the reforms of the new regime. Despite their unwillingness to accept the many reforms he now introduced, Muhammad Ali found ways to impose the hated innovations *(bidah)* within a limited governmental circle.

The regime's attacks upon the political influence of the *ulama* and its seizure of most of the revenues which sustained the vast system of schools, mosques, *takiyah*s and ceremonies of the religious community had a devastating effect upon the religious institutions in Egypt. Deprived of most of their revenues and ignored by the new regime, religious institutions entered a period of rapid and continuous decline. Numerous *kuttab*s fell into ruin during Muhammad Ali's reign, and by 1875, when Ali Mubarak Pasha made his famous survey of mosques and schools, decay was widespread. "The majority of the schools," he reported, "have become mosques."[9] He also noted that there were no more salaries for *ulama*, except at al-Azhar, and that many mosques, unable to support the personnel necessary to sustain public services, were turned into occasional meeting places for small groups of dervishes. The very function of many mosques and schools had therefore been abandoned. Other institutions such as the guilds and the dervish orders experienced a similarly disastrous century of decay.

The *ulama* found it inadvisable to challenge Muhammad Ali once he insisted upon imposing his will upon them. The best they could do was to attempt to limit the scope of the modernizing trends their Pasha now set in motion or through their own tactics surround, isolate, and eventually suffocate the hated innovations. It was difficult, though, to oppose successfully the introduction of new practices or organizations at the level of the state, where the Pasha was supreme. Muhammad Ali did not openly challenge the traditions and concepts of the *ulama* nor totally abandon the basic concepts of Islamic government. He recognized the supremacy of the *shariah* and continued the bald charade of consulting the *ulama* and gaining their official approval for his programs, even if this meant forcibly securing a necessary *fatwa* (legal opinion) for an unwilling *alim* of the second rank. Above all, he made no attempt to challenge their control of religious education, the law, or their moral dominance of society.

One of the key relationships between the *ulama* and the military elite, between religion and the state, was nevertheless missing from the new pattern of relationships which was being forged by Muhammad Ali. Where once the military elites had respected the *ulama*, patronized their activities and institutions, where they had solicited (and generally obeyed) their counsel and made them virtual partners in government, the new regime saw them as obstacles to modernization, rivals of power, and teachers of sciences, attitudes and practices that were responsible for the social, economic, and intellectual backwardness of the nation. They and their teachings were increasingly seen as major factors in the military weakness of Muslim states.

The strategy that each side adopted in the struggle to modernize appears in retrospect to have greatly facilitated the institutional modernization of the state and to have permitted the substitution of one belief system for that of another among a small segment of society without totally disrupting traditional socioeconomic institutions and beliefs in general. Early modernizers such as Muhammad Ali felt they could borrow just the "cutting edge" of Western civilization, such as military technology, new drills and formations, without disturbing society's basic equilibrium. Modernization was felt to be a simple operation of grafting onto traditional society a narrow range of Western borrowings, in particular a new military organization and technology.

Muhammad Ali therefore made no attempt to modernize society in general. The many innovations he introduced into Egypt were meant solely for the aggrandizement of the state, particularly its military arm. The factories he founded produced items essential to the military, such as weapons, ammunition and uniforms. The schools he established were military schools. Even the famous medical college which was placed, like so many other new programs, under the direction of a European, was meant to train medical specialists for the armed forces alone. The Pasha's programs, the new techniques, the new skills, and the institutions he introduced therefore were to benefit only a small segment of society clustered around the military-bureaucratic institutions of the modernizing state.

Despite the necessary public approval the higher *ulama* were obliged to give to their Pasha's innovations, they joined the rest of their corps in maintaining an unrelenting hatred for and opposition to virtually all the new programs. Though they were powerless to halt their introduction at the level of the state, where even their own theories told them the ruler was supreme, their public opposition successfully confined the reforms within a narrow governmental circle.

The results of this mutual policy have been disastrous for the *ulama*, for their institutions, concepts, political influence and self-image in particular, and for Islamic society and its belief system in general. Having usurped their former revenues, curbed their political influence and destroyed their inner cohesion, the regime abandoned all religious institutions to their own devices. Deprived by their alienation from the government of necessary financial support, the *ulama* saw their institutions fall into a physical decay and intellectual stupor from which they have not yet recovered. The policy of permitting innovation at the level of the state, while trying to block its spread to society, moreover, appears very much like permitting the introduction of a virus into one part of the body and then working frantically to contain its spread to other parts.[10] The strategy of isolation is therefore responsible for the wide cultural and political gulf that now exists between the still relatively small modernized sector of society organized around new institutions and concepts and the vast majority that still clings tenaciously to traditional beliefs and practices. The latter remains organized around decaying socio-economic institutions and continues to follow an impotent religious leadership that clings to traditional concepts and practices.

Though most of Muhammad Ali's actual reform programs disintegrated in the decade of the 1840s, the essence of secularization survived. While his military factories and armed forces were dismantled, his schools closed, and his state monopolies abandoned, the spirit of reform continued to guide the policies of a small elite bent upon further modernization. Secularization during the first half of the nineteenth century was confined largely to the expansion of nonreligious functions by the government, the growing centralization of authority, the casting adrift of religious institutions, and the creation of the skeletal institutional framework of a modern state bureaucracy. Secularism appeared to make no penetration of society's beliefs or institutions and remained confined to a handful of reformers intent upon borrowing only a narrow range of western military technology or bureaucratic practices. Yet secularization seemed to break through the barriers thrown up against it and to overwhelm Egyptian state and society in the latter half of the century. Secularism was expressed not merely as a changing set of institutional relationships, but as a coherent ideology and style of life.

THE TRIUMPH OF SECULARISM

The second half of the nineteenth century appears to be the key period of secular gestation, for it is the period when socioeconomic change developed the momentum to destroy the equilibrium of Egyptian society and when new institutions, concepts, and elites coalesced to form the basis of a modern state and society. All systems by which Egyptians ordered their lives were profoundly affected during this period by the frenetic attempts of the Khedive Ismail (1863–79) to make Egypt "a part of Europe," by the extensive activities of a vastly enlarged foreign community that founded new businesses, opened modern schools, brought Western technology and introduced new habits, values, and attitudes, by the policies of a reforming British administration that controlled Egypt after 1882, and by the efforts of a modernizing native elite. The course of secularization was now largely determined by three interdependent forces: the continuing trend toward the expansion of government functions and the centralization of authority, the disruptive nature of socioeconomic change, and the spread of Western political concepts among the new political elite.

The trend toward institutional secularization begun by Muhammad Ali continued as the government expanded its functions and centralized its authority. It was not always disruptive of the rhythm of traditional institutions because much of the government's expansion was into areas of only marginal concern to the religious community or into entirely new areas such as public health and sanitation. Ultimately, however, the evolution of a state bureaucracy performing a wide range of non-religious functions developed an inertia of its own that impelled the state to seek control of *all* institutions and to perform functions normally left to religious groups.

Ismail was the first ruler in modern Egyptian history to attempt to revive decaying religious institutions. He made a modest effort to bring order to the chaos within al-Azhar's educational system, gave lavishly of revenues and lands to reinvigorate the dervish orders, supported public religious ceremonies, and sought to make structural changes in the organization of the *shariah* courts. But all his programs, and those of succeeding regimes, no matter how well intentioned, have been viewed by the *ulama* as a threat to their remaining political and economic influence and have been successfully blocked or deflected by the stubborn defense they have made of their positions.[11] Because education and the law together form such an indispensable part of the institutional and philosophical framework of any society the struggle between modernists and conservatives for their control has been particularly intense and drawn out. Though they suffered the gradual secularization of other areas, the *ulama* made successful (until the 1950s) stands to safeguard the autonomy and content of religious education, *shariah* law, and *waqf.*

Finding it impossible to impose reform upon the *ulama,* Ismail returned to the policy of Muhammad Ali by creating entirely new institutions to duplicate the functions of the religious ones still under the control of the conservatives. Secular law codes slowly took their place alongside *shariah* law, secular court systems (consular, minority, and mixed) increased in number, and modern schools belonging to the state or to religious and/or national minorities began to compete with the *kuttab*s and *madrasah*s. Over the course of the next century these institutions gradually expanded their functions at the expense of traditional institutions until the scope of the *shariah* was reduced to personal status law (marriage, divorce, inheritance, etc.) and the *kuttab-madrasah* system had fallen to a secondary status behind the secular system of primary, secondary, and university schools developed by the state and the non-Muslim minorities.

The duplication of functions and institutions permitted reformers to work around the opposition of conservative forces, but it led to a painful cultural bifurcation in all fields. Two societies, the one modernizing around imported institutions and concepts, the other clinging tenaciously, but often in bewilderment, to traditional values and habits, were now locked in constant competition. Two societies touching at every point but having virtually nothing in common now co-existed alongside one another. The result was cultural chaos.

Religious institutions might resist the expansion of governmental functions and the imposition of central authority from without, but the force of socioeconomic change was completely shattering from within the cohesion of Islamic state and society. As Manfred Halpern has pointed out, socioeconomic change was generating forces *outside* traditional systems, forces over which the *ulama* had no control.[12] Once these forces gained enough momentum to penetrate the traditional systems, they sundered the links that had bound the various elements of Islamic society together for centuries. One by one, the institutional, economic, social, psychological, and ideological links that bound together such institutions as the sultanate, guilds and dervish orders, *kuttab-madrasah* education, and the *shariah* were loosened or lost altogether as socioeconomic change began the inexorable transformation of Egyptian society. While the *ulama* saw modernization as the imposition by government of administrative reform, as the spread of a foreign belief system, or as the diminution of their own influence and successfully defended their own institutions from infection, socioeconomic change was rapidly destroying the intricate pattern of relationships upon which their own influence, functions, and concepts were dependent.

The same forces that were destroying the ideological, social, economic, and institutional bases of traditional society were slowly giving birth to a new combination of forces. Entirely new social groups emerged to perform a vast range of skills not found within traditional society. The lawyers, doctors, journalists, novelists, professional politicians, engineers and others, themselves both the product of socioeconomic change and the chief motive force for further development, now challenged the political, intellectual, and social leadership the *ulama* had always enjoyed and forced them ever farther away from the center of the political arena.

Socioeconomic change also gave impetus to secularism in the changing attitudes, values, beliefs, habits, even in the dress and style of the modernizing urban social groups, Secular ideas and attitudes found their way into literature, formed the basis of new fields of study, were popularized in a burgeoning native press, and taught in modern schools and courts. Secularism even found expression within Islamic reformist circles when such modernists as Muhammad Abduh tried to relocate the boundaries between religion and science, between reason and faith.

The twin goals of the emerging social and political elites, nationalism and liberal reform, were explicitly framed on the basis of secular principles derived from the West. The liberal-nationalists developed the same disdain that Muhammad Ali had shown for the *ulama* and conservative religious beliefs and practices, but, unlike Muhammad Ali, they were willing to contest the control of religious institutions with the *ulama* to challenge their concepts and interpretations in open debate, and to engage them in a struggle for the moral and cultural leadership of the masses. Though they expressed clear secular principles, it would be wrong to call the liberal-nationalists anti-religious; many, such as Sad Zaghlul and Taha Hussein, were themselves the product of the Azhar system. They realized that only the state could impose reform upon the *ulama* and their institutions and therefore sought to gain political control over them in an effort to revive them, not to destroy them, for they felt religious principles ought rightly to continue to form the moral basis of society. It was the successful defense that the *ulama* made of their institutions and beliefs that forced the state to develop secular institutions alongside the unreformed religious ones while the regime continued to seek control over the latter. This drive by the liberal-nationalists to subject the Islamic educational, legal, and charitable institutions to state discipline and control is of no less importance for the emergence of a modern national state in Egypt than the struggle to obtain complete independence from England, but it has unfortunately not enjoyed as much study as the latter.

By concentrating on the emergence of Western political theories and institutions, Western scholars have had a tendency to exaggerate the pace of socioeconomic change in modern Egypt, assuming that socioeconomic change was racing hard on the heels of ideological and institutional change. Though traditional society was beginning to show signs of disintegration, modernization had transformed only a very small segment of urban Egyptian society.

In his annual report for 1899 Lord Cromer, the British Resident, offered a sobering reminder that modernization remained confined to a small socially prominent minority clustered in Cairo and Alexandria. Discussing the crucial field of education, he remarked that the total number of students in schools under state direction was only 7,735. Against that figure he offered an estimate of 180,000 students enrolled in approximately 9,000 *kuttabs* spread across the country. Al-Azhar alone contained more students than all the state-directed modern schools and remained the only "university" in Egypt.[13] Cromer also estimated that 91.2 percent of males and 99.4 percent of females in Egypt remained illiterate.[14] All other statistical indexes would indicate that secularism had made little headway in Egyptian society.

Gabriel Baer's many studies on Egyptian social history also offer a counterbalance to the studies on Egyptian ideological or political change. In one study he concludes that

> the contact with Europe and the economic and administrative development in the nineteenth century changed only partly the life and organization of Egyptian society. The traditional family and religious community remained intact and the position of women in society did not change. Neither wealthy Egyptians nor the lower classes acquired the mentality of an industrial society. The social change brought about consisted almost entirely in the destruction of the traditional socio-economic framework: the dissolution of the tribe and the village community, the disappearance of the guilds, and the abolition of slavery. Most of these developments occurred during the last two decades of the century. But the creation of modern groupings, such as modern parties or labour trade unions, was left for the twentieth century.[15]

Despite the limited scope of socioeconomic change, a secular political theory, derived entirely from the West and resting on the concepts of constitutionalism, consultative or representative government, nationalism and popular sovereignty, evolved in the latter part of the nineteenth century and gained rapid acceptance among the emerging social groups. The separation of the Ottoman Empire into independent national states in the aftermath of World War I marks a significant turning point in Islamic political history, for it signals the triumph of radical political concepts over classical Islamic ones. Together, these concepts laid the conceptual basis for a secular state.

Nationalism redefined the community in terms totally inimical to classical theory by substituting in place of the universal *ummah* or the dynastic empire a greatly reduced entity composed not of Muslims and *dhimmis* (non-Muslims having protected status, but unequal right and duties), but of men of all faiths sharing a common citizenship, equal rights, and common duties. As understood by those responsible for giving nationalism articulation, many of whom were themselves of the Christian or Jewish minorities, nationalism has been a powerful secularizing ideology in the Muslim world by eliminating altogether emphasis upon the religious bonds holding the polity together.

By far the greatest blow to the classical theory of the Islamic state was the acceptance of the Western concept of popular sovereignty as the basic organizing principle of the new national state. In his review of the attempt to create an Islamic constitution for Pakistan Leonard Binder remarked that "Islamic legal theory does not recognize the authority of any human legislation."[16] Yet the modern national states that emerged claimed the right, based on the popular sovereignty of the nation, to organize their own affairs and make their own laws.

The popular will was expressed in the written constitutions, and the legislation that flowed from the newly established parliaments was legitimized not by the *ulama* (who in general obstinately opposed the flood of reforms now legislated by the liberal-nationalists), but by secular politicians claiming to speak in the name of the popular sovereignty of the nation. Though they did not totally abandon the classical concepts, their actions virtually replaced the sovereignty of God with the sovereignty of the people and raised the national state to the level of divinity.

The emergence of national states based on Western political institutions and theories was a remarkable triumph for the liberal-nationalists and secured the victory of secular principles at the level of the state. The liberal-nationalists, finally in control of the government, now sought to complete the modernization of Egyptian state and society by pushing reform into all areas. But they first had to gain control of the bases of their own state.

A continuous battle was fought between the *ulama* and the liberal-nationalists on a myriad of fronts. Issues such as the liberation of women, the freedom to think and write as one chose,[17] and a host of other questions involved the *ulama* in constant political conflict with their modernizing government. The *ulama* showed little willingness to depart from traditional political theories or even to understand fully the new political concepts that formed the ideological basis of the modern state.[18] They let pass the opportunity to brand the concepts of popular sovereignty and nationalism as totally reprehensible to Islam, and instead have clung tenaciously to the classical theory of the Islamic state, whose major institution (the sultanate-caliphate) no longer exists, faithfully keeping up an implicit criticism of nationalism by teaching that the only true unity is that of the universal *ummah* of believers.

Despite the recalcitrance of the *ulama*, the drive by the liberal-nationalists to create a modern state and society in the image of the West was giving great impetus to the force of secularization. Politics was the first area to approach almost complete secularization. The state was organized around secular institutions on the basis of Western political thought. Political parties, parliaments and an expanding national court system had usurped virtually all the remaining political functions of the *ulama* and forced them into headlong political retreat after independence. Religious principles and practices were under constant attack, liberal-nationalists denied the *ulama* the right to "interfere" in the affairs of government, and few serious attempts were made to derive political concepts or to legitimize economic or social policy, administrative reform or foreign policy by reference to religious principles. Liberal-nationalism continued to borrow almost exclusively from Western thought, maintained a determined confidence in the superiority of a Western belief system and its appropriateness for Egyptian society, and kept up a constant pressure and criticism of traditional concepts, beliefs and practices. Though they strove mightily to impose reform upon the *ulama,* even employing the weight of government legislation against them, they failed in their attempts to reform *awqaf,* Islamic education, or *shariah* law, or even to subject Islamic institutions in an unambiguous manner to central authority. It nevertheless appeared only a matter of time until Western beliefs and institutions would totally displace Islamic ones and when Islamic society in Egypt would accept the separation of politics and religion as the West had done. Secularization appeared to be a unilinear force heading toward a predictable goal.

THE RETREAT FROM SECULARISM

Liberal-nationalism had not yet achieved its secular goals when the Revolution of 1952 introduced a radical new factor into the Egyptian political equation. Now the trends towards the differentiation of function and the centralization of authority that had been set in motion by Muhammad Ali were brought to a speedy conclusion as the Free Officers created a highly centralized authoritarian state around their Revolutionary Command Council, the executive committee of the Revolution.[19] Religion posed an immediate and dangerous political problem for the Free Officers because of the power and appeal of the Muslim Brotherhood *(al-Ikhwan al-Muslimun)*, a broadly based religio-political organization of a fundamentalist nature that was making a serious bid for power behind the banner of Islamic revival.[20] A brief period of flirtation between the Free Officers and the Brotherhood ended in the unsuccessful attempt by the latter's extremist arm on the life of Nasser in 1954. The subsequent destruction of the *Ikhwan* organization was no less a rejection by the new leaders of its fundamentalist ideology and programs, which the majority viewed as disruptive and anti-modern, than of its politics. Its elimination permitted the Revolution to subject all religious institutions to the discipline of the state and to develop its own solutions to Egypt's complex religious and cultural problems.

Waqf had been the first of the remaining semi-autonomous religious institutions to fall under the complete control of the state. It had been seen by the new regime as inextricably intertwined with the general question of land reform and, following suggestions proposed by the liberal-nationalists in the debate on *waqf* reform in the 1920's, the state began in 1952 a series of reforms, including the abolition of all personal foundations (*awqaf ahliyah*), that have brought *waqf* under firm government control.[21]

The Revolution also developed a radical solution to the questions concerning *shariah* law. The confusion that had characterized Egypt's legal structure since the days of Muhammad Ali was ended dramatically in 1955 when the regime suddenly announced the abolition of all religious courts, including those of the minority communities. As of January 1, 1956 *shariah* and other courts were to be absorbed into the secular state system. Henceforth a single system of courts would apply a unified code of laws, a code in which religious statutes would cover only the area of personal status.

The last remaining bastion of autonomous shaykhly (and Islamic) power was finally breached in 1961 when the regime imposed upon al-Azhar a sweeping reorganization of its educational system.[22] The reform reduced the Shaykh al-Azhar to the position of a mere figurehead, placed al-Azhar's various administrations into the hands of laymen appointed by the government, reformed its curriculum, and added four modern (secular) faculties. Simultaneously with the announcement of the Azhar reform the government opened a withering propaganda attack against the *ulama* in the nation's press, a campaign whose aim was not only to make it difficult for them to mount a defense of their institution by throwing them off balance, but to silence them completely, to drive them from the political arena, and to wrest from them the control of religion itself.[23]

Perhaps the most telling charge leveled against the *ulama* was that their inability to reform their own institutions or to make religious ideals compatible with modern science or conditions was turning the nation away from Islam and bringing into question the validity of the Prophet's revelation. Herein lay the seeds of the regime's evolving activist religious policy, for implicit in this criticism is a rejection of liberal-nationalism for its heavy reliance upon a belief system derived from the Christian West and its banishment of religion and religious principles to the domain of private concern. The military leaders were moving toward a religious solution which had eluded the *ulama,* Islamic reformers such as Muhammad Abduh and Rashid Rida, the Ikhwan, and the secular liberal-nationalists. The state itself would assume responsibility for the revival of Islam.[24]

The high water mark of the liberal-nationalist secularist tide was reached in 1962 in the debate on the Charter, the document that was to be Egypt's blueprint for future development. The regime did not want to give prominence to conservative religious forces or ideas at that time, so it refused to submit to the vociferous demands by the *ulama* to have the Charter designate Islam the religion of the state.[25] The Revolution reversed itself, however, when in 1964 the constitution designated Islam the state religion, as did the constitution of 1971. The Revolution's policies towards Islamic institutions might have given the impression that the regime was working to secularize the state by separating the religious and state institutions, but in reality it was seeking to break the independent political power of Islamic institutions so it could use them for its own reformist purposes.

The Revolution has sought to achieve cultural unity no less than institutional unity, for it has viewed social and cultural problems just as seriously as those of a political nature. Liberal-nationalism had spent its strength by the 1930s as Britain's refusal to grant Egypt true independence, growing disillusionment with corrupt democratic institutions, and continuing poverty and social injustice led Egypt's intellectuals to reconsider their former support of rationalism and secularism. As P. J. Vatikiotis has observed:

> Such leading modernists as Taha Husayn, Muhammad Husayn Haykal, and Mahmud Abbas al-Aqqad, were, by the 1930s, already in hasty retreat from their earlier positions of secular liberalism and the adoption

of European culture. Their reverential studies of the early fathers of the Islamic Community smacked of frantic and solicitous apologia for their earlier rationalist-secular attacks upon religion and its cultural heritage. A romantic proclivity for the epic quality of early Islam now became a major characteristic of their writings.[26]

This trend has carried right through the Revolution. The Charter of 1962, for instance, marks a clear turning away from total reliance on the West and begins a search for native cultural roots, for it acknowledges that "the real solutions to the problems of one people cannot be imported from the experience of another."[27] Reformed Islam is to mold the values, habits, and norms of society and provide the source of its economic and political principles.

The revolutionary regime took an important, but abortive first step toward reviving the power of religion in 1954, when, after a Meccan pilgrimage by its leaders, it founded the Islamic Congress in partnership with Pakistan and Saudi Arabia. The work of the Congress was quickly paralyzed by political disputes among the three governments, but Egypt, sensing the importance and potential of such an organization, proceeded to create its own Supreme Council for Islamic Affairs. Among its more important activities is the publication of a highly respected journal, *Minbar al-Islam,* which has become a leading voice of religious reform in the Muslim world. It is significant, moreover, that its most important articles dealing with the reinterpretation of Islamic principles are consistently written by lay intellectuals, such as university professors.[28]

The Revolution has not been hesitant to use religious symbols and has reinterpreted Islamic principles to legitimize its revolutionary programs. "This policy was strengthened," wrote Morroe Berter, "as the regime seemed to recognize more and more that Islam remained the widest and most effective basis for consensus despite all efforts to promote nationalism, patriotism, secularism and socialism."[29] Besides offering its own interpretations of Islamic tradition the regime has solicited from the *ulama* formal legal opinions (*fatwas*) on the entire range of its activities, including birth control, land reform, nationalization, scientific research, foreign policy, and social affairs. The most serious attempt to date to use Islam for the benefit of the regime came in the 1960's when it sought to create a socialist ideology on the basis of reinterpretated Islamic principles.[30] By an imaginative reconstruction of several incidents from early Islamic history and of such fundamental concepts as *zakat* (almsgiving) the ideologies of Islamic socialism tried to use religion to legitimize the regime's socialist economic programs, particularly the nationalizations of the late

1950s and early 1960s. During the course of the 1970s this attempt at the radical reinterpretation of Islamic principles gave way under Sadat to an approach that once more gave prominence to traditional interpretations.

All this has made religion once again an important factor in the politics of the nation, but Islam is introduced into political debate by the regime, not by the *ulama*. Religious discussion is carefully monitored by a regime that seeks to maintain the unity of religion and state *(din wa daw-lah)* so essential to an Islamic society without permitting Islam to become a political vehicle for religious groups the regime considers troublesome.

The Revolution has taken a seemingly paradoxical approach towards Islam. Both the regimes of President Nasser and President Sadat have politically repressed Islamic institutions and religious groups and denied the men of religion a meaningful political role, fearing that religious politics could destroy the fragile harmony of Egyptian society and give political power to fundamentalist groups whose programs the Revolution long ago rejected as unworkable. Yet the regime has embraced Islam, has consciously used it to legitimize its foreign and domestic programs and has repeatedly called upon Islamic religious leaders to provide cultural, moral, and spiritual leadership for the nation. President Nasser saw Egypt's foreign relations circumscribed by three circles—Arab, African and Islamic—and sought to couch his relations with the Muslim states of sub-Saharan Africa or Southeast Asia in a religious context. At the same time that the regime called upon Egypt's religious leaders to support its "Islamic" foreign policy or "Islamic" socialism, it denied the men of religion any role in shaping these policies. This dual approach was made apparent again in August 1979 when President Sadat warned a meeting of *ulama* and representatives of religious organizations not to involve themselves in politics or to use Islam for their own narrow political purposes. He remarked that religion and politics should be kept separate and was particularly critical of the continued activities of the Muslim Brotherhood. He warned that he would not permit in Egypt the type of religious strife that has torn Lebanon apart. But at the same time he suggested the formation of a broadly based new Supreme Islamic Council to deal with religious problems.[31]

The Sadat regime has adopted a paternalistic attitude towards Islam. It has appropriated for itself responsibility for the "correct" interpretation of the faith but has at the same time undertaken programs to revive and strengthen Islamic educational and cultural institutions. It gives its support, for instance, to the officially recognized Sufi orders while simultaneously attacking the excesses of ecstatic Sufi practices. It has also countenanced the evolution of a conservative social movement whose chief visible manifestation is the modest dress of a growing number of (seemingly young) women, but whose clandestine political acts of terror have brought down on some of its splintered political groups the full wrath of the government. This rededication to conservative Islamic belief and practice by a highly visible segment of Egypt's population reflects trends that are sweeping the Islamic world and forcing the Sadat regime into a series of political concessions to traditional groups.

The same social and economic forces that have carried secularism forward for more than a century are still at work, but traditional Islamic groups within Egypt are also strengthening their position despite the regime's reformist nature. A new polarity within Egyptian society could be evolving as the conservative elements gain in strength. The *ulama* remain a latent barrier to the Revolution's reformist programs, but pose no serious political threat to the regime. But were the regime to ease its control of religious institutions and drop its surveillance of religious groups such as the Muslim Brotherhood and the new *Jamiyat Islamiyah* it would quickly be faced with a fundamentalist movement of considerable size that could conceivably introduce into Egypt the type of social and political conflict that has torn both Lebanon and Iran apart. These latter groups, whose increasing activities are easily observed on university campuses, in mosques, on streetcorners and even in public buses, have few ties to al-Azhar or the official religious bureaucracy and are therefore freer to express their opposition to secularism and the policies of the regime. Growing pressure from the Brotherhood and these new fundamentalist Islamic groups has already forced the regime to take a more conservative religious stance. These domestic pressures, moreover, are reinforced by the foreign pressures brought to bear on the entire Islamic world by those conservative or revolutionary regimes that are presently attempting to forge an Islamic alternative to the Western or Communist systems that have served as models for development in the past.[32]

′ Several of the oil-rich states, notably Libya, Saudi Arabia and Kuwait, have given to Islamic conservatism a new legitimacy as their great wealth has permitted them to create Islamic welfare states, to impose *shariah* proscriptions (such as those against alcohol and the eating of improperly slaughtered animals) in their own societies, and to give financial and political support to conservative movements throughout the Islamic world. The revival of Quranic punishments has also been received as visible proof of the workability of the "Islamic way." The examples of revolutionary Iran and Afghanistan, which are seen to be struggling against Western cultural, economic, and political imperialism, have also injected a new militancy into the international Islamic resurgence. These states are therefore creating a new Islamic standard by which other states can measure their own degree of adherence to traditional forms. By their example the conservative states represent a critique of Egypt's Westernized lifestyle, her basic orientation, and her westernized legal and parliamentary systems. The night clubs, bars, liquor stores, and cinemas around which much of Egypt's night life revolves can be an obvious source of embarrassment to a regime whose standard of public morality is being increasingly questioned by the morally strict regimes on Egypt's borders and by a growing domestic religious opposition. These criticisms and pressures for change are clearly felt by the Egyptian regime, for the parliament, which contains conservative Islamic spokesmen as well as secularists, is already studying ways in which specific *shariah* laws, especially Quranic punishments, might be revived. Plans to restrict the sale of alcoholic beverages (if not to outlaw them altogether), and to close the bars and night clubs are also frequently mooted, but to date no restrictive action against these institutions has been taken by the regime.

Despite its stated secular goals, the use of religion by the revolutionary regime has done little to spread views on the separation of politics and religion among the polity. Morroe Berger has also observed this failure on the part of the Revolution to complete the secularization process. He noted that "the military regime's denial of political influence to the ulama is not secularism. Secularism means separation of church and state and the latter's supremacy; it does not call for the state's control of the intimate details of religious teaching or the harnessing of religion to the purposes of the government of the day."[33]

It is therefore difficult to agree with Donald E. Smith's assumption that the dominance of the polity over religious beliefs, practices, and ecclesiastical structures in itself is a form of secularism.[34] It is not the institutional relationship between religion and state (whether or not the polity dominates the religious structure) that is important, nor even who introduces religious considerations into political debate, but the character of the issues themselves that constitutes the essence of secularism. Secularism of necessity therefore demands the ability by the individual and the state to make that subtle psychological distinction between religion and politics, to be able to accept willingly a public sphere where rational, secular concepts and principles are dominant and a private sphere where religious principles prevail — to be able, in short, to know what to render unto Caesar and what to render unto God. But this is a concept indigenous to Western Christian civilization and cannot be transferred to Islamic civilization without completely transforming the spirit of the entire civilization.

Most studies on the process of modernization or secularism recognize the necessity for all systems by which man lives, the psychological
and intellectual no less than the political or economic, to undergo transformation.[35] We do not find this change in Egypt, whether at the level of
the state or society, except among a small minority of Westernized individuals. Traditional beliefs, practices, and values reign supreme among
Egypt's teeming village population and among the majority of its urban
masses. It should be emphasized that adherence to tradition is not confined to any single class or group of occupations, but is characteristic of a
broad spectrum of all Egyptian social classes. The modern Egyptian state
has regained control of religious institutions and religion in the manner of
some of the classical Islamic states. It assumes responsibility for religious
interpretation, determines what role Islam will play in political life, and
organizes the religious life of the nation. Egypt has gone as far as any Islamic state but Turkey towards Westernization, but does not reject the
theoretical supremacy of the *shariah* nor the fundamental political unity
of *din wa dawlah*. Though having many of the institutional forms of a
Westernized secular state, Egypt remains an Islamic state in form and essence, just as its society remains faithful to traditional religious beliefs
and practices despite more than a century of evolution towards secularism. As the conservative religious revival continues to gain momentum,
both in Egypt and throughout the rest of the Islamic world, pressure will
mount on both the regime and society to draw closer to traditional Islamic practices and concepts. How many concessions the Egyptian regime
will be forced to make to the conservative forces will depend not only
upon the stability or instability of the regime itself, but also upon the
strength and achievements of the revivalist movement in key countries
such as Iran and Pakistan and upon the political influence of conservative
Arab states such as Kuwait, Libya, and Saudi Arabia. One must wonder,
therefore, whether the new Islamic revival is only a temporary phenomenon that will dictate only a momentary pause in the evolution of Islamic
states and societies towards modernism and secularism or whether the
religious movements will develop the strength to completely reverse the
modernist-secularist trends to which they have always felt antipathy and
do serious damage to the achievements of an earlier generation of liberal-
nationalists. Certainly modernists are not as confident about the amount
of further progress towards secularism their societies will achieve as they
were only a few years ago.

☙ 4 ❧

Veiling in Egypt as a Political and Social Phenomenon

John Alden Williams

*S*INCE THE ELEVENTH CENTURY the women of Egypt have been noted to have strong characters. First Muslim geographers and travellers, then European travellers and oriental writers observed with consternation or with approval that Muslim Egyptian women were more fearless than women in other Muslim countries, more likely to scold and use strong language, more likely to dominate their husbands and their families, even more likely to demand sexual gratification, despite the obvious difficulties put in their way by their society. In this century, Egyptian women were the first in the Arab World to call for putting aside the veil (in the 1920s), for admission to universities (in the 1930s). In the face of their determined and expert insistence, most occupational and professional restraints on women have since been removed.[1]

While Egypt at first led the way in family law reforms to improve the status of women, the legal position of Egyptian women has recently fallen behind that of the women of Tunisia, Syria, Jordan or Iraq. Until June 18, 1979, an Egyptian woman was not protected against her husband's marrying another wife against her wishes, or against his suddenly divorcing her, paying her token maintenance for one year only, obtaining custody of the children over age nine and forbidding her to see them.[2] Nonetheless, the social gains of Egyptian women have been impressive. American women might find them enviable in several ways. Egyptian women are not only doctors and professors, but also engineers, architects, managers of companies, deans of university faculties, and cabinet ministers. They receive equal pay for equal work, find redress when they complain of male discrimination at their jobs, and many of them choose to retain their maiden names after marriage. They are also admitted to

71

higher education entirely on the basis of their academic merits, in a fully competitive way with men.

The cause of *tahrir al-mara* (women's liberation)[3] was already well-launched among upper-class women by the time of the Egyptian Revolution of 1952, and it spread to the middle and lower classes of women, especially in the cities, during the Nasserist period, from 1953 to 1967. Women took a more public role in a society dedicated to modernization, and many of them laid aside traditional dress. This tended to be especially true among the youth, on the campuses of the universities, and in business and professional sectors, which were Egyptianized by requiring businesses to correspond and keep their records in Arabic rather than in French or English. Here Egyptian Muslim women stepped into roles only just vacated by the most Europeanized segment of the society.

During this period it became rare to see a veil and common to see Egyptian imitations of contemporary "Western" costume. At the same time, men were abandoning the traditional *galabiya* for trousers, shirts, and suits. Women advertised their attachment to modernity even in the smaller provincial towns by adopting forms of dress regarded as contemporary and modern, including the mini-skirt. Nowhere else in the Arab World, except perhaps in Lebanon, did Muslim women seem less to present the traditional image of swathed, mysterious beings from a second, private world only just impinging on the public world of men.

Of course, in many parts of Egypt, especially the Delta region and near Cairo, women had always worked alongside men, when extra hands were needed, in the fields. Within limits set by tradition, women of the lower classes could come and go, buy and sell at the market, fetch water; and while their forms were cloaked from wrist to ankle and their hair covered, their faces were bare.

Perhaps this long tradition helped account for the ease with which women seemed to adapt to international costume, but in any case, it was widely assumed that Egyptian women were demonstrating how the Arab woman of the future would behave and dress: that things were as they were because they should be so, and would be so generally. Women who continued to go out with black *milaya* cloaking their forms or drawn over their heads were likely to be women "too old to adjust," or if not, were regarded pityingly or patronizingly as simple provincials with quaint, disappearing manners. It scarcely occurred to anyone to claim that such women were *better Muslims* for dressing in outmoded clothing. Women in international dress were not regarded as "less Muslim" than others, providing it showed modesty and restraint. Such women were often seen to be pious and observant in such matters as prayer, fasting, pilgrimage and reading of scripture; the quality of their commitment to God was not judged on whether or not they wore traditional dress.

If questioned by a naive observer as to their views on costume, women who wore international dress denied that there was anything un-Islamic about it, provided it was not gaudy and did not expose too much of the person. In practice, they chose subdued colors and costumes that did not go above the knee or much above the elbow. They argued that early Islam had not segregated women or veiled them, except perhaps the Prophet's wives, and that this had been because they had lived in a very public place; rooms along the side of his mosque, in which there was constant coming and going. In this situation there might have been some fear that they would distract the worshippers, but also, they would otherwise have had no privacy at all. In fact, the language of the Quran makes it appear that only a curtain over the door, not a veil, was intended.

> O you who have faith, do not enter the apartments of the Prophet unless leave is given to you for a meal, without watching for its time. But when you are invited, then go in; and when you have had the meal disperse, without seeking familiarity in conversation; that is hurtful to the Prophet, and he is ashamed before you, but God is not ashamed to tell the truth. And if you ask his wives for any object, then ask them from behind a curtain [hijab]; that is purer for your hearts and theirs [Quran 33:52]. O Prophet, say to your wives, and to your daughters, and the women of the faithful, they shall draw their robes [jalabib] close about them; thus it is likelier that they will be recognized, and not hurt. [33:58]

Such ideas—that early Islam did not make women veil and that international contemporary dress could be fully compatible with Islam—were made available to women in the popular press and on the radio, which was becoming more and more accessible through transistor sets, even in the remotest villages.[4] The trend for women to adopt contemporary international dress was especially strong between the War of Suez (also known as the Tripartite Aggression) of England, France, and Israel against Egypt in October 1956, and the June War of 1967. These years were accompanied by an almost total state control of the economy, by closer political and economic ties with the Soviet bloc and with "progressive" and neutralist states in Africa and Asia. State control of the economy had been facilitated by the Agrarian Reform Bill of 1952, further implemented by that of 1961, which broke the power of the land-owning classes. New job opportunities were created for all Egyptians by industrialization and by encouraging the emigration of the minority groups

(Maltese, Greeks, Italians, Syro-Lebanese, Jews, and Armenians) who had once played so active a role in urban business life.

Socialism was smart, and imitating the customs of decadent colonial societies was not, but the modernization of the role of women (and their dress) was a part of the socialist ethic. Egyptian middle-class women took hearty advantage of it.

The facts I have set out so far are generally known, and they do not prepare one for the dramatic change in women's appearance that is apparent to any visitor to Egypt today. Observable in the streets and in public places are numbers of women in costumes rather similar to those of Catholic nuns before Vatican II; although their flowing dresses, coifs and long wimples are usually in light rather than dark colors. Other women are dressed in pantsuits, often with long jackets, and with a wimple or at least a large kerchief tied on their heads. The old-fashioned *yashmak*, or face-veil, is rarely seen. What Edward Lane observed a hundred years ago is still true: "The women of Egypt deem it more incumbent upon them to cover the upper and back part of the head than the face;"[5] yet the form is disguised, and only the face and the hands are uncovered. This costume is not traditional, but in its specific form it is new, and it is intended to satisfy the strict requirement of the Islamic Law on the veiling of women written in the books of *Fiqh*. Take for example the Hanafi work *al-Hidaya* of Marghinani: "It is not permitted men to look at strange women, except in the face and palm of the hands. . . . It is reported from Abu Hanifa that it is also permissible to look at the feet of a woman, since there is sometimes occasion for it. From Abu Yusuf there is also a tradition that the seeing of the shoulder is also allowed, since from the influence of custom it may be exposed. If however a man is not secure from the stirrings of lust, it is not allowable to look even at the face of a woman, except in cases of absolute necessity."[6] The medieval authorities agree that veiling the body and hair of women from the sight of men is the primary objective, and the veiling of the face is a secondary importance.

Since the new costumes arise in response to an interpretation of the *Shariah,* the Law (and ironically enough the citation and many like it are more concerned with the impropriety of men's gazing lustfully at women than with what women should wear), they are referred to in modern Egypt as *al-ziyy al-shari:* "lawful dress."

The women who adopt such dress come from the middle class, exactly those who until recently followed the drive for modernization, and they include numbers of university students and graduates. Many women students in the national universities make an effort to persuade their classmates to adopt *ziyy shari,* and it even appears in the American University in Cairo, which, as a private institution charging tuition, is

usually regarded as a bastion of upper-class and cosmopolitan pretensions. The costume appears at a time when President Sadat has proclaimed the "open-door policy," a return to a greater measure of private
initiative, when Cairo is thronged with foreign visitors and business people, and when Egyptians have more opportunity to travel abroad than
they ever had in the Nasser years.

Both the name of the costume and the declarations of the women
who adopt it make the claim that this is a religious gesture, that it con-
forms more to the religious Law of Islam than any other available costume. Now, it can be argued that an orthodox Muslim woman could with
just as great propriety wear a simple dress of modern type, with long
sleeves, black stockings, and a nylon scarf tied over her hair, especially if
she did without jewelry or make-up. Indeed, many educated Muslim
Egyptian women have so dressed during the last decades, and do so still.
Their dress has identified them as observant Muslim women but not made
them conspicuous; many of them are models of piety, active in prayer and
good works, fast during *Ramadan* and also the supererogatory fasts such
as *Ashura,* making the Pilgrimage and seeking religious knowledge. Yet
increasingly, such simple and modest modern attire is seen as no longer
good enough: the woman who appears in *ziyy shari* is evincing an aspiration to dress counter to recent norms of clothing, and claiming to be more
observant of the Law than other women. To this extent, then, we may
perhaps label this *fundamentalist* behavior. A fundamentalist in Islam, as
in Christianity and perhaps in other religious traditions as well, sees him/
herself as trying to right a wrong turn in history; as sitting in judgment of
his/her society, and critical of the way it appears to be going. In a developing country like Egypt, this could easily become a reaction against
modernization generally and a force for violent revolution.

The modern *shari* dress seems to be largely a middle-class, urban
affair. In villages the traditional *tarha* or head-scarf and the black *milaya*
or wrapper or the full long *thawb* still prevail, in all their local variations.
These of course cover everything that the new *shari* dress is supposed to
cover, and satisfy the requirements of the medieval legalists. In small
towns, women still seem to be discarding traditional dress for modern
dresses or pantsuits. Even in the cities, the daughters of poorer families
save their piasters in order to have a dressmaker make them something
modish and foreign-looking, rather as middle-class women did ten years
ago. If the family can save enough money to go to the seashore for a week
or two in summer, they go to the beach in attractive bathing suits. The
woman who wears *shari* dress, on the other hand, wears it to the beach,
and at the most does a little wading in her long costume.

The *shari* dress can certainly be called a reaction against international style, or what is called (with increasing inaccuracy) Western dress. It is not so clear, however, that it is a reaction against *modernization,* because in its specific form it is innovative, not a return to the traditional costume worn by Egyptian grandmothers. Also, it is a modern phenomenon. It is hot, uncomfortable, and costs more than a simple dress; it takes more work to launder and is hardly convenient for many of the jobs Egyptian women have been adopting. Rightly or wrongly, it appears to some segments of Egyptian society as a retrograde step, an exaggeration of religious principles, and an attempt to be conspicuous. But is it also a reaction against the wider, more liberal and more cosmopolitan life available to Egyptians under the "open door policy?"

In Iran before the revolution against the Shah there was a very notable turning to *shari* dress among educated women and university students. In the Iranian case, women put on the traditional *chadar,*[7] sometimes in black, the color for mourning. They did not develop a new form of *shari* dress, but returned to an old one, as part of a very broadly based movement against a regime held to be tyrannical and corrupt. Some of the students involved were so-called "Islamic Marxists"; many were inspired by the lectures of Dr. Ali Shariati, which popularized the ideas of Franz Fanon among Iranian youth, and explicitly urged a rejection of "this Europe that always speaks of humanity, but destroys human beings wherever it finds them."[8] While the Shah's government and the American press dismissed this airily as an incomprehensible wave of religious reaction against modernity generally, Iranian women insisted that it was the Shah and the slavish imitation of the West that was outworn in Iran; the veil was still valid. And in the *Shii ulama* Iranians generally found a source of legitimization for their social and political aspirations. The Ayatollah Khomeini certainly dislikes the old style fundamentalist Wahhabis of Arabia, and they in turn have no use for Shiis. Yet in today's context, the Wahhabis appear as conservatives,[9] and the Ayatollah Khomeini's most devoted followers appear indeed to be Shii fundamentalists.

There have also been returns to the veil in Turkey and in Tunisia: certainly a rejection of the secular republic has been involved in the Turkish case. In both, as in Iran, there must be particular as well as general reasons. We may note that the Egyptian case is paralleled by a more fundamentalist orientation in Muslim lands generally in recent years and by a more *shari* costume among women all the way from North Africa to Central Asia. But one does not learn much about trees simply by observing that they grow in forests. When a woman chooses to put on a distinctive *shari* costume or the veil in a modernizing Muslim country, there is always some personal choice operating: she is making a personal statement,

usually connected with her faith. It does not illuminate her choice for u
we simply ascribe it to a worldwide wave of Islamic fundamentalism. O.
the other hand, if we can understand what is going through her mind and
in what climate her choice operates, we may possibly get some useful insight about a worldwide wave of Islamic fundamentalism.

The *Shariah* and the *Fiqh*[10] have been in existence for hundreds
of years: why are Egyptian women, who once led other Muslim women in
a desire for "liberation," choosing this time to demonstrate in this conspicuous way an affirmation of *shari* norms of dress? Political scientists
and anthropologists have noted that nationalistic periods usually see a
swing to conservatism in morality: why did the *shari* costume not surface
in the more nationalist Nasserist period of Egyptian society? The Sadat
period has brought a resurgence of Egyptian national feelings, as opposed to pan-Arabian: Why are Egyptian women now dressing in a manner more likely to conform to ideas about the place and proper behavior
of women in other Arab countries, such as the Arab peninsula and Libya,
than to those recently prevalent in Egypt?

Egypt is a distinct country. It is necessary to insist on this. However much they may share with their Arab neighbors, Egyptians are aware
that in some final sense, they are themselves: a special people with a
special land and country. They may sympathize keenly with other Arabs,
but they will not be ruled by them, and they are well aware that in many
past periods Egypt has ruled or led her neighbors. If women in modern
Egypt decide to adopt a new *shari* costume, it is for reasons to be found in
Egyptian realities, not in a fashion originating elsewhere, or because
women in Iran or Tunisia have done something similar.

Some of the problems of modern Egypt play an important role in
the decision of women to adopt *shari* dress. In the last quarter of a century, the population of the country has more than doubled. Cairo has
grown from a city of about two million to a city of nearly nine million. It
is a city bursting at the seams, beset with traffic problems, public transportation problems, housing shortages, with a telephone system that
scarcely functions any longer (though it is being improved), with problems of distribution; an infrastructure inadequate for the demands that
are being made upon it. It is in fact a showpiece of all the problems that
beset a primate city in the third world. Its problems have been aggravated
by the constant necessity over the last twenty-five years of being in a posture to defend itself against the threat, thrice-realized, of war with Israel.
The available resources of the country have had to be given to arms, the
army, to paying the debt to the Soviet Union for the Aswan High Dam,
and to industrialization.[12] Cairo has had to be left to shift for itself, for

the most part. Alexandria, though only half the size of Cairo, has been in a similar situation. As a result of the 1967 War, the whole population of the Suez Canal Zone, nearly a tenth of the population of Egypt, became refugees, and most of them poured into Cairo and Alexandria. Attempts to send them back, made since the disengagement agreements with Israel, have not yet met with much success. In the rural areas, overpopulation has now passed the point where it can be absorbed by labor-intensive agriculture. For example, from 1937 to 1970 the active male rural population grew from 2,976,000 to an estimated 4,048,300, but the cropped area (one land unit that is cropped three times a year counting as three units of crop land) grew from 8,302,000 *feddans* (a *feddan* is about one acre) to only 10,700,000.[11] As the countryside becomes more crowded, villagers are forced to leave it and seek what employment they can find in the overcrowded cities. Moreover, the rising expectations of a better life that the revolution fostered among the people could only find satisfaction among the amenities of the larger cities.

To an unhealthy degree, the new industries have been located near the major cities in order to take advantage of the infrastructure that was already there. They have also brought industrial pollution. Social problems have naturally proliferated, and although these may seem mild to Americans because actual crimes of violence are rare, crime occurs frequently enough to make Egyptians wonder what they are coming to and to make them fear the future. People also do not have as much time as formerly to be courteous, to visit neighbors, relatives, and friends, and are often too short of money or of space to offer much hospitality to friends when they come to visit. Egyptians still impress foreign observers as remarkably patient, amiable, generous, and sunny people, but all things are relative: Egyptians complain of the greed that besets modern society, of the decline in morality, of wild behavior among the young, and of corruption in high places.

During the Nasser period, the State adopted socialism and turned to the Soviet Union. This was at first greeted with general public approval, and much hope was placed on the new orientation. After a few years, however, Egyptians began to complain that socialism was undermining their economy, their educational system, and their moral values. The official hangers-on of the regime advocated socialism and lived like lords, while the masses continued to live in almost unbearable conditions. When President Sadat turned from socialism, expelled the Russians, adopted *infitah* or "being open" as a policy, and turned to the U.S., people were for the most part delighted, and once again, expectations ran high. Currently after a few years have passed, people are beginning to ask in what way life has really changed for the better. Peace would be welcome, but aspects of the new relationship with Israel seemed fearfully like capitulation: would Israel really evacuate all of Egypt's land, and would the Palestinians have a homeland?

Very troublingly, at home in Egypt, prices soared. The government threatened to withdraw the subsidies on basic foodstuffs which kept millions from going really hungry. Huge fortunes have been made in a very few years by protégés of the regime, by people engaged in export-import trade, and by those who helped Arabs from the oil-rich states invest or spend their money in Egypt.[12] In short, a few people have a great deal of money, secured in ways which are questioned, and they flaunt it shamelessly — a thing that was never possible under Nasser.

For ordinary people, it is harder than ever to make ends meet. Most men have to take a second job, and wherever possible, their wives work too. (The girl who can bring in a second salary in the city is more likely to find a husband these days, a factor which should be borne in mind when discussing the behavior of women. There is still little place for spinsters in Muslim society.) One may meet government minor officials or teachers who drive a taxi or keep a shop when they are not in the office. Mothers and fathers worry about their children's education constantly and try to afford to send them to the few, overcrowded, private schools, or send them with misgivings to a class of fifty to seventy in one of the three daily shifts at a government school. They may live in cramped small apartments in enormously crowded popular quarters, with no place but streets for their children to play in, with highrise apartments on every side. Even upper-class families are often driven to live with their married children and their grandchildren in one house or apartment, because housing is simply not available, except to the very affluent. The lack of housing means that marriages must be postponed, a situation which is socially more threatening for women than it is for men.

The purpose of this chapter is to examine reasons that women give for returning to the institution known as *hijab,* or veiling — though as we have seen, this means veiling not the face, but everything else; and not the seclusion of women, but their participation in urban life while wearing a distinct and local costume. Central to the inquiry is a conviction that the choices that women believe they are making when doing this are illuminating in terms of Islam and modernization. Yet women make these choices in the context of a society where men have always played a very strong role. There is a vigorous religious movement going on among young middle-class men. In every national university a group has been formed called "*al-gamiya al-islamiya,*" the Islamic Association. These associations have not been benevolently regarded by the authorities of the university or by the police, but the greater the attempts to hamper them, the greater popularity they have enjoyed. They are largely made up of zealous young men, eager for more knowledge of their religion, and eager to belong to a collectivity that is both visible and larger than themselves. In most cases, they are joined by a number of earnest young women students, no less eager than themselves, and garbed in *ziyy shari*.[13]

The constitution of Egypt states that Islam is "the official religion" of the State. Why, these people ask, is Islamic Law, the *Shariah* not being implemented? Why does the State allow nightclubs to flourish where alcohol, gambling, and prostitution are easily available to those with money? They are not satisfied with the answer that such things have often happened in officially Muslim states before.

Television and radio allot much time to religious programs, with lectures and sermons on Quran, Hadith, and early Islamic history. Private owners of new buildings frequently have unofficial, privately built mosques, called *zawiyas* (though they may have no affiliation with any Sufi brotherhood), set up on the ground floors of their apartment houses. It is said that it is much easier to get a permit to build an apartment house with a *zawiya* than one without. These furnish a locus for neighbourhood men to gather in during the evenings, and thus also help nurture popular piety.

The government, too, has taken steps which nurture this movement, even though it is not popular with the authorities or with the police, who see how easily it could become a powerful political instrument or even the seedbed of a new revolution. The Ministry of Education includes "Religion" in the curriculum, which must be passed like any other course. The Ministry of Waqf allots prizes for memorizing the Quran and prizes for compositions on religious subjects. Most important of all, the government has promised to recodify all secular laws into *Shariah* laws. This promise, even though its practicality is highly problematic, has been repeated several times, and it sets the seal of legitimacy on the demands of fundamentalists.

When asked why *shari* dress is increasing among women, many educated Egyptians are apt to shrug their shoulders, look embarrassed, and reply that they can't imagine. Pressed, they often reply that "it's all because of the Saudis." Yet many Saudis, if they come to Cairo at all these days, come to enjoy themselves, and are not interested in the sort of girls who wear *shari* costumes. True, Egyptians may reply, but the Saudis, and the Libyans, give money to writers and *shaykhs* who will further a fundamentalist version of Islam. There is at least something in this.

A woman student at Cairo University has stated that she received a small sum of money to hand out head-kerchiefs to her classmates, and more money for every woman she converted to wearing *shari* dress; money which came from a Saudi source. It is said that girls who announce their intention to change dress may have a contribution for the cost of their new clothing from various fundamentalist organizations with mysteriously large supplies of money. But although such stories are pointed to by Egyptians to explain the movement, they do not suffice. Egyptian women, we have suggested, are no sheep. No one is likely to persuade them to exchange cooler, more comfortable dresses for *ziyy shari* unless they wish to.

In fact, however, Egyptians who say that the Saudis are responsible for *shari* dress have something else in mind than the tips which women who change their clothing may or may not receive: they usually mean that the revived and powerful Muslim Brotherhood is behind it, and that the Brotherhood is subsidized by the Saudis, and perhaps by the Libyans as well. (There is no quicker way to move a Brotherhood member to rage than just this assertion.) Men who join the Brotherhood have been known to threaten to divorce their wives if they did not adopt *shari* costume. A prominent Egyptian who is a devout Muslim told me how his niece along with other young women at Cairo University had received threats at the university to the effect that if they did not adopt *shari* dress, they would have acid thrown on them. When his niece asked him what to do, he replied that she must know who she was and act according to the conviction: if she adopted *shari* dress only with the thought of pleasing God, she would have done a good deed. If she wore it only out of fear of acid when it went against her convictions, she would not be acting in accord with Islam. In this case, at least, the young woman and several of her friends elected to continue to wear regular international dress.

It appears, therefore, that male fundamentalist pressure on women to conform does occur, but it would still be wrong to imagine that behind almost every woman in *shari* dress there is some stern member of the Brotherhood or its offshoots.

I recall a student of mine in Cairo, the very pretty daughter of a prominent father (this may be worth mentioning, in case anyone thinks that only homely girls, or girls of humble background, are attracted to the covering), who appeared one day in class wearing *shari* costume. I congratulated her on her new dress, and she volunteered that she was now very happy and had a real sense of peace with herself. She said that she had often not known really who she was before, had felt "pulled this way and that," to "act like other girls." Now, she felt, she had taken her stand;

she knew who she was—a Muslim woman. Also, she said, young men would not mistake her for an easy mark; they could see what sort of girl she was. Thus she had solved some sort of personal identity crisis, and she had protected herself to some extent against the attentions of the persistent men who annoy women on the streets and in the crowded trams, trains, and buses of Cairo. Protection against unwelcome attentions is often advanced by women as a reason for adopting *shari* costume; I have even known of Western girls and women who in desperation resorted to *shari* dress to avoid unpleasantness. It is a reaction against the aggressiveness of young men who as a result of the alienation of life in the crowded, faceless city behave in unacceptable ways, and it is also a reaction against urban alienation among women.[14]

As I became interested in the question of why women adopt *shari* dress in modern Egypt, it became ever clearer that women who did felt that they were "solving problems." Even those who tended to defend it on fundamentalist grounds: "I am a Muslim woman; this is what my faith demands of me," responded somewhat differently when they were asked what had conditioned this response to a demand that, after all, Islam has appeared to make for a long time, and which has not always been so clearly heard. I began to ask Egyptian friends and colleagues to ask women in their own circle of acquaintances how they came to put on *shari* dress.[15]

Some of the reasons were personal and rather superficial. Some women said that they had put on *shari* clothes as a result of a vow that if God would give them a son or the husband they hoped for, or in some way respond to them in their personal problems, they would put on *shari* dress. A significant answer commonly given was: "I did it to reject current behavior by young people and contemporary society." Other answers were: "I began to look for something to do after the 1967 War. This seemed to me to be the right thing. When I saw some other women putting on *shari* dress, I decided that that was what I wanted to do too."

"Up until 1967, I accepted the way our country was going. I thought Gamal Abd al-Nasir would lead us all to progress. Then the war showed that we had been lied to; nothing was the way it had been represented. I started to question everything we were told. I wanted to do something and to find my own way. I prayed more; and I tried to see what was expected of me as a Muslim woman. Then I put on *shari* dress."

"1967 was the rude awakening. Then in the 1973 War, it seemed that God was answering our prayers. We had become too careless before. Now we want to respond to God with faith."

Another response often heard was that women had put on *shari* dress because they were afraid of *inhilal,* which may be rendered as "dissoluteness" or "disintegration in society." The personal affirmation involved in *shari* dressing thus seemed a way of applying at least some remedy to a society falling apart.

Another woman said "Once we thought that Western society had all the answers for successful, fruitful living. If we followed the lead of the West, we would have progress. Now we see that this isn't true; they (the West) are sick societies; even their material prosperity is breaking down. America is full of crime and promiscuity. Russia is worse. Who wants to be like that? We have to remember God. Look how God has blessed Saudi Arabia. That is because they have tried to follow the Law. And America, with its loose society, is all problems."

One middle-aged woman responded with a frank and significant explosion. "Really, I wonder what people expect us to do. Nasser put us under Russia's armpit. The Russians didn't want to help us; they wanted to dominate us. Then we were lied to and put in the 1967 War. Then Sadat comes and turns to America. The Americans didn't want to help us; they exploited our longing for peace to make us give concessions to their pet dog, Israel, and humiliate us. And the prices went up and the thieves made fortunes and we said 'that's capitalism.' And our rich 'Arab brothers'; did they want to help us? Did they care about all we had suffered for thirty years for the 'Arab Nation'? No, they wanted to measure out their *riyals* and their *dinars* and keep Egyptians boys fighting for Palestine. To whom shall we turn for help, if not to God? In Him alone I will put my trust!"

Many women who still wear Western clothing said that they were seriously attracted by *ziyy shari*. They might put it on in the future. They admired the women who had done it. They thought these women had demonstrated strength of character.

Nearly all the women questioned felt that industrialization, technology, and education in the sciences were good, and *also culturally neutral*. They saw no reason at all why a change of dress should impede the appreciation of these goods, though they often spoke of "false progress" and corruption in society.

One of the striking comments — which other women agreed with — was by an intelligent woman who said "There are so many problems in Egypt today that we don't know the solution for. It seems that only God can change them. We have problems with housing, with budgets, with the schools, with transportation, with electricity, butagas and water, and the telephone doesn't work. When we put on *ziyy shari*, we feel that at least here is one problem we can solve for our families and society for ourselves. At least we've done something." Other women spoke of wanting to be, or do, something authentic (*asìl, haqiqi*).

What can one gather from all of this? Certainly that no one single reason for adopting *shari* costume is given, but that circumstances conjoin to move women to do it.

Urban alienation, fear of the future, desire to protect the family, turning to God in problems that appear insoluble, and a desire for authenticity in a rapidly changing society all appear to play a role in the decision of matrons. What is one to conclude about young unmarried women who become fundamentalists and adopt *ziyy shari*? As we have suggested, it does not appear to stop them in the pursuit of a job, or in finding a husband: it may in fact put them in contact with a large group of potential husbands, e.g., the men of the *gamiya islamiya*.

There is another reason, one which none of the women questioned directly mentioned, but one which we may infer. We have alluded to the concern of Egyptians about "the wild behavior of youth," and a desire of women to "repudiate contemporary morality." The smoke that these veiled and general terms allude to rises from real fire, though it often escapes the notice of members of the sexually permissive societies of America and Europe. It is also a phenomenon hard for Muslim conservatives to come to terms with, because they do not like to admit that it is there, except as an example of the corrupting influence of "the West." Nonetheless, the factors which produce it are rooted in contemporary Egyptian social realities, and perhaps also in the well-known strength of Egyptian femininity. Simply stated, it is this: lack of available housing and economic difficulties make it necessary for the young urban people to postpone marriage, or at the least postpone the consummation *(dukhla)* after the formal contract of marriage (the *aqd,* which in this context functions much like a betrothal). Girls who study or work and who leave the house have freedoms and temptations denied to those kept at home until the wedding night of an arranged marriage. Men are traditionally allowed some freedom by the double standards of Islamic custom if they must postpone marriage, women are not. Yet today some girls (by traditional Muslim standards, far too many girls) solve the problem thus posed by having illicit relationships. Others solve it by rigid self-repression and religious fundamentalism. It is their way of dealing with a modern problem, and one which is socially and religiously acceptable.

It is to be hoped that we have suggested that *ziyy shari* in modern Egypt is not simply part of a fundamentalist revival of Islamic rigor, or of an obscurantist reaction against modern civilization, but one highly nuanced way in which women in this society are trying to deal with real problems: a rational response to an intolerable situation.

The social problems encountered among the urban middle classes of Egypt have produced an overwhelming sense of frustration, despair, and loss. The strains impel many Egyptians — men and women — to try to reconsider their lives and reconstruct them.

The problem of identity, the continuing social debate over identity — Egyptian, Arab, modern Mediterranean, Islamic — looms especially acute for Egyptians today. The search for identity and for authenticity turns people to the Law, just as social frustration turns them to God.

Certainly modernization and political development in the Islamic world do not seem to follow the pre-ordained patterns of America, or Europe, or the Soviet Union. The social models of the West and of Russia are less attractive than ever. Modernization is not being questioned; false models and false friends are being questioned. Though one woman spoke admiringly of Saudi society, very few would see it as a model for Egypt; indeed, the identification of these new ways with Saudi Arabia seems usually to both critics and fundamentalists a damaging one to make. A new Egyptian revolution is very possibly in the making. If the present government cannot respond to people's needs and longings, there will certainly be a reckoning, and the Muslim Brotherhood will try to win as much advantage for itself as it can from the new situation. One concludes that in the materially poor and traditionally rather hedonistic society of contemporary Egypt, women though seemingly powerless continue to have opinions and to mold opinions, and that in matters regarding the family and the structure of society, Muslims will continue to tinker with what they borrow from abroad until it feels right.

∞ 5 ∞

Islam in Pahlavi and Post-Pahlavi Iran: A Cultural Revolution?

Mangol Bayat

*T*HE 1978–79 IRANIAN REVOLUTION is too often perceived by the superficial observer, the uninformed media representative as well as the religiously inclined Iranian himself, as symbolizing the rise of Islam and the Muslims against its enemies from within and without. To many Western readers such a "resurgence" marks the end of the era of modernization and progress in Iran, since the new leadership of the nation aims at "turning the clock backward." To their mind Islam is synonymous with the fundamentalist, black robed, "turbaned" religious leaders. Clerical authorities in Iran seem to justify such perceptions. This monolithic view of the Islamic revolution also reflects misconceptions of Islam and Islamic history perpetuated by a certain type of Western scholarship and uninformed Muslims themselves. Thus it is too often argued that the *ulama* (plural of *alim,* men learned in the religious sciences) have, throughout the centuries, been the sole spokesmen for Islam, and that they have always constituted a distinct, socially and ideologically cohesive class of their own. Such views need rectification if one is to understand the full implications of the current revolution.

SHIISM IN PREMODERN TIMES

Ideally Islam recognizes no separation of "church" and state, since the original Muslim community, as set up and led by the Prophet Muhammad himself during the last ten years of his life, demanded both religious and political commitment on the part of its members. To profess faith in

87

Islam required not only a profession of faith in the oneness of God and in the prophethood of Muhammad, but also to abide by the latter's religious, moral, legal, and political commands. For he was both the Prophet-Legislator and the executor of divine directives. However, the actual implementation of this theocratic ideal ceased soon after Muhammad's death in 632, as the state that succeeded him failed to attract universal Muslim allegiance. Since he left no specific instructions regarding his succession, problems of legitimacy and authority, with far-reaching repercussions on the religious and sociopolitical development of the Islamic societies generations later split the community from the start into rival factions. Furthermore, neither the Quran the revealed scripture which is believed to be the source of all knowledge and encompassing all rules necessary to regulate the life of the faithful, nor the Prophet's *sunnah* (practice) as recorded in the *hadith* (compiled words and deeds attributed to him by reliable transmitters), provide specific answers to questions that Muhammad did not raise or face himself or that did not exist in his time. Yet, the expansion of Islam shortly after his death into vast Asian, African, South and East European territories, raised complex issues which required immediate solution. Generations of Muslim leaders, confronting the dilemmas of integrating conquered peoples with definite sociopolitical and cultural patterns of their own, absorbing alien ideas and world views imported from the conquered lands, dealing with socioeconomic forces that constantly threatened to shake the very foundation of the Muslims unity, saw themselves forced to compromise the theocratic ideal. Different sects, different dynastic or individual centers of localized power fragmented the Empire into separate religious and/or geo-political entities. The degree of compromise and its resulting effect on the society varied according to time, place, the sect, and/or the political leadership the particular society followed. With the exception of a few extremist sectarian cases, Muslims in general came to accept the de facto secularization of politics and to grant a certain measure of legitimacy to rulers who had seized power through sheer force.

With time, temporal power more and more fell into the hands of the mightier and not necessarily the most pious or most qualified by religious standards. The social and spiritual influence of a group of men who had established for themselves a solid reputation as specialists in the religious sciences proper, correspondingly increased. While not interfering with the authority of the temporal state, the *ulama* came to conceive of themselves as the guardians of religion and the protectors of the Muslim law, without, however, giving themselves exclusive or overpowering rights as a dominant class. In fact, while reserving for themselves the practice of private and commercial law, they generally accepted the state's judicial prerogatives over questions of public law based on local customs and not on the *shariah* (Muslim law). Though confronted with the discrepancy between the theocratic ideal of single leadership over a united community, and the reality of political fragmentation and pluralistic views, the *ulama* made no attempt at doctrinal reforms. Instead they continuously maintained the ideal while, paradoxically, justifying and rationalizing the historically established facts. They merely counselled the rulers to follow the "just" path, enjoin the good, and forbid evil. In no Muslim society had this compromise had such remarkable effects, positive as well as potentially explosive, as in Shii Iran.[1]

Imami or Twelver Shiism, claiming that succession to the Prophet is a divine right inherited by his direct descendents, recognizes no legitimate leader other than Ali (d. 661), his cousin and son-in-law, and eleven of Ali's descendants. However, no *Imam* (lawful leader of the Shii community), aside from Ali, ever acceeded to power as head of the Islamic state, despite several early attempts which invariably ended with crushing defeats and bloody massacres. Consequently the sixth *Imam* in line, Jafar as-Sadiq (d. 765), ordered his followers to give up armed struggle and adopt instead an attitude of acquiescence towards the Sunni state. In 874 the depoliticization of Imami Shiism was completed when rival claims to the Imamate and internal strifes induced the Shii *ulama* to declare the twelfth *Imam,* who apparently had died in his infancy, occulted (alive, ever present in this world, yet invisible—the "hidden Imam." By 940, it was officially declared that the occulted *Imam* shall not return till the end of time. This practical doctrine enabled the leaders to postpone indefinitely the realization of the Shii claim to political power. For, implicit in the doctrine of Occultation, is the conviction that the time was not yet ripe for the "true believers" to establish the reign of the "just." More importantly, it meant that temporal rule is not one of the necessary functions of the *Imam,* thus further accentuating the spiritual and theological priorities it had chosen earlier. The theoretical separation of temporal power from divine authority, a necessary consequence of the doctrine, became an established fact.[2]

Outwardly abiding by Sunni political rule, the Shii *fuqaha* (jurists) enjoyed a certain measure of freedom to further develop their theology and jurisprudence. Anxious as they were to safeguard this freedom and, at the same time, to firmly consolidate their position as the religious leaders of the sectarian community, they felt compelled to restrain the revolutionary, millenarian impulses inherent in original Shiism as it developed in the first two Muslim centuries amongst the politically active opponents of the Sunni state. To do so effectively, they defined the term *ilm*, knowledge of the divine, as knowledge of the religious sciences and declared the gate to *ilm* in the former sense closed until the return of the Imam at the end of time.

Knowledge, *ilm*, in Islam has an exclusively divine meaning, God being its only source. The Koran is not only the source of religious knowledge, but also the definitive sum total of all knowledge men need to know. Though Shiism accepts this view that Muhammad's revelation was final and complete, it expects a further perfection of its understanding. The task of "unveiling the esoteric meaning" of the holy texts was regarded as the exclusive function of the *Imams*. This notion of esoteric truth, as opposed to the exoteric or literal understanding of religion, provided the early Shiis and other more extremist sectarians with a rationale for their respective deviation from majoritarian norms. It justified their conception of a special category of beings entrusted with the sacred duty of gradually revealing to the initiates the "esoteric truth" hidden in the Koranic and traditional texts. Through highly elaborate devices, texts could be reinterpreted in such ways as to provide legitimacy to the nonconformists while helping them maintain their faith in the Koran. A possible consequence of this belief in *ilm* as an omniscience, the exclusive property of the "chosen ones," is the conviction that they would also be the ideal political ruler, the deliverer from distress. Thus amongst some radical Shiis, this messianic belief in the perfect human leader who would restore true order and justice by establishing the ideal rule of the Sage, initiated independent political revolts against existing regimes. The medieval history of the Muslim world in general, and Iran in particular, offer ample evidence of the threat such messianic movements brought to the sociocultural and even political establishments.

Contradictions inherent in original Shii millenarianism and the *fuqaha's* apolitical stand surfaced when in 1501 Ismail, founder of the Safavid dynasty, came to power as a result of such a messianic revolutionary movement. He declared Shiism the state religion of Iran, and lay claim to the *Imam's* vigerency *(niyabat)* through alleged descendency from the line of the eighth *Imam*, while assuming the ancient Persian kingly title of shah. Thus by fusing into one what had officially developed as two separate functions, he revived the old Islamic ideal of theocracy. The Shii *ulama*, resident of southern Iraq and the Persian Gulf area, who were invited by the Shah to settle in the country and promote the Shii creed, accepted the political sovereignty of the Safavids to whom they owed their very raison d'être in Iran. Nonetheless, they failed to grant the shahs legitimacy over religious affairs. In the eighteenth century the traditional secularization of politics was effectively restored when the *mujtahids*, the highest ranking *fuqaha* (jurists), who had by then firmly consolidated their socio-religious influence, directly challenged the Safavids claim to the *niyabat* in order to collectively assume the title themselves. However, claiming religious authority as vicegerents of the Imam in no way entitled the *mujtahids* to political rule. The jurisdiction of the *mujtahids* as interpreters of the Imam's will, "was tantamount to specific matters covered in the corpus of the Shiite *fiqh* (jurisprudence); these did not include normative provisions regarding rulership."[3] On the other hand, the Shah was compelled to abide by the sacred Islamic law. As guardians of the *sharia,* the *fuqaha* acted as advisers, judges, teachers, financial trustees of charitable and private endowments, custodians of the orphans and the poor. They thus succeeded in institutionalizing their influence which, though totally dependent on the Safavids in the beginning of their reign, gradually separated itself from the state.

The concept of the *Imamate,* formulated and enforced by learned theologians of the seventeenth and eighteenth centuries, came to be defined in eschatological, other-worldly terms, having lost its original connotation of political leadership.[4] Consequently Safavid Shiism emerged as the religion of the quiescent, pious, inner-worldly faithful who, shunning politics, patiently awaits the return of the *Imam,* his Saviour, which would mark the end of time. He dutifully submits to the authority of the state which regulates his public life, and of the theologians who guide his private and religious life. Shii orthodoxy, however, was constantly challenged from within the ranks of the *ulama* themselves. The intellectually restless and speculative thinking *ulama,* who rebelled against the *fuqaha*'s legalistic approach to religion, devoted their studies to the "forbidden" disciplines of philosophy and mysticism. The philosophers stressed the primacy of reason over faith, the mystics that of divine inspiration and/or spiritual initiation. Both developed ideas and theories which orthodox *fuqaha* condemned as "heretical," either because such ideas did not strictly adhere to their own prescribed views, or because they were too dangerously close to refuting some fundamental doctrines of Shiism. Both the philosophers and the mystics, the *urafa,* emphatically challenged the *fuqaha*'s notion of the gate to *ilm* being closed. To the *fuqaha*'s conception of *ilm* as knowledge of the religious traditional sciences, they opposed the original meaning of the term as knowledge of the esoteric truth. Reminiscent of the extremist sects is their insistence on the right of the "chosen qualified ones" who possess true *ilm* to initiate their adepts. However, unable to openly espouse some theologically controversial ideas without risking *takfir* (to declare someone an infidel), the "deviators" reverted to a

rather abusive use of esoteric writing destined to a very select private audience, while publicly professing orthodoxy. This cautious compromise,
time honoured in the Muslim world, allowed the speculative thinkers a
certain measure of freedom to develop truly non-orthodox views of religion. Despite the relentless war waged by the orthodox *fuqaha,* Shii mysticism, philosophy, and speculative theology escaped the stifling confine-
ment imposed by the latter and, through the centuries, flourished as an
alternative to "official Shiism."

The fall of the Safavids from power in 1722, the half-century of
political instability and chaos that followed, and in 1779 the accession to
the throne of the Turkic Qajar tribe whose monarchs, though assuming
the title of "shadow of God on earth," neither sought religious sanctions
nor claimed descent from any *Imam*'s line, enhanced the chances of the
fuqaha to further institutionalize their religious authority. They ensured
their influence by making *taqlid* (following the religious guidance) of a
living *mujtahid* incumbent upon all believers, regardless of their rank and
position in society. They did not hesitate to use coercive means to enforce
their views and suppress any other that might have contradicted, hence
challenged, their position as the sole exponents of religion and its protectors against any kind of "innovation." However, it is worth noting here
that the resulting centralization of the religious leadership was not aiming
at "modernizing" the "national church," as some erroneously maintain.[5]
Similarly, throughout the greater part of the nineteenth century the
ulama's concern was not the nation. Their religious policy was not a national policy, nor was it meant to be. It is also important to stress here
that the *fuqaha* were not "deemed the leaders of the nation."[6] To attribute
to this group's activities at that time any kind of nationalist, modernist
ideology, would be entirely misleading and anachronistic, to say the least.

Contrary to the commonly held view, the *ulama* in Qajar Iran, or
even before then, did not constitute a uniform, ideologically cohesive,
distinct class of their own with binding allegiances and loyalties. Internal
factions, divergence of religious outlook, conflicts of interests that often
shifted some *ulama*'s concern from purely religious to economic and political considerations, seriously divided their ranks. For after all, even in
the nineteenth century when the *mujtahids* emerged as a viable powerful
group, broadly speaking, the *ulama* formed a loosely defined association
with no clearly marked delineation. A number of them owned land and
shared common interests with the landowning class as well as the wealthy
merchants. Some were related to the royal family or to some tribal chief-
tains. Many held government appointments, including the powerful position of *Imam juma* (chief religious leader in a town or city), and received

stipends from state officials, royal patrons and wealthy individuals. Similarly the *ulama* included within its ranks not only *fuqaha,* but also philosophers and speculative theologians, mystics of all sorts who formed their own respective orders with separate hierarchical organizations, "deviators" heading a variety of movements more or less openly active. Dissatisfied elements from within these different groupings often built up intricate networks of communication and means to promote their views over rival ones. A highly elaborate system of expedient alliances, more or less short-lived, was developed among them, attracting the patronage of some powerful members of the ruling classes who had common vested interests. One important theme gained ascendency in the nineteenth century among groups and individuals representing different layers of the social structure. It stemmed from an old conception of religion and religious laws as progressively evolutionary, continuously undergoing change. Such a view of religion naturally constituted a radical deviation from orthodoxy. Yet the idea that religious laws have to undergo constant adjustment to times and social conditions proved supremely attractive to many who wished to remain loyal to Shii Islam yet were committed to reforms they deemed vital, as well as to the revolutionary-minded who thought more in terms of socio-political changes.[7] Since education was almost exclusively religious, received in the *madrasa* (schools administered and taught by the *ulama*) where religious studies formed the bulk of the curriculum, practically the entire educated class of the nation who had not joined civil service was considered as *ulama.* These individuals wore the turban as a sign of distinction indicating their "learned" status. Yet, paradoxically enough, the most virulent anti-*fuqaha* stand came from within the ranks of the *ulama* themselves, among those who defied official orthodoxy. Shii dissidents, periodically encountering the relentless hostility of the orthodox *fuqaha,* continuously rejected, albeit mostly in private secluded circles, the authority of the religious establishment. Charging the latter with anti-intellectualism, they maintained an attitude of resistance to religious conformism, and sought to widen their intellectual horizon. In fact the most lasting and fiercest feuds that divided the society into several enemy camps and often plunged whole regions into bloody civil strifes involved, not the secular state and the religious leaders, but orthodox *fuqaha* and religious deviators, or two rival schools of theology. The secular state was not only tolerated but condoned by the *fuqaha* themselves as a religious necessity, since it formed an integral part of the entire Islamic social structure of Iran and not a separate evil force. In pre-Pahlavi Iran when religion, based on Shii ethics, permeated all aspects of national life, intellectual, political, and even economic, nothing would be

further from the truth than to claim that the *fuqaha* were the sole exponents of Islam, or that they represented the collective voice of religious
conscience.

MODERNIZATION

The Constitutional Revolution of 1905–11 best illustrates this point.[8] It
did not rally all members of the merchant and *ulama* classes together with
the nascent group of secular intelligentzia in opposition to all members of
the Qajar state. Men and women belonging to diverse interest groups and
religious affiliations were loosely associated to a single common cause for
totally different reasons. They formed alliances that were not intended to
outlive the immediate goal once it was accomplished, namely the establishment of a national assembly that would check the despotic power of
the Qajars. Some leading *mujtahid*s gave their support to "deviators" or
to followers of "deviators", such as Malkom Khan, Talibzada, Mirza Aqa
Khan Kirmani who were partisans of a secular state and of far-reaching
social, political, and cultural reforms aiming at severely curbing the influence and authority of the *fuqaha*. Similarly, the Constitutionalists
included "turbaned" individuals (Malik al-Mutakallimin, Sayyid Jamal
ad-Din Isfahani, Majd-ul-Islam, Nazim ul-Islam Kirmani, all followers
of Jamal ad-Din "Afghani") who ideologically were closer to the secularists than to the *fuqaha*. On the reactionary anti-Constitutionalist side, influential *mujtahid,* such as Fazlullah Nuri, gave their support to the
Shah's effort to safeguard his dynastic interests. The Kirmani members of
an important school of theology, Shaikhism, considered controversial by
orthodox *fuqaha,* stood by the Qajars side, while a rival branch in Azer-
baijan declared itself in favour of the Constitution. It is worth noting here
that, even from amongst the most zealous Constitutionalists, rare were
those who called for a republic or another dynasty to replace the Qajars.
Neither the institution of the monarchy itself nor the secular state were
questioned. Only the Qajar policies were.

The Constitutionalists were unable to save the National Assembly from its enemies for too long. Their feuds, purposeless and unideo-
logical, proved even more disruptive than their naive belief that they
could build a modern political system based on a traditional society.
Nevertheless, they left one lasting contribution that deeply affected the
future course of Iranian social history: the secularization of Iranian social
thought. Despite the vital leadership of some *mujtahid*s, the revolution
marked the ascendency of the anti-*fuqaha* intellectual element in the po-

litical scene. Prominent decision makers not only demanded the secularization of the educational and judicial systems which previously were
under the control of the religious establishment, but, more importantly,
divorced their sociopolitical views from Islam. Most of them sought their
source of inspiration in the Western European model. With them the concept of *ilm* (knowledge), which in pre-modern Iran was understood to
mean knowledge of the divine in the tradition of the *urafa,* or knowledge
of the religious sciences in the tradition of the *fuqaha,* and which the first
generation of nationalist dissidents (Afghani, Malkum, Talibzada and
others) had broadened to include all the sciences, was thoroughly secularized. It became synonymous with the Persian root word *danish* with no
religious connotation. Similarly the term *danishmand* was used to distinguish the man learned in the secular sciences from the *alim,* the man
learned in the religious sciences. Also with the Constitutionalists the anti-
fuqaha stand, which had previously expressed the *urafa*'s resentment of
the orthodox jurists' intransigent anti-intellectualism, turned into frank
anti-clericalism. Whereas the earlier generations of reformers had cautiously demanded religious reforms that would help religion adapt itself
to new sociopolitical conditions, and even attempted to reconcile their
new ideas with Islam, the Constitutionalists wished to confine religion
and religious views within the walls of the mosques and *madrasas* turned
seminaries. Doubtless a great number of them were fully aware of the fu-
tility of doctrinal reforms, given the experience of ill-fated movements
that marred the history of the nineteenth century. Iranian constitutionalism and liberalism at the turn of the century had no room for religion. On
the other hand, some of the *mujtahids*' efforts to accommodate constitutionalism, sovereignty of the people, to Shii Islam proved to be nothing
more than a justification, rationalization of the proconstitutional stand
of the liberal *ulama.*[9] It was not accompanied by a new view, or a new
conception of the role of Islam and of the Shii dogma in twentieth-
century Iran. Thus the doctrinal conflicts with aspects and theories of the
"new learning" and new sociopolitical systems that were nationally
adopted in the Constitutional period, were left unresolved. Furthermore,
the dismissal of theological restraints and taboos which the *fuqaha* had
imposed for centuries upon Iranian thought, broke down the fences that
had artificially contained different groups of intellectuals and professionals within the loosely defined class of the "turbaned." A new class of intellectuals and professionals, writers, journalists, lawyers, teachers, politicians, orators, philosophers, came into being, with separate interests and
group allegiances. Their anti-clericalism did not mean they were anti-
religious, or that they wished to eradicate religion from society. Rather
their secular nationalist ideal transcended their Muslim identity which for

them had become a matter of private conscience. Similarly, the *ulama* were, for the first time in Islamic Iran, emerging as a separate professional class of *fuqaha,* theologian specialists of Islamic *fiqh* (jurisprudence), and as *ruhaniyyum,* spiritual guides. Thus limited by their traditional expertise, they proved themselves vulnerable in comparison to the secular professionals whose education prepared them better to assume political and social leadership.

The stripping of the clerics' traditional role and function was gradual. For the Constitutionalists had proven themselves powerless in constructing the new society with well-founded modern sociopolitical institutions. It was not until the Pahlavis came to power in the 1920s, and implemented the secular socio-cultural policies as first defined by the Constitutionalists, that the *fuqaha* suffered major setbacks and were finally pushed further back to their mosques and *madrasa*s. With the exception of the brief interlude (1941–53) of political freedom when they, and other secular groups, vehemently protested against the dictatorial regime, the religious opposition was ineffectual in having its voice heard. Education was made compulsory in the state secular schools, and the judicial system was brought under the jurisdiction of a Ministry of Justice headed and staffed by secular educated lawyers and jurists. The modernization of the educational and judicial systems, using mostly western models, was the most effective weapon manipulated by the Pahlavi regime to undercut clerical influence which it considered as the most resisting obstacle to its radical nationalist reform policies. To further undermine the role of the religious leaders, the Pahlavis sought to give the nation a cultural identity which, though not totally displacing Islam, at least lent their state a semblance of legitimacy. Thus in pre-Islamic Iran they found a rationale for their imperial designs and their basically modern secular views, as well as authenticity for the "Aryan" self-image they wished to project in contrast to the Islamic one.

These trends had already been revived in the past. In the tenth and eleventh centuries the Buyids had restored the ancient Persian concept of kingship (a term Islam theoretically rejects since incompatible with its conception of God as the sole "king") which helped them acquire legitimate status as lawful temporal rulers paying nominal allegiance to the Sunni Abbasid Caliph.[10] Successive minor dynasties in Iran followed suit until the Safavids fully restored it as an integral part of the Iranian Shii theory of government. Similarly, ancient Iranian kings and legendary heroes provided motives for literary and artistic expressions throughout the Islamic period, thus keeping alive a nostalgic attachment to ancient traditions. Nauruz, the Zoroastrian festive holiday celebrating the begin-

ning of the spring equinox, had survived as a national feast observed annually. The Pahlavis fully integrated these cultural traditions, giving
them official status. Nauruz, adopted as the day marking the beginning
of the Iranian new year in a revised calendar, was declared the most important national holiday, thus displacing Muslim festivities. School textbooks stressed ancient Iranian history and the role of the shahs in the
Islamic period, emphasized "the genius of the Aryan" culture, and linked
the Iranian cultural and historical continuity from pre-Islamic times to
the present with the institution of monarchy. However, whereas in earlier
times the *fuqaha* had acknowledged the necessary existence of kingship,
leading clerical opponents of the Pahlavis adamantly refused to sanction
their authority. They now rose in defense of Islamic law and morality, so
severely displaced by modern reforms.

It is important to note here that the messianic and eschatological
features so characteristic of original Shiism and which orthodox theologians kept checked for centuries was reactivated. Thus modernization
finally provoked the *fuqaha* to reverse the long tradition of waging war
against extremist Shii millenarianism, and raise the banner of the *Imam* in
self-defense against a state so determined at annihilating their social role.
All the main traits of Shii millenarianism were fully invoked: *jihad* or
holy war against the infidel; the readiness to die a martyr for a holy cause;
the strong conviction that a true and pure Islamic order would and should
replace the corrupt and evil government; the charismatic appeal of the
leader who lays claim to the *niyabat-i Imam* (vicegerency). The *fuqaha*
who previously were instrumental in the depoliticization of Shiism and
the secularization of politics, now turned into messianic figures aiming at
establishing a theocracy, the rule of the Sage on earth. In the 1960s and
70s the revolution of the *fuqaha,* who, as a result of the Pahlavi policies,
had emerged as a distinct, socially defined, ideologically cohesive class of
its own, was more than just a revolution for the sake of religion. It was a
social and cultural revolution as well. The message of Khomeini's often
quoted work[11] leaves no doubt as to its author's aim: to restore the lost
power of the *faqih* while updating and reformulating his function in
society.

The role Khomeini attributes to the *faqih* is truly revolutionary
not only in the context of Pahlavi Iran, but essentially in the context of
Imami Shii political theory as written down and upheld by successive generations of *fuqaha.* In Khomeini's view, the *faqih* is both the interpreter
of the Islamic law and the only legitimate political ruler of the community
in times of occultation. Thus he declares un-Islamic the concept of kingship and the Constitution of 1906, which recognized the legitimacy of the

monarchy while giving legislative power to the National Assembly. In Islam, he argues, God alone is the Legislator. The Prophet and, after him, the *Imam*s were the executors who implemented the divine law. In the period of occultation, the *fuqaha* assume their task. Thus the old theocratic doctrine which, since the death of Muhammad, had survived only as an ideal theoretically supplemented by a pragmatic justification of secularized politics, now threatens to overthrow the balance, even though strained at times, between the religious and political forces. Ironically, the lay ideologists of the past two decades helped the *fuqaha* to advance successfully their claims.

CULTURAL MALAISE AND THE EMERGENCE OF LAY ISLAMIC IDEOLOGY

The harsh coercive means the Pahlavis used to implement their policies eventually succeeded in alienating not only the *fuqaha* but also the lay professionals themselves who began to view the lack of political freedom as too high a price for the secular programs they, and their precursors at the turn of the century, had hopefully called for. Already in the 1920s and 30s nationalist liberals, strongly resenting Riza Shah's police state, turned against him. Men like Ahmad Kasravi, the historian-journalist-lawyer, whose modernist and secularist ideology, at least in spirit, was so close to the Shah's; Sadiq Hidayat, novelist and amateur scholar of ancient Iranian languages; Malik al-Shuara, the poet laureate; found the new dictatorship morally repellent. As men of the pen, as enlightened thinkers, *raushanfikran,* they commanded respect and a large following among the educated youth who studied in the state schools and universities.

　　With other politically-conscious nationalist professionals, opposition to the Pahlavi regime acquired a religious undertone. Mihdi Bazergan,[12] who was a member of the first group of students sent to Europe on government scholarship, best represents this category. Upon completion of his engineering studies in France where he had the occasion to learn to admire and respect Western social and scientific achievements, he returned to Iran with a heightened awareness of himself as an Iranian and a Muslim. Convinced that religion and faith alone constitute the driving force behind individual and national progress, he challenged the modernists' view that Westernization would rescue the nation from "backwardness." Proclaiming that, to the contrary, the root of all national problems lay in the government's disregard for Islamic laws and principles, he set up religious and professional organizations which he used to propagate his ideas. He also joined other associations bringing together clerical as well as religious-minded lay dissidents fighting for the same cause. Most of these organizations, banned during the reign of Riza Shah, came out into the open in 1941 when the latter was forced to abdicate in favour of his son, and political freedom was granted.

Two important features characterize Bazergan's thought as expressed in most of his writings: 1) his differentiating the "real Islam," a socially and politically committing ideology, open to necessary reforms, from what he termed the traditional stagnating Islam. 2) though he collaborated with politically-committed clerical figures, his Islamic political views did not reflect the theocratic ideal of a state. While championing Islam and Islamic moral values, Bazergan was revealing a deeply-felt disillusion and disenchantment with the West and Western values, so symptomatic of the sociocultural malaise that gripped the nationalists as a result of Western economic and political encroachment in Iranian affairs. In Islam he saw a moral bond, a vital cultural identity that would help rejuvenate the patriotic zeal needed for the nationalist struggle against the imperialists, their lackeys at home, and the morally corrupt materialists. Though in his lectures and in his writings he displayed the moral tone of a traditional Muslim preacher, politically he chose to side by Mossadegh, the prominent secular nationalist leader of the 1940s and early 50s, even when Ayatollah Kashani, the then most important clerical opponent of the Shah, withdrew his support. Moreover, Bazergan's political views did not offer a new conception of the state, but rather suggested the revival of the 1906 Constitution, with some amendments and the guarantee that the clause specifically calling for a council of clerical experts as advisory board would be implemented. Thus the government he wished to see established in Iran was a secular government enjoying the blessing of religious sanction. Neither Bazergan, nor any other contemporary liberal lay intellectual (*raushanfikr*) who nurtured similar anti-western political sentiments and simultaneously rose in defense of traditional national values and culture, ever contemplated a return to the old socioreligious order.[13] Their view of society and their conception of knowledge, thoroughly modern and secular, differ from and, more often than not, oppose the *fuqaha*'s. They are in tune with the secular spirit of social change deemed necessary and innovated by the Constitutionalists at the turn of the century. However, whereas the latter group looked up to the West as a source of inspiration, contemporary nationalists wish to redefine, reformulate the whole process of modernization and no longer to equate it with Westernization.

The emergence of radicalized Islamic ideology in Iranian politics can be viewed as an inevitable consequence of the fall of Mossadegh from power following the CIA staged coup in 1953. Political and economic factors account for domestic crisis that led to the 1978–79 revolution and the emergence of the *fuqaha* as leaders of the opposition: an increasingly dictatorial regime outlawing all independent political parties; following the death of Mossadegh in 1967, his National Front party, which had gone underground, rapidly disintegrating into several ideological factions though remaining under the same umbrella; the secular nationalists' inability to produce a single national secular leader of a stature comparable to Mossadegh's. In contrast, the religious hierarchy, despite heavy social and economic setbacks inflicted upon them by the government, had remained virtually intact, producing capable leaders. In addition a widening economic gap separated the few rich from the vast majority of poor, and a growing number of middle and lower middle-class youth despite their secular education in the state institutions, are religious-minded and resentful of the privileged Westernized upper classes, identify more closely with the Islamic opposition.

It is the economic and cultural alienation of this important segment of the population, educated, increasingly self-aware, mainly urban, middle and lower middle classes, that constituted a formidable power base for the Islamic revolutionaries. Impatient with the secular liberals and the moderate *raushanfikr,* restless and demanding, eagerly awaiting the signal for them to rise for a "just cause," the Iranian youth of the 60s and 70s looked elsewhere for leadership that would totally commit them to radical political action. In 1963 Khomeini showed them the way, only to be arrested and then exiled. Ali Shariati,[14] the Sorbonne educated sociologist, who had perfectly understood the mood of the young, was then able to provide them with an ideology that fulfilled both their desire to remain loyal to their faith and their urge to undertake a revolution. Shariati's particular genius lay in his ability to fuse into a single ideology seemingly contradicting social, economic, and cultural ideals, and thus offer to all types of politically committed Iranians a united cause. Three predominant aspects of Shariati's thought are worth analyzing within the context of the present paper: his anti-clericalism, Islamic reformism, and third-worldism.

Like Bazergan, though in a more radical fashion, Shariati differentiated the "true Shiism," liberating, future oriented, progressive, from the reactionary religion of the corrupt, oppressive, power-thirsty "official clergy." In addition to the political despotism of the kings, and to the economic exploitation of the property owners, Shariati depicted the deceit of the "long-bearded official clergy"[15] as the main source of evil that plagued the masses throughout the centuries. Islam, he argued, recognizes no mediation between man and God; hence the existence of a clerical class of *ruhaniyyun* is unIslamic. The Muslim learned men in religious sciences possess no official status, no inherent power or hereditary rights. They are ordinary individual scholars who have come into being in Muslim societies "out of necessity and not officially," deriving their influence from the people who gave it to them on their own free will.[16] Implicit in this definition of the Muslim *ulama* is Shariati's categorical refusal to grant them any authority beyond that acquired as scholars and teachers of their special discipline. He even denied them the right to consider themselves as "vicegerents of the Imam" since the *Imam* has not appointed any.[17] Elsewhere he firmly argued that the *ulama*, who have reduced Islamic sciences to the narrow discipline of *fiqh,* are not learned in the true comprehensive meaning of the term.[18] Here then, Shariati followed the traditional argument of the *urafa,* the philosophers and mystics who, in reaction to the *fuqaha*'s denunciation of their "deviating" views, claimed the latter group had no knowledge of "true *ilm.*" It is no accident that his works are replete with praises for the Muslim mystics. Such praises reflect both his own emotional attachment to and intellectual affinity with the *arafa,* as well as the influence of his father, Muhammad Taqi Shariati, a scholar and admirer of Persian mysticism. In the introduction to one of his works, Ali Shariati's eloquent reference to Ayn al-Quzat, a Persian Sufi sentenced to death in 1132 for his heresy, is most enlightening. "Seeking refuge in history, out of fear of loneliness, I immediately sought out my brother Ayn al-Quzat, who was burned to death in the very blossoming of his youth for the crime of awareness and sensitivity, for the boldness of his thought. For in an age of ignorance, awareness is itself a crime. Loftiness of spirit and fortitude of heart in the society of the oppressed and the humiliated . . . are unforgivable sins."[19] Bearing in mind that the mystics, the philosophers, speculative thinkers in general who refused to abide by established orthodox norms, were persecuted by the *fuqaha* and not so much the secular state; one can understand Shariati's violent condemnation of the orthodox religious leaders such as Baqir Majlisi (d. 1699). For he held the latter and other fellow Safavid *fuqaha* responsible for stifling "true" Shiism and establishing instead "official" religion.

Perhaps Shariati's most lasting achievement lies in his attempt to present a new, invigorating, inspiring, conception of Islam. By resurrecting the old spirit of revolt and martyrdom which characterized original Shiism, and reactivating the millenarian tradition, he succeeded in turning the religion of the pious faithful into a viable political, revolutionary ideology. As already stated, revolutionary *fuqaha* like Khomeini, Talighani, Shariatmadari and others, had also turned to the millenarian tradition their predecessors had persistently waged war against. However, while making use of messianic language and metaphors, the militant clerics were primarily interested in a revolution that would help them and fellow clerics come to power and restore their lost influence in society. In contrast, Shariati, the lay revolutionary ideologist, relentlessly emphasized his Islam is a "reformed and renewed Islam."[20] He constantly wrote and talked about the need for an "Islamic Protestantism" to help make Islam once more a positive sociocultural force that would abolish the dark age and usher in the age of the renaissance.[21] Though he respected the revolutionary and "true" theologians who did not collaborate with the despised Pahlavi regime, Shariati conceived the "reformer" as a member of the *raushanfikr* group, and not the *ruhaniyyun*. It is the *raushanfikr,* he again and again asserted, the committed, enlightened intellectual, who is best qualified to lead and reform. For, in modern times, the *raushanfikr* replaces the prophet of earlier times, since he gives birth to new social movements, even new cultures.[22] Whereas Khomeini addressed himself to the "real good Muslims" within Iran and beyond its frontiers, Shariati deliberately appealed to "enlightened" men and women, be them believers or non-believers, pious or not. In fact he directed his message to "any enlightened mind who thinks independently and wishes to serve his society as well as relate to his generation and his time."[23] His own religious view, Shariati told his audience, is not based on the belief in the superiority of Islam over other world religions; nor is it based on a particular religious idea or sentiment. It is a social faith.[24]

Whereas Khomeini proclaimed the religious right of the *faqih* to rule the nation, Shariati spoke of the *raushanfikr* and the *mujahid* (fighter for a holy cause) whom he contrasted to the *mujtahid* (high ranking religious official).[25] Khomeini proposed a *vilayat-i faqih* (the rule of the religious jurist) to be entirely founded on an all-encompassing Islamic law; Shariati called for Islamic reforms he deemed vitally needed to enable the Muslims to follow the path of progress, reforms which only the *raushanfikr* could initiate. Whereas Khomeini insisted on reinstating the *fuaqha*'s hold over all the social institutions they controlled in the past, Shariati defined Shiism as the "religion of protest."[26] *Intizar* (expectation of the Imam), he wrote, is the opposite of reactionary traditionalism; it means "futurism," that is, to look forward with hope and not backward, no matter how golden the past seems to have been.[27]

The cultural malaise and the resulting crisis of identity which a number of educated Third World men and women experience simultaneously left its deep mark on Shariati's thought. He was fighting a war on two fronts: the political establishment, and the culturally Westernized segment of the population which, though numerically insignificant, had assumed an influence of disproportionate magnitude. In addition, he was engaged in a bitter denunciation of Western imperialism both at home and in other Third World countries. Of all the different facets of imperialism, political, economic, cultural, he feared the latter most. Thus he never failed to sound the alarm and warn fellow Iranians of the evil consequences of such cultural dependence on the West.[28] To combat imperialism, he argued, the Third World youth who are committed to their respective nationalist causes, must strive to "return to their roots" as determined by the history, the culture, and the language of their society. His own search for cultural authenticity led him to Islam; it alone lies at the root of the Iranian culture. He pleaded with the "committed" Iranians to "go back" to their Islamic roots to find the necessary strength to defeat Western imperialism, and ensure national independence. Here too, Shariati's view of Islam fundamentally differed from Khomeini's. He openly admitted the Islam he had in mind is not Islam the tradition, or a particular doctrine, or a social order, but an ideology, a faith generating social consciousness. The search for one's roots, he claimed, is not restricted to religious believers alone. In fact, he added, the issue was first dealt with by "progressive, non-religious intellectuals," such as Aimé Cézaire, Franz Fanon, Sanghor, Katib Yassin, Al-i Ahmad. Neither of them were of the "religious type." They all belonged to one world-wide movement led by "anti-imperialist leaders of the third world," accepted by all ideological wings.[29]

To anyone acquainted with Shariati's writings, the wide divergence separating his religious views from Khomeini's, or other religious leaders, is striking. His stand, by far more radical than Bazergan's, alarmed even the revolutionary-minded *ulama* who could not fail to foresee the potential danger of his implicit deviation from religious orthodoxy and of his relentless denunciation of, not only the clerics who collaborated with the Pahlavis, but also of the traditionally-minded *fuqaha* in general. However, while the revolution was in the making, these differences, consciously or unconsciously, were minimized practically by all those who were involved in the revolution. Shariati's immense popularity could not be overlooked, or dispensed with. Throughout the 60s and 70s, his voice rang loud and clear in university and public halls; his transcribed lectures were distributed and widely read throughout the nation and abroad, thus drawing an audience which, numerically as well as in the diversity of its class composition, certainly surpassed Khomeini's in the pre-revolution period. The years he spent in prison, and his premature death in the summer of 1977, far from decreasing his popularity, provided him with a halo of martyrdom so necessary for an Iranian hero to achieve immortality.

THE AFTERMATH

To understand the current problems of the revolution and the fierce power struggle among the various religious-minded groups, one must perceive the Islamic ideology in its proper perspective. For the deep division that has now split the ranks of the various leaders and their respective followers into rival factions represents more than the inevitable sociopolitical convulsions and upheavals that normally accompany any revolution once its first target is accomplished. Rather it is symbolic of the dichotomy that has traditionally existed in Imami Shii circles among proponents of the *fuqaha*'s orthodoxy and those of the speculative thinkers, the "deviators." Just as, throughout the past centuries the two opposing camps fiercely fought for the right to promote their respective views of religion, presently the clerics and their supporters on the one hand and the "radical" or "militant" Muslims on the other are engaged in a battle the outcome of which might decide the fate of, not only Islam in Iran, but the political future of the nation. For the struggle involves more than just two rival parties striving to control power. It underlies the adamant determination of one social group, the "turbaned," which had lost its influence as a result of three-quarter of a century of modernization, to regain ascendency at all cost and, once again, establish its hegemony firmly based on religious populism. To do so successfully, it must revert to its traditional stand as protectors of "orthodoxy" and mercilessly wage war against the "deviators"—in other words, resume the position of official religious authority so vehemently denounced by Shariati in all his works as one of the three oppressive forces that dominates society and "oppose God and the people." In pre-Pahlavi Iran Shii speculative thought and orthodoxy coexisted within a large, loosely-defined association of *ulama* with a secular state acting as a "neutral" outsider regulating, even manipulating the interaction of the two trends. Hence differences of opinion and pluralistic religious outlook survived the *fuqaha*'s persecution, as long as the "deviators" outwardly professed orthodoxy. The current politicization of Shiism and the fusing of political and religious authorities into one leave no room for religious dissent not even Shariati's Islamic reformism.

There is no doubt that, at least for the time being, the *fuqaha* have to crush all dissent in order to maintain themselves in power. The modern educated lay professionals who refuse to accept their politics are their prime target. To aim effectively, the *fuqaha* must turn anti-modern, anti-secular, and fundamentalist, since currently their very raison d'être in Iranian politics is religion as interpreted in its most literalist fashion. For instance, the doctrine of *ghaibat* (occultation of the *Imam*), never before seriously taken advantage of, provides their newly-acquired political power with a rationale. Literally understood, the doctrine alleges that in the vacuum created by the absence of the "true leader," only the "learned" in Islamic law are best qualified to rule in order to protect the community and the Law from the "infidels'" design. The Law must therefore be restored and fully enforced literally. Polygamy, male-biased divorce procedure, even the veil for women, and other aspects of laws pertaining to private lives of Muslim men and women which need reform, are reinstated. Education must return to the Islamic fold, hence the entire system is to be "purified" and purged of its corrupt, corrupting elements. Although Khomeini claims that he does not intend to divide *ilm* (knowledge) into two separate categories, Islamic and non-Islamic, he insists it must be founded on Islamic morality and values. The cultural revolution of the Islamic Republic, aiming at freeing the university system from its past bond to the West, is in fact establishing severe clerical censorship which the Constitutionalists at the turn of the century had eliminated. In the last analysis, the clerics, acting as the champions of Islam, symbolize the erosion of national secular values, and the enlargement of the religious in the realm of human loyalty and devotion. Shariati's followers and the anti-clerical nationalists view this stand as a sacrifice of socioeconomic issues which demand priority.

For Islam to survive destructive fundamentalism, doctrinal reforms are necessary. Only then could one speak of cultural revolution. Such was the message of Shariati and other religious-minded ideologists and politicians. In the past the *urafa* rescued Shiism from fundamentalism by challenging the *fuqaha* from within their ranks, using the same religious sources and arguing within the framework of speculative theology. At present, there exists no reform-minded theologian willing to undertake seriously the task of doctrinal reforms. In fact, at the turn of the century and throughout the Pahlavi era, philosophers and theologians alike were dislodged by politicians. Politics, political ideologies, took over philosophy and theology. More often than not the *raushanfikr* himself was nothing more than a polemicist, a light weight thinker committed to an immediate political goal which distracted his attention away from more creative, more constructive analytical thought. An intellectual like Shariati succeeded in ideologizing Islam, yet drastically failed actually to reform the dogma. He had no program to offer, only fiery revolutionary rhetoric and inconsistent sociological analysis of religion. Anxious as he was to prepare the way for the revolution, he was left with no time, or he could not produce solid theories. He did not live to see the revolution, and his followers, the *raushanfikran* (plural of *raushanfikr*), were left with no solid, concrete foundation to build on what he had started.

At present the *raushanfikr* has acquired the vague, loosely defined, ideologically heterogeneous, multi-functional character the *ulama* had in pre-Pahlavi Iran. The religious-minded lay intellectual or professional might find himself in an increasingly isolated position, left without the support of the scientists and other modern types of intellectual "deviators." For, unlike him, they have chosen a clear-cut secular path, feeling no longer, if they ever did, the need to speak the language of religion now associated with the political establishment. If pushed against the wall for too long, the religious-minded *raushanfikr* might then wish to close ranks with the secular dissidents. And the circle would then be completed. For the *fuqaha* would once more prove themselves vulnerable in comparison to the modern educated professionals. Islam, the faith, would survive as it has survived the sociopolitical upheavals of premodern times, and the secularization process of the Pahlavis. Islamic ideology might not, since it supports the politics of totalitarianism.

The Arab-Israeli Wars, Nasserism, and the Affirmation of Islamic Identity

Yvonne Haddad

A VISITOR TO THE ARAB WORLD cannot but note the intensification of Islamic identity that has taken place in the past several years. The Islamic nature of the area is apparent in the flood of conservative religious literature in the bookstores of Egypt, the availability of Muslim Brotherhood publications in Bathist Damascus, the rise in the number of veiled educated "liberated" women, and the general tenor of the society. The militant actions of Jamiyyat al-Takfir wa-al-Hijrah, the attempt to enforce Islamic laws of reform in Egypt and Kuwait, the permission for Maruf al-Dawalibi to visit Syria, the rising academic respectability of writing texts from the Islamic vantage point – these and many other phenomena can be cited as illustrations of the increased measure of Islamic identity.

The writing of texts from a specifically Muslim perspective, of course, is in part due to the competition among faculty at Egyptian universities for the highly remunerative teaching positions at the many new institutions of higher learning in the Arabian peninsula. Also influential are the academic conferences on Islamic subjects sponsored by these Arabian universities and by the Muslim World League. By focusing on Islamic topics, they have directed historical and social science research into specific channels, and have fostered a network of authors and professors committed to the pursuit of such research.

The rise of Islamic consciousness is in no small part the result of the Arab-Israeli wars of 1967 and 1973. It is also the result of political and military realities, realignments and perceptions of these confrontations as well as the end of the Nasser regime and its policies. The existence of Israel in the heart of the Arab world has had a dramatic effect on the growth and development of modernity, reform, and Westernization in the area.

107

Western historians and social scientists will never be able to understand fully the Arab/Islamic interpretation of the current state of affairs in the Arab world as well as the Muslim view of historical process without coming to terms with the meaning of the existence of Israel for Arabs. Although Israel and its supporters may perceive its existence in the heart of the Arab world as a purveyor of modernity and technology for the area, for Arabs both Muslim and non-Muslim it serves as a constant reminder of their impotence and failure. It is crucial to the understanding of the Islamic view of history to see that for Muslims the existence of Israel is a condemnation and a sign that the forces of darkness and immorality, of wickedness and apostasy, have for reasons yet unexplained, taken the ascendancy in the world.

After thirty years of pain and struggle, of sacrifice and suffering, the Arab cannot fathom why Israel continues to prosper and become stronger while his people are weaker and more helpless. Israel is seen as part of the confrontation and effort at domination of the Arab world by the Western colonial powers. Many publications refer to Zionism as a modern version of the Crusades,[1] an insidious conspiracy of the Western Christian world in its continued hatred and enmity toward Islam. Recent publications about the role of the city of Jerusalem and its central place in Muslim piety echo the concerns of medieval writers who saw in the Crusades an infidel incursion against Islam. Jerusalem must be under Muslim domination in order to guarantee the worship of the true God. Both the Christians and the Jews have deviated from the true way; control of this sacred city must therefore be in the hands of Muslims whom God has appointed to be the guardians of His truth.[2]

The religious significance of the Arab-Israeli conflict was enhanced by the loss of the holy city of Jerusalem (al-Quds). This loss was aggravated by Israel's attempts to Judaize the city through the systematic eradication of its Arab influence.[3] This was carried out by the policy of expropriation of Arab land and the demolition of Arab housing, the expulsion of eminent intellectuals and leaders of the Arab community, and the imposition of the Israeli curriculum on Arab schools which distorted the historical claims Arabs have for Palestine. Israeli policies also encouraged Jewish settlement of the area by providing subsidies for settlers as well as the construction of high-rise apartments "the Cement Jungle" around the Arab sector of Jerusalem aimed at truncating it from other Arab communities and rendering it into a ghetto.

The activities and speeches of Rabbi Shlomo Goren of the Israeli armed forces alerted many Muslims to the possibility of the destruction or expropriation of the Muslim holy places. Besides holding services in the

Aqsa Mosque, Rabbi Goren affirmed his intent to rebuild Solomon's Temple[4] (on the grounds where the Mosque now stands). These fears were also fanned by the archeological excavations around the mosque which precipitated the weakening of the existent structures and necessitated the installation of supportive beams. The several Zionist conferences calling for the restoration of Jewish places of worship and the high-handed manner in which the Judaizing policy was and continues to be implemented did little to allay the fears in Arab minds that the Israeli government would seek the eradication of Muslim holy places, especially the Aqsa Mosque because of its historical significance. Thus, the burning of the Mosque on August 21, 1969, by an Australian Christian fanatic escalated the fear of what was perceived as part of the Zionist conspiracy.

The religious significance of the Israeli occupation of the Holy Land and the burning of the Aqsa Mosque in 1969 was reflected in a letter written by Nasser to the armed forces in which he said:

> I have waited and thought a great deal about the terrible crime inflicted against the holy of holies or our religion, our history and our civilization. At the end, I did not find anything but the new affirmation of the meanings that were evident to all of us from the first day of our terrible experience. There is no alternative, no hope and no way except through Arab force, using all we are able to muster, to allocate and to pressure with, until the true victory of God is achieved.
>
> We have opened every door to peace, but the enemy of God and our enemy closed every door in the way of peace. We left no means untried, but the enemy of God and our enemy obstructed the means, blocked the roads and made evident to the world what was hidden about his nature and intent.
>
> We are before an enemy who was not satisfied by challenging man, but through his arrogance and insanity transgressed by challenging the sacred places that God blessed and willed as houses for Himself.
>
> I want our men, officers and soldiers to understand the feelings of the last two days and be aware of their meaning, to appropriate in their conscience the conscience of their nation and to know in their depths that they shoulder the responsibility not carried by any army since the descent of revelations from heaven as guidance and mercy for the world.
>
> They, in their next battle are not the soldiers of their nation only, but the army of God, the protectors of His religions, His houses, and His Holy Books.
>
> Their next battle is not a battle of liberation only, it has become necessary for it to be one of purification.

Our vision is focused on the Aqsa Mosque in Jerusalem as it suffers from the forces of evil and darkness.

Whatever our feelings at this moment may be, we pray to God as believers, in awe, that He may grant us patience, knowledge, courage and capacity to remove evil and darkness.

Our soldiers shall return to the courtyards of the Aqsa Mosque. Jerusalem will be returned to what it was prior to the age of imperialism which strove to spread its hegemony on it for centuries until it (Imperialism) gave it to those who play with fire.

We shall return to Jerusalem and Jerusalem will be returned to us. We shall fight for that. We shall not lay down our arms until God grants His soldiers the victory and until His right is dominant, His house respected and true peace is restored to the city of peace.[5]

A flood of literature appeared as an essential response affirming the centrality of Jerusalem for Islam.[6] The Fifth Conference of the Academy of Islamic Research of Al-Azhar in 1970 devoted a substantial part of its proceedings to the topic of the Islamic nature of Jerusalem and Palestine.[7] In his opening speech, Muhammad Fahham, Rector of al-Azhar, affirmed that historically, the Arabs were the first to inhabit Jerusalem (3000 B.C.). Jewish settlement in the area came later (1200 B.C.). Consequently, if historical precedence is used as an argument for right of possession the Arabs were the original inhabitants.

Moreover, the religious arguments that Palestine is the promised land for the Jews is rejected as obsolete since God's promise had been fulfilled in history and the Jews had forfeited their right to the land having broken the covenant and committed evil.[8] Thus, Jerusalem's religious significance for the Muslims is contingent on the Muslim concept of prophecy which sees all prophets as Muslim since they were sent by God to affirm His guidance for humanity which He initiated with Adam and fulfilled in the Quran as revealed to the Prophet Muhammad.

Also, of unique importance is the fact that God has blessed Jerusalem with special significance since He has repeatedly chosen it as the place where His revelation was made manifest. In the case of Islam, its centrality is heightened through its being the place from which Muhammad ascended to heaven during the Isra and Miraj.

Crucial to an understanding of the wars with Israel is the perception of victory and defeat within the Quranic context. The Quran is very explicit that victory will be given to those who are with God. Israel's victories then stand as a condemnation of the Muslim *Ummah*. The Arabs apparently have lost because God has forsaken them. This gives rise to a series of related questions: Has God given the victory to Israel because she has been found more zealous in commitment to His purposes? Is it possible that Judaism is the more correct way of life? Has God forsaken the Muslim nation? What are the reasons for the apparent victory; have the Muslims been tested and found wanting? Each war with Israel has elicited different justifications and reasons, depending on the particular perceptions Muslims have had of themselves.

It has been relatively easy to justify the debacle of 1948. The loss of Palestine can be blamed on the colonial powers, especially Britain, that nursed the Jewish immigrants into a sizable community in Palestine and provided them with training and armaments, while decimating the Arab resistance and bleeding its human and material resources during the disturbances of 1936–39. The Jordanian army in the meantime was led by British officers who deliberately disobeyed the orders of King Abdullah in favor of England's command to cease fighting once the demarcation lines were reached. Jerusalem, which had already surrendered to the Transjordan army, was granted as a gift to the Israelis by Glubb Pasha.

The defeat of the Syrian forces, meanwhile, was clearly due to their disorganized condition, lack of leadership, and the treasonable behavior of some government officials. During the French occupation, which had ceased only three years earlier, the Syrian army was led by Christians, Alawis, and other minorities due to France's policy of ruling the majority (Sunni Muslims) by the use of minorities. Upon gaining independence the Syrian government had removed the core of officers, who had been pawns of the French regime, rendering the army ill equipped with no trained officers and in no way ready to fight the Israeli forces. The Egyptian army was in no better condition. Egypt itself was occupied by British forces, and the king and government were puppets administering the policies of the resident British High Commissioner.

Thus, although the 1948 war ended in defeat of the Arab armies by 1949, genuine reasons and excuses were found to cope with its disastrous impact.[9] Given the condition of the Arab forces, it has been easy for Arab historians to understand the ease of the Israeli victory, especially given the duplicity of the colonial powers in providing Israel with arms while denying the Arab troops any such assistance during the armistice. The defeat was not only proof of the present military impotence of the Arab nations; it also provided a dramatic end to the romantic period in which the West was perceived by many modernizers as primary representative of a system worthy of emulation in the search for full participation in the modern world.

Events had been leading in that direction for decades. The occupation of the Arab world by Western forces, the failure of Britain to live up to its agreement after the First World War, the mockery made of parliaments by occupying forces, the travesty of the human rights of indigenous citizens, and the steady and insistent support of Western nations for the creation of the state of Israel put an end to the dreams of the romantics. Any student of the careers of literary and reformist figures such as Taha Husayn, Abbas Mahmud al-Aqqad, Sayyid Qutb, and Ahmad Amin can find in their writings the shock of realization that the West they loved and championed had spurned them again as unfit partners. These and other authors turned back to their roots in an attempt to find a more authentic existence and a reliable *raison d'être*. For each one the creation of the state of Israel was incomprehensible. The West that had promised so much had in the end jilted them, not because they did not measure up to its requirements but for the specific reason that they were Arabs. By treating them as nonpersons the West not only violated Arab faith, but in effect invalidated their very existence.[10]

The revolt of 1952 in Egypt was welcomed by the masses and the army because it eliminated the discredited leadership under King Farouk that was a puppet of the British and had proved impotent in Palestine. Also backing the revolt was the Muslim Brotherhood organization, then in its heyday of power. It rejected the West not because it had failed to live up to its promise as did the romantics; rather it rejected it because of what the West was, alien, and therefore potentially leading Arabs astray from the true path of Islam. The Brotherhood, along with the conservative Muslims, maintained that the Muslims were weak because they had abandoned Islam. The Muslims were in the condition they find themselves in, defeated and backward, because they had ceased to strive for God's purposes and consequently God had abandoned them. For the Arabs to regain their position of leadership, of ascendancy, and of power, they must cease to champion alien ideologies, put away the worship of the gods of materialism and technology, and return to the true faith and a life committed to the way of God in obedience and humility. Only then would God give victory over the enemies of Islam. The Muslim Brotherhood was not opposed to technology. It established factories in different areas of Egypt to provide sources of employment, and was progressive to the point of organizing unions for workers and championing their rights. Its main creed was that to be modern is not to be Western, but to be truly Muslim, recognizing the traditions of Islam and its authority over all aspects of life, seeking answers to today's problems from within the Quranic revelation which is eternally sufficient and valid.

Others reacted to the creation of Israel by calling for a rearmament program that could match Israeli power and be able to replace the foreign rule that was established on Arab land. What was most galling to them was the fact that while most colonies were winning their freedom from colonial rule, the British with the might of the Americans planted an alien people in the heart of the Arab world. The Israelis were seen as tools by which the colonial powers would suppress the hopes and wills of the burgeoning Arab nations.

Rejection of the West, of course, was not the only response to the 1948 war. Some actually called for a renunciation of all Arab culture and the total appropriation of Western technology on the grounds that Israel's victory is the proof that to be modern one has to be Western. In this understanding traditional moral and ethical considerations must be renounced and the "new morality" of might over right adopted. Israel has provided the perfect example of this kind of modern morality in which people count only insofar as they can successfully fight for their rights. The United Nations, on which was pinned all hope for the ushering in of an era of brotherhood, human rights, and equality, turned out to be a tool in the hands of the imperialist Western forces. True justice was ignored in favor of force and the might of arms as thousands of Palestinians were thrown from their homes in order to make room for the European Jews that Europe and the United States did not want.

The second major confrontation between the Arabs and Israel occurred in 1956. It confirmed for the Arabs Israel's role in the area as an agent of imperialism and colonialism. The confrontation came as a result of collusion between the governments of Britain, France, and Israel as a response to Nasser's nationalization of the Suez Canal. Rebuffed by John Foster Dulles because he had purchased arms from Czechoslovakia, Nasser saw no alternative but to seek Russian help in building the Aswan Dam. Once again the Arab world became a victim of the Cold War which was then at its peak.

Although Britain, France, and Israel occupied the Sinai and the Canal areas in a very short time, the outcome of the war was perceived as a victory for Nasser. For centuries the Western powers had pressured the Middle Eastern nations to follow policies that are beneficial to the West. They had removed rulers who refused to do their bidding, formulating legal and economic policies favoring Westerners over the native peoples. They had used their armies and navies to eradicate all resistance. Thus Nasser's ability to stand up to the dictates of the West and insist on making decisions that benefit the interests of the Egyptian people was hailed as a great achievement. Whether he won or not in practical terms was insignificant. The important thing was that he was able to withstand pressure and to tell the aggressors that the Arabs will not be pushed around any longer. Despite the fact that the tripartite aggression resulted in extensive devastation of Egyptian land, and that the army was routed and the economic loss was huge, Nasser came out of the war with the image of a hero who saved the world of Islam from another humiliation. He had led Muslims, therefore, to what was perceived as a moral victory.

Political events following the 1956 war led to the further growth of Nasser's prestige and power and his increasing use of Islam. These included union with Syria and the insistence on a policy of nonalignment between East and West. Nasser was also successful in obtaining Russian aid in building the Aswan Dam and in training and supplying the armed forces. The union with Syria encouraged socialist planning for the United Arab Republic. When Syria broke away, Nasser set in motion socialist reforms that were meant to fashion a new Egypt, a program that was to remove it from its backwardness and bring it into the twentieth century. The landowner class was legislated out of existence through the Land Reform Act that limited the acreage any person could possess. The land was distributed to the farmers and cooperative agricultural societies were initiated.

Western occupation of Egypt provided the opportunity to rid Egypt of its resident entrepreneurs. As agents of Western influence on the economy, they were perceived as a threat to Egyptian interests. Thus Nasser nationalized both Western companies and large indigenous businesses. The effort was concentrated on the development of a new Egypt and its citizens as persons who could proudly raise their heads among other men.

In this brave new world of the revolution that was to lead Egypt to its longed-for goals, there was no room for critics or dissidents. The Muslim Brotherhood was silenced through the execution of a few of its leaders and the imprisonment of a substantial number of its members. Al-Azhar and Islam were reformed by several decrees, leading to virtual nationalization of the religious institution. Thus the religious leaders and most religious literature became an effective agency legitimizing the government and its policies. These reforms were instituted in 1961 under the leadership of Mahmud Shaltut, the new reactor of al-Azhar whose reformist ideas coincided with those of the Revolutionary Council. They were expounded in Law 103 that reorganized that venerable institution.[11] A ministry of al-Azhar was begun, making religion one of the areas supervised and maintained by the government. Official academic recognition was extended to graduates of al-Azhar, placing them on a par with graduates of secular institutions of learning. Furthermore, the title Rector was changed to the more religious one of "The Grand Imam and Shaykh al-Azhar." It was also determined that the Vice-Rector and all the college deans were to be appointed by presidential decree.

Through the action of this reform, the Azhar was divided into five institutions. These included:

(1) Al-Azhar Higher Council, which was to function as the general administration of the complex.

(2) The Islamic Research Academy, perceived as the highest body for Islamic research, whose function was "to work to revitalize Islamic culture, purify it from unwelcome foreign accretions and traces of political and sectarian fanaticism, and restore it to its pristine condition."

(3) The Institute of Islamic Missions designed to provide trained religious leaders to help spread Islam abroad.

(4) Al-Azhar University, which was to consist of several colleges concerned with Islamic Studies as well as colleges for Arabic studies, business administration, engineering, agriculture, medicine, and industry (Art. 34). The law provided for free education and an equal opportunity to all Muslims.

(5) Al-Azhar Institutes, including the al-Azhar Institute for Women, providing primary and high school education for women in preparation for university training.

Also in 1961 the government nationalized the press and the news media. All writers and authors, even literary artists, as well as any person involved in the dissemination of news, became employees of the government. With this kind of tight control the government was able to censor anything not in line with its own propaganda. In 1962 further consolidation of governmental authority was attempted. A charter entitled *al-Mithaq* was published outlining the guidelines of the revolution and presented to the National Conference of Popular Forces for deliberation. Whereas the Constitution of 1956 declared Islam as the state religion,[12] the draft of the charter of 1962 advocated religious freedom and gave equal status to all religious faiths:

> In their essence all divine messages constituted human revolutions which aimed at the re-instatement of man's dignity and his happiness. It is the prime duty of religious thinkers, then, to preserve for each religion the essence of its divine message. . . . The essence of the religious message does not conflict with the facts of our life; the conflict arises only in certain situations as a result of attempts made by reactionary elements to explain religion—against its nature and spirit—with a view of impeding progress. These elements fabricate false interpretations of religion in fla-

grant contradiction with its noble and divine wisdom. All religions contain a message of progress.[13]

Besides elevating other faiths to the status of Islam, the *Mithaq* emphasized national consciousness. The true expression of Arab national consciousness was "unity, liberty, and socialism;[14] Islam was merely a component of Arab nationalism.[15] It was recognized as an element in the achievements of the revolution in the past ten years, but ranking only fifth in importance.[16] The *Mithaq* also proposed socialism as the direction of the state.

With the al-Azhar reforms of 1961, the government relegated the religious institution to an arm of its own operation. A great number of *ulama* became government functionaries, and a substantial amount of their literary output was a religious justification or apologetic of the regime. An article in *Majallat al-Azhar* explained that "the task of al-Azhar in its new era is to inculcate the new, revolutionary thought and understanding in the people's mind."[17]

Whereas orthodox Muslims have always believed that the Islamic state "would protect and propagate Islam, would strive for the realization of Islamic ideas, and would apply Islamic laws,"[18] under the Nasser regime its function became one of providing Islamic apologetics and interpretations for the policies of the government in order to propagate socialism and implement its goals.

Nasser's use of Islam to legitimate his Arab nationalist/socialist ideology and to enhance his status as a leader in the Arab world did not go unchallenged. Saudi Arabia was also looked upon by many as a concrete example of God's favor precisely because of its rise in power and prestige. Wealth and progress, as we have seen, are regarded in Islam as signs of God's approval and potency as a gift of His mercy. Thus Saudi success provided an impetus to a re-emerging sense of Islamic identity for all Muslims at the same time as its financial support of other Arab states tempered their socialist zeal. Saudi Arabia did not come into this role suddenly. Faysal's efforts at combating the influence of Nasserism date to the early sixties. The formation of the Muslim World League, Rabitat al-Alam al-Islami, and its efforts at propagating the Islamic way of life through sponsorship of conferences and lectures on Islamic subjects were aimed at providing an Islamic alternative to Nasserism.

Nasser's involvement in the war in Yemen[19] set him against Saudi Arabia and its ally, America. His emphasis on "Islamic socialism" enabled Nasser to attack Saudi Arabian Islam as reactionary and stifling. True, Islam was that which would lead to the modern victory of the Arab people and not to retardation and decline. He further criticized King Faysal's calling of an Islamic summit which was co-sponsored by Faysal and the Shah of Iran. Nasser attacked this "Islamic Pact"[20] in a speech on February 22, 1966, and condemned it as an imperialist conspiracy "using religion as a tool with which it can restore its influence."[21] The "Islamic Pact" was portrayed as a move away from Arab unity. "The imperialist reactionary alliance aimed at spreading the idea of Islamic unity to counter Arab unity. It agreed that the Islamic countries of the Baghdad Pact should work for Islamic unity. . . ."[22] Nasser saw this stress on Islamic unity as a threat because it would of necessity include non-Arabs, thus diffusing the efforts that were needed in addressing the immediate problems of the Arab world—Israel.

In the spring of 1965, the Muslim World League held its second conference in Mecca,[23] agreeing to espouse Islam over against nationalistic considerations. This was, of course, contrary to the Egyptian ideology of Arab nationalism. Nasser perceived in the League's goal an imperialist conspiracy to eradicate the gains of the revolution.

Relations between Egypt and Saudi Arabia worsened. While Egypt supported the Yemeni Republicans, Saudi Arabia gave aid to the Royalists. Both nations worked to undermine each other's ideologies. It is as a result of the sharpening of this controversy between the Islamic and the Nationalist ideologies that we find the most intense debate about the present and future of Islam. In the context of this debate, particularly on questions of allegiance and destiny, one finds the focus of the ideological concerns of the seventies. The debate, of course, was in effect the continuation of the 1952 Egyptian revolution, for manning the agencies of the Muslim World League and editing its publications were many of the members of the Egyptian Muslim Brotherhood who had sought asylum in Saudi Arabia when their society was banned.

Egyptian attacks on Saudi efforts continued. Saudis were accused of championing imperialistic causes and of impeding the liberation of the struggling Islamic nations.[24] Besides attacking the reactionary forces (*al-rajiyyah*), the Egyptian government sought to insure that its employees supported its ideology.[25] Thus it embarked on a thorough program of indoctrination that included the *ulama*[26] to prepare them for their revolutionary role in society.[27]

The fear of subversion or the teaching of unauthorized interpretations of Islam led to the Egyptian government's censorship of the Friday sermon[28] and insistence on focusing on pertinent topics. Among the themes expounded in the literature was the affirmation that the revolution was based on faith, *thawrah muminah.* It did not draw its ideas from posited theories or rational philosophies, but rather was inspired by the *shariah,* "one that is whole, eternal, and valid for every time and place."[29]

The ideology of the revolution was presented as the heart of the Islamic *dawah* (mission). Islam was seen as identical with socialism,[30] and deviation from socialism in Islam as one of the causes of retardation. Other expressions of the intricate relations between socialism and Islam led to interpretations such as that which said Muhammad's message was a socialist response to a capitalist society in Mecca which had a class structure. "Muhammad forbade usury because it is an expression of the capitalist system,"[31] thus suggesting that the Quran may be of human rather than divine origin. Even Sufism was seen as socialist in origin by the head of the Sufi orders.[32]

Besides being socialist, Islam was presented as revolutionary. It was seen first and foremost as a revolution against corruption,[33] and the revolution of July 23, 1952, was said to have "materialized the heart and content of Islamic revolutionism in a practical manner."[34] It came into being "for spiritual values and the revivification of the religious heritage of the Arab person."[35] In fact, not only was Islam presented as revolutionary and as a driving force, but Nasser even said that "Islam *is* revolution."[36]

The literature on Islamic socialism is extensive. Various efforts were made to reinterpret the life of the Prophet and his Companions so that one finds titles describing the socialism of the Prophet *(Ishtirakiyyat Muhammad)*,[37] of his wife *(Umm Ishtirakiyyah: Khadijah Bint Khuwaylid)*,[38] of Umar *(Ishtirakiyyat Umar)*,[39] and of Abu Bakr *(Ishtirakiyyat Abu Bakr)*.[40] Typical are works such as that by Ahmad Farraj entitled simply *Islam, the Religion of Socialism.*[41]

Under Nasser Islam continued to provide the aura of divine legitimation and validity for proposed social, political, and economic reforms. Even though the programs failed, Islam survived precisely because of the Nasserite emphasis on the Islamic aspect of this brand of socialism which kept radical groups from introducing extreme proposals for change. Through suppression of dissent and a carefully orchestrated propaganda machine (which included the religious leaders and institutions) Nasser maintained a feeling of developing power, or potency, of belonging to the modern world. A sense of pride was growing, an identity as a people who could no longer be described as "the mat over which powerful nations wipe their shoes."

The third Arab-Israeli war in 1967 came at a time of the recapturing of Arab/Muslim pride, of great hope, and of a feeling of maturity. The internal and external causes of the war for both Israel and Egypt are not crucial for an understanding of Arab/Muslim response. What is important here is that the defeat was total and catastrophic. While the Israelis felt bolstered in confidence and powerful in their strengthened position and holdings, the Arab world, defeated, stood once again naked, vulnerable, the laughing stock of all the world. Less agonizing than the humiliation of the present defeat was the collapse of faith in the future and despair over any means of survival.

For the conservative Muslims, the war of 1967 proved a vindication of what they had been saying all along. The ways of "Islamic socialism" are not the ways of God. The defeat came as a punishment from God because the Muslims once again had placed their faith in alien systems and devoted their energies to the posited purposes of these systems rather than zealously working for the purposes of God. They had marshalled their efforts for the pursuit of materialism, not only ignoring God, but manipulating His revelation to serve their own purposes. The only way to recapture ascendancy and victory is by a total renunciation of man-made ideologies and a reorientation toward an unwavering commitment to the realization of Islam in the world. Israel did not get the victory because it represented a better system or a truer religion or a more perfect response to God's revelation; rather God used Israel to punish His errant nation and allowed the forces of evil to conquer the Muslims because they had strayed from the Straight Path. The defeat was thorough because they had deviated so greatly.[42]

Other Muslims, less conservative yet just as painfully feeling the defeat, ascribed it to lack of preparation and planning. The causes of the defeat, they felt, were in the inability to mobilize the masses and bring them into the twentieth century. Still others felt that the defeat was a failure of the Arabs to modernize. Ascendancy in the modern world comes only through creative inventiveness and technological know-how. Unless the Arabs were willing to discard their worn-out heritage, irrelevant to the modern world, they would never be able to join the ranks of the civilized nations.

Some of the more radical socialists[43] felt that this defeat may have brought an end to the socialist experiment in the Arab world. What they regretted was that socialism had been neither radical enough nor sufficiently influential to bring about its purposes. It had compromised itself by allowing the revolution to be colored with an Islamic aura which rendered it vulnerable in several areas. By maintaining the influence of religion over people's lives, it thus restricted the liberating forces of revolutionism from implementing drastic changes to produce the new Arab person.

Thus after the initial shock of defeat, self-criticism and condemnation became common responses. No one, of course, was satisfied with the state of affairs, but while all advocated some kind of definitive action, there was no unanimity concerning what that course of action should be nor what role the Islamic heritage ought to play. There was again division, in other words, over the constitution of the ideal society for which they were striving as well as what means were to be used to arrive at that goal.

The Arab world descended into a kind of psychological morass while struggling with these questions, from which it did not emerge until the 1973 war with Israel, referred to as the October or Ramadan war. As if the pendulum had again made its swing, Arabs viewed this conflict as a clear victory over Israel. That is, had not the United States intervened so decisively and replaced Israeli armaments, the Arabs would surely have defeated their opponents.

The portrayal of the "Crossing" *(al-ubur)* has acquired Exodus dimensions in the recounting of the war. In the religious literature that is produced by the Sadat propaganda organization there is a definite indication of an Islamic victory. This is supported in the first place by the Sadat maneuver of ridding himself of the socialists in 1971, referred to as the Rectification *(al-tashih)*. Seen from the perspective of political science as a move to the right, this action had a strong religious connotation; President Sadat in announcing the Rectification program made it clear that the nation would henceforward be built in *iman* (faith) and *ilm* (knowledge, science). *Ilm,* being validly open to interpretation as religious knowledge, has been seen as a clear support of the role of religion in the state. Even Sufi orders that had gone underground during the Nasser regime now operate in the open and hold their Mawlid services in season.

The religious significance of the October 1973 War was obvious since it occurred during the Islamic holy month of Ramadan. The code name for the war was Badr, a reminder of the first Islamic victory under Muhammad in A.D. 623 over the forces of apostasy which, like its twentieth-century counterpart, was fought against seemingly overwhelming odds. In the 1967 war the battle cry of the Arabs was "Land, Sea, Sky," implying faith in equipment and the tactics of military engagement. In 1973 the cry was more explicitly Muslim, the call of "God is great *(Allahu Akbar)*," with which Islam has spread the message of God through major portions of the world.

It is not unusual to find Muslim writers who specifically ascribe the 1973 victory to God and His forces. One even wrote that "white beings" were seen aiding in the fighting on the side of the Egyptian army, an obvious reference to the angelic assistance rendered according to the Quran to the early Muslims in their battles against apostasy. The 1973 war is also seen as an Islamic victory because it was the result of the oil boycott by Saudi Arabia. God thus has favored Saudi Arabia because it is the only nation among Arab/Muslim countries that declares itself to be truly Muslim in that it is the only place where religious law and the tenets of the Quran are literally implemented.

Enhancing the newly emerging image of Islamic identity is the evident failure of the Western experiment as perceived not only in the Arab world but also in the West itself. The West that in the last century Arabs idealized as ethical, honest, and enthusiastic is flawed by racism, by corruption, by a degenerate "pornographic" society in which every person seems to strive for his own interests rather than for the collective good. The disenchantment with the West is due not only to its treatment of Arab hopes and goals *vis-à-vis* Israel, but also to the apparent inconsistency of Western ideals and what is perceived as the imminent collapse of the West. Such an image frees Islam, purified and committed, to resume its sacred role of spreading the faith to all corners of the world.

The events of Lebanon during the last few years, which have pitted Christian against Muslim and revealed a collusion between the Maronites of Lebanon and the Israelis, has led to the disenchantment of some of those who believed in Arab nationalism as a unity that transcends religious identities. These events, especially recently in Syria and Jordan, have led to an increasing stress placed by many on religious identity as the identity *par excellence,* over against regionalism, nationalism, or socialism.

In February of 1970 the Supreme Islamic Research Council in its Fifth Conference addressed itself to the question of Palestine and the occupied territories. In its published findings it says, The Palestine Question is not a national issue nor is it a political issue. It is first and foremost an Islamic question.[44] This is clearly true if one realizes that the military fortunes of the Arab people in relation to Israel are directly involved in the ways in which Muslims perceive themselves, the world, and history, and that that perception is intricately involved in the question of how they marshal their efforts in order to formulate the goals they seek and the methods they use to achieve these goals.

The Roles of Islam in
Saudi Arabia's Political Development

James P. Piscatori

$\mathcal{J}$N A PERIOD WHEN RELIGION seemed politically anachronistic, Saudi
Arabia was curious; in a period of "Islamic revolution," it is preoccupy-
ing. If we once cast Arabia in the soft hues of the romantic explorer,
today we paint it in the dramatic colors of the crisis manager. However
different our depiction, there has been a common belief that the Kingdom
will be short-lived, either, in the first instance, because the noble and
devout Badu is no match for the man in the gray flannel suit or, in the second, precisely because the former is becoming more and more like the latter. The Saudi way seems to be either too simplistic—i.e., out of touch
with the rigors of modern life, or too complex—i.e., confounding the adherents of traditional sentiments. Conceding that everyone's days are
numbered, especially those of political regimes, it is more instructive to
consider how it is that a monarchy espousing centuries-old values has survived so long in a turbulent era and unsettled region.

ORIGINS OF THE SAUDI STATE

In the mid-eighteenth century the meeting of belief and purpose of Muhammad ibn Saud and Muhammad ibn Abd al-Wahhab provided the
spark still animating the Saudi state. It proved indeed to be an historic
alliance, although the principals were a small and not particularly influential *amir* and a puritanical and carping reformer. Yet the effect of harnessing temporal ambition to spiritual vision yielded, as it did in the seventh century, territorial conquest and social vitality. As John Burckhardt

123

suggested, the campaign to reform the religious practices of the nomads had a corresponding impact on their political folkways: "The merit, therefore, of the Wahabys, in my opinion, is not that they purified the existing religion, but that they made the Arabs strictly observe the positive precepts of one certain religion; for although the Bedouins at all times devoutly worshipped the Divinity, yet the deistical principles alone could not be deemed sufficient to instruct a nation so wild and ungovernable in the practice of morality and justice."[1] The predictable result was centralization of authority in the quasi-caliphal figure of a Saudi *shaykh*.

The Islamic scimitar, however, cut both ways, for the alliance proved to have not only the weight to subdue a peninsula but also the sharpness to arouse the enmity of many. Shiites took to assassination to avenge the attack on Karbala by the stern disciples of Abd al-Wahhab who thought inappropriate the veneration there of heroic men; the Ottoman caliph and *sultan* took umbrage at the arrogance of these new, nominally subject crusaders; local leaders resented the growing limitations on their authority and the constant aspersions on their probity; and the Egyptians and Syrians grew antagonistic when the Sauds prohibited their pilgrims from carrying, as was their custom, the mahmal or national standard into Makka.[2] The agent of their wrath was Muhammad Ali who, taking his charge from Istanbul and relying on the resources of his base in Cairo, exploited family infighting among the Sauds and razed their capital in 1818. Not until fifty years later was there a revival of Saudi vigor, but, as in the early period, it lasted only long enough for the opposition of the Ottomans and their Arabian surrogates and for fraternal rivalry to sap it.[3]

From his exile in Kuwait at the turn of this century, the young Abd al-Aziz set out to realize the family destiny. Initially, his reliance on the old religious-political alliance was slight since his chief rivals in the Najd, the central region of Arabia, were also *muwahhidun,* followers of *shaykh* Abd al-Wahhab. But when he carried the campaign to al-Hijaz, the home of Islam's holiest cities, the invocation of pristine Islam had three benefits: it *delegitimated* the rulers of Makka and al-Madina who seemed profligate by comparison to the austere *muwahhidun;* it channelled the natural restlessness of the tribesmen into a holy and a dynastic cause; and it provided an ideological base for a new order, at once more righteous and, in contrast to predecessors, more sure-footed.

Abd al-Aziz's most notable instrument was the *ikhwan* or Brotherhood whereby he organized the Badawin to combat the evil innovations Muslims in Muhammad's peninsula had adopted. To that end he urged their settlement in agricultural communities and their consequent organization into a militia unswervingly loyal to him. Organizing it in

1912, he is supposed to have been able to assemble a fighting force between 75,000 and 150,000 strong from a variety of tribes, including the Mutayr, Utayba, Harb, and Ajman, but he probably relied heavily on a multitribal phalanx of 25,000 to 30,000 warriors.[4]

The movement is noteworthy for having lived by an unmistakably Islamic dynamic. Proudly calling themselves Brothers, these sometimes antagonistic tribesmen came together in *hujar*—the plural of the term for "flight" *(hijra)*; this time the movement was from the nomadic and otherwise errant life to the sedentary and otherwise virtuous life. In addition, like the early warriors of Islam, the Brothers found motivation partly in the power of the Word and partly in the lure of booty, and, like their ancestors again, they saw to it that they received their legal allotment. The *ulama,* the religious scholars, also played a central role in their lives, including sanctioning the resort to fighting in certain circumstances. Finally, like the true believers of the seventh century, they were often immoderate in the means to their goal. Indeed, Abd al-Aziz's "following of intrepid and semi-savage wild men from the desert"[5] often played the devoted knights to the *amir*'s Henry II and, at other times, failed to heed his restraining voice. The result was a number of atrocities, leading a British observer to exclaim even before the terrible excesses at al-Taif in late 1924: "They spare neither man, woman nor child and are as destructive as a horde of locusts."[6]

Although one direct observer in 1917 thought the Brothers' loyalty to the Sauds was certain,[7] the examples of their rambunctiousness should have suggested that sedition was possible. The presence of two factors warned of the tenuousness of the ties to the new capital of al-Riyad: first, tribal leaders remained to exercise their natural and sometimes contrary influence within the *ikhwan,* and second they told that they were the true defenders of Islam; the Brothers insisted that everyone, even their Saudi overlord, prove his faith. The two, in fact, combined in the revolt of Faysal al-Dawish, leader of the Mutayr, when Abd al-Aziz courted the infidel British and adopted some of their satanic machines. Openly disobeying the Saud's commands by the mid-1920s, many of these dissident Brothers attempted to carry their crusade into the British mandates of Trans-Jordan and Iraq. A few demonstrations of the Royal Air Force's accuracy against the raiders helped to persuade Abd al-Aziz that the *ikhwan* rebellion was doubly menacing: it threatened to bring British intervention if he was not able to right his own house and, at the same time, he seemed even weaker to his own people because of the external threat. But, finally at Sabala in 1929, he reestablished his supremacy by a clear victory over al-Dawish's forces.[8]

While the history of the *ikhwan* suggests that a self-image of ideological purity added to tribal restlessness makes for volatility, it also demonstrates that the combination makes a mighty political engine. By the deft handling of the Brothers, the Sauds were able to oppose their enemies, particularly *sharif* Hysayn who, to the horror of the Arabian puritans, awarded himself the title of caliph in 1924. The *ikhwan* proved extraordinarily useful, for it not only provided the enthusiastic manpower to do battle with them but also provided the pretext for doing so. In the case of the Rashids, in the central region, the *ikhwan* claimed to be more Wahhabi than they; in the case of the Hashimites, in the west, it claimed that being true Muslims was more important than being fellow Arab nationalists; in the case of the Shiites of the East, it claimed to bring them witness of the Prophet's unadulterated message. The result was a peninsula unified, a family promise realized, and a nation-state proclaimed.

THE POLITICAL RELEVANCE OF ISLAM

Structure

Among those who emphasize that the Saudi kingdom is indeed a fabrication *ex nihilo,* few believe that it is greatly reliant on brute force for its existence. But even among those who accept that Islam is the greatest national adhesive, a growing number believes that its strength is rapidly declining as modernization renders the conservative Islamic ideology irrelevant.[9] The trend is not yet clear, but it is important to take note, first, of how crucial Islam has been to date in molding the very institutions of state.

In an important sense, Islam had to seem central when Abd al-Aziz made himself king and deemphasized his title of *Imam.* The development was portentous not only because the basis of kingly rule was uncertain in classical theory but also because it had the effect of equating the regime with governments, like those in Britain or Egypt, whose example could hardly have been acceptable to the conservatives of Arabia.[10] The Sauds' response was to insist that in their country, the *sharia* governs all, even the king. It is this comprehensiveness of Islamic law that rescues the monarchy from charges of absolutism and theocracy.

It was a kind of masterstroke for them to offer no other constitution than the Quran and the other sources of the classical law, for it confirmed their religious credentials at the same time it gave them considerable flexibility in policies not specifically forbidden by the scriptures.

There has been as well the political side effect of leaving the royal family unrestrained by formal checks and unburdened by concrete pledges to the people. In times of unusual dissent, however, the Sauds have found it expedient to promise a more standard constitution. For example, Faysal did so in 1962 when he assumed the powers of Prime Minister after the combined shocks of external conflict and internal unrest.[11] Egypt under Nasser went on the ideological offensive against the Sauds and more directly threatened them by intervening militarily in the Yamani civil war. With the prodding of Cairo, several prominent members of the government in al-Riyad pressed their drive for liberalization and set up, later in exile, an Arab Nationalist Front dedicated to the overthrowing of the royal family. In this unstable environment the promise to allow the creation of national and regional assemblies gave Faysal the sympathy of his domestic audience and strengthened his hand in the struggle with Nasser.

A constitution with a small "c," to paraphrase Fuad al-Farsi,[12] had promulgated the Council of Ministers in 1954, yet no general constitution or assemblies in fact came into existence, even when there was a hint of doing so after Faysal's assassination in 1975.[13] It took the shocking events of November-December 1979, when an armed group invaded and occupied the Grand Mosque of Makka *(al-masjid al-haram)*, for Crown Prince Fahd to stir. Within a month of the mosque seizure, he announced that "a basic law of governance" *(al-nizam al-asasi lilhukm)* was forthcoming. While studiously vague, he did indicate that there would be a consultative assembly *(majlis al-shura)* and new "modes" *(asalib)* of government.[14] To indicate the seriousness of the pledge this time, he and the king created a constitutional committee in March, 1980. It is under the chairmanship of Prince Naif, the Minister of the Interior, and composed of conservatives and moderates, with the overwhelming majority, however, traditionally educated.[15] At the time of writing, the committee is continuing to deliberate on some two hundred articles of the proposed fundamental law in order to verify their Islamic content and utility.

If the Sauds can call on Islam to render kingly rule acceptable and to devise a national constitution, they are obligated to turn to it for the panoply of judicial institutions and officials charged with the task of implementing the *sharia*. Unlike in other Islamic states, *sharia* courts in Saudi Arabia have jurisdiction in all civil, criminal, and family cases. There is now an appellate court and a supreme judicial body, but final word remains, theoretically, with the king directly or through his agents, the *amirs*. It is the kind of executive interference that worries political scientists imbued with the theory of separation of powers, including judicial independence. Contrary to their fears, the system has worked well with the courts maintaining their freedom, due, largely, to the reputation for probity of the *qadis*. They are key figures, expected to be prudent and concerned, known to be stern and generally incorruptible. Their integrity makes their advice prized, their access gives them some of the resources of the ward boss, and, for both reasons, the government contradicts them at its peril.[16]

Islam also accounts for the importance of the religious scholars in national decision making. Advising on appeals and making inputs in the content of royal decrees, they are a formidable force in Saudi society. For instance, in the transfer of powers to Faysal in 1964, the *ulama* issued a *fatwa* that eased the transition by declaring it to be in "the public interest," a *sharia* principle.[17] Though they have become bureaucratized to some extent, as Minister of Commerce Sulayman al-Sulaym suggests,[18] they are still an elusive group to Westerners and to most Saudis as well. Without the public visibility of a Khomeini, they provide much of his monitoring function. In this sense, they represent an institutionalized conscience, a kind of brooding omnipresence with which the would-be modernizer must contend.

It is noteworthy, finally, that the Sauds have used Islam to justify the absence of several institutions. In addition to a legislature, Saudi Arabia lacks political parties and trade unions. Parties are, on one hand, superfluous since justice prevails throughout the land because of the *sharia*'s sway, and, on the other hand, antithetical to the scriptural prohibition on divisive sects.[19] Trade unions, for their part, are rejected as dangerous to a fledgling economy and unnecessary in a country like Saudi Arabia where the law of the land is fully protective of the worker. The Saudis suggest, moreover, that we reflect on the history of Marxism, premised on the liberation of the world's workers yet leading to their complete subjugation everywhere that there is a Communist state.[20]

Policy

In addition to drawing the main contours of their policy with an Islamic pencil, the Saudis find a second importance in Islam: it affects the formulation of particular policies as both a determinant and a constraint. While it is difficult to discern motivations behind policy, it is not unreasonable to suggest that the Saudi leaders take Islam into account when shaping some of their plans for society. A notorious example of Islamic values determining policy concerns the role of women. Though they are now allowed to pursue segregated education and to assume limited kinds of jobs, the fact remains that they are prohibited from driving, working freely, and dressing publicly as they please — all in keeping with the spirit of *muwahhidun* puritanism. The letter of Islamic law is also applied in matters of divorce, inheritance, and testimony, whereby women are at a judicial disadvantage.

Under the influence of his wife Iffa, Faysal took on the most conservative of the religious establishment when he insisted that Islam prohibit the wasting of any mind. To soften the criticism against his 1960 decision to allow women to attend school, he placed women's education under the special protection of the Grand Mufti's office where a Department for the Education of Women was set up. The original budget, covering fifteen schools, was 2 million riyals, and it increased to 93 million riyals eight years later. In 1963–64 there were 23,683 females at all levels of school, whereas ten years later the number had risen to 200,786 (compared with 497,733 males).[21] Still, probably only one-sixth of the eligible girls were in elementary school in 1975. The government anticipated, somewhat rosily, that that number would rise to 50% by 1980 and that over 460,000 females at all levels would be at school then. One mark of accomplishment is that the Kingdom is now able to provide its own teachers to cover the primary school level for girls.[22]

But obervers who pointed to these developments as harbingers of radical change have misunderstood the depth of Islamic feeling on the subject. There were only 27,000 women at work, mainly in social service sectors of the economy, in 1974–75, with 48,000 expected to be at work by 1980.[23] Despite severe manpower shortages, there is continuing suspicion of women in the work force. An indicator of this suspicion is the statement of a government official at the time of a 1975 royal decree offering monetary rewards to large families: "The Kingdom needs more males for work and more and more females to bear and rear children."[24] Indeed, in keeping with their interpretation of Islamic theory, the Saudis seem committed to a policy of "separate but equal." For instance, women in al-Riyad now have the option of banking in an establishment run by and for women[25] and they have a library for their exclusive use.[26] While there is some concern that the idea of segregation might go to impractical extremes,[27] the prevailing official and popular attitude is that the traditional faith ordains still a special — and different — status for women.

Islamic teaching also accounts for the Saudi imposition of hudud penalties. It is a long-standing policy that is being reconfirmed in the reign of Khalid and defended as essential to maintaining an Islamic society and a low crime rate. "Why, (Saudis) ask, should we adopt western liberal laws and reformist penology if they lead to the murders, muggings, and drug scandals of London and New York?"[28] Criminal deterrence is served by the occasional beheading or amputation, and political deterrence by the extraordinary execution of rebels, such as the sixty-three beheaded for their part in the Grand Mosque takeover.[29]

While foreign Muslims have never been exempt from the hudud, non-Muslim aliens are now also subjected to them. In earlier practice the need for technical assistance had outweighed the sensitivity to enforcing the penalties impartially, and, consequently, most serious crimes of Westerners in particular resulted in their deportation while lesser ones were ignored. Khalid's strong feelings on the subject and the regime's nervousness over the large number of foreign workers have put Americans and Europeans in an involuntarily intimate contact with the *sharia*. The authorities, for instance, have flogged several British citizens for selling alcohol to Muslims.[30]

So committed are the Saudis to the traditional punishments that even members of the royal family are not spared. Abd al-Aziz reportedly thought one of his sons, who, in an intoxicated rage, shot a British diplomat, should himself forfeit his life.[31] More recently, officials beheaded a nephew prince for assassinating King Faysal, and, in 1978, they executed a woman of the blood royal for committing adultery. The latter event's depiction in the "docudrama," *Death of a Princess,* has stimulated a worldwide controversy on the ways of Islam and of the Saud dynasty. In criticizing the Anglo-American movie, a member of the royal family reaffirmed its commitment to carrying out the *sharia* sanctions.[32] In light of the growing resentment of the privileged few's wealth and coming shortly after the unexpected rebellion in Makka, the statement was doubly politic: it demonstrated the Sauds' readiness to defend the faith against vilification, and it reassured that no one is above the law. The *ulama,* condemning the distortions abroad, also brought the message home by pointedly arguing that the guardians of law and order prove their fairness by the willingness to act against the guilty among the noble. After all, they noted, the Prophet indicated his intent to sever his own daughter's hand if she committed theft.[33]

Death of a Princess has also reminded us that values sometimes play an important part in foreign policy. In this instance, the Saudis' outrage at the British showing of the movie led them to delay sending a new ambassador to London, to request that the British ambassador leave the Kingdom, and to review economic relations between the two countries.[34] In other cases as well, the Saudis have shown that Islam is sometimes a determinant. Examples include their long-standing demand for the liberation of Jerusalem, the faith's third holiest city, and their encouragement of pan-Islamic institutions and the autonomy of Muslims in places like Eritrea and the Philippines. Moreover, the Soviet invasion of Afghanistan has only confirmed their antipathy to the godlesssness of Communism and the prudence of their policy of little contact with Eastern bloc states.

It is perhaps easier to pinpoint the constraints Islam places on policy formation. Abd al-Aziz, for example, faced early opposition to the introduction of the wireless and to allowing non-Hanbali law in newly conquered al-Hijaz. There was similar opposition to the policy of inviting non-Muslims into the country. Abd al-Aziz's father issued this warning on public opinion in the 1920s: "The people have become angry and you know the Ikhwan and their cause for anger. . . . Among other things they say that you are conniving [with the British] . . . ; even the *ulama* are beginning to doubt."[35] Under Faysal's stewardship, there was opposition to the introduction of schooling for women and of television. None of these innovations, it turns out, was cancelled, but each was delayed and its defense recrafted along Islamic lines, thereby testifying to the impact on decision making.

Perhaps the most notable examples are current. It is clear that deference to Islam or, put differently, anxiety over preserving ancient values has induced moderations in the Five Year plans. I do not mean to suggest that development is unIslamic or even that the religious leadership has objected to particular projects; rather, my point is that the fear of loosing currents of modernization so vibrant that they erode traditional mores has had a natural inhibiting effect on essentially conservative rulers. Finally, the Islamic prohibition on usury continues to govern official Saudi attitudes towards economic transactions. Any suggestion that a modern economy would do better to have banks charging interest is condemned as tempting infidelity. It is a message *shaykh* ibn Baz, the chief *alim,* reiterated to readers of a Saudi newspaper that had printed a Cairo bank's offer of interest on deposit certificates. Reminding them of God's certain punishment for those who engage in usury, he hoped that press officials would have the good sense not to publish material vexing to Him.[35]

Change

There is a third political role of Islam: it provides a framework for facilitating change. The stories of Abd al-Aziz's cleverness in persuading the *ulama* and his people to accept modern contraptions are legion, and their general outline is his reliance on deduction from the Quranic and traditional texts to justify innovation. He legitimated photography as the bringing together of light and shadow, both divine creations, and thus acceptable despite the idolatry of pictorial art. Similarly, the radio became acceptable after the King arranged for a demonstration of Quran reading over the air; because they witnessed the faithful transmission of the holy words, the religious leaders concluded that the radio could not be the devil's work and hence ought not to be banned.[37]

Since then, astonishing changes have occurred in the Kingdom through ostensibly the most orthodox means. The changes are considered valid precisely because the vocabulary of Islam frames and expresses them. Jurists, for instance, invoke a convenient legal fiction to avoid even the slightest appearance of encroaching on the divine prerogative of legislation. Rather than referring to an innovative royal decree by the presumptuous word *qanun* (law), they label it *nizam* (rule); more than rhetorical quibbling, this distinction allows for legal and social change without transgressing fundamental beliefs. Authorities, moreover, presented the workmen's compensation law in the context of the traditional Islamic system of social welfare, and the Mining Code proclaims itself consonant with *maslaha* or the "public weal."

One reason why there is flexibility of expression is the reliance on *ijtihad* or independent reasoning, once precluded in Islam but now accepted by all jurists in Saudi Arabia as the fourth general legal source. The *ulama* may call on analogical thinking and make informed judgments on matters on which the Quran and the *sunna* are silent. One Saudi has argued that Faysal institutionalized the reliance on independent thought by creating the Judicial Council to reconcile the conflicting demands of modern life and traditional teachings.[38] *Shaykh* al-Yamani, the oil minister, has emphasized that Islamic law is able to change with differing circumstances precisely because of the use of analogy and reason as well as the invocation of the notion of public interest.[39]

Another reason, paradoxical, is the conservatism of the Hanbali school, which prevails in Saudi Arabia. Contrary to popular perceptions about its medieval rigidity, this school is conducive to changes so long as they are not expressly prohibited. The fundamental thrust of Hanbali thought, indeed, is to demand evidence of a restraining norm. Although Saudi jurists are to rely principally on this school of thought, they are not exclusively limited to it if there is no adequate guidance in the six predominant texts, particularly *Kitab Sharh al-Muntaha* and *Kitab Sharh al-Iqna*.[40]

Instead they may, in the exercise of *ijtihad,* call on the opinions of other schools of thought, thereby providing them greater latitude for judgment.

One other reason for the flexibility is the well-established tradition of Islamic law whereby the ruler is able to take administrative action to add to the bases for judgment in the existing legal system and to create new institutions. With regard to the former, the government has promulgated the Regulation on Commerce (1954), the Regulation for Nationality (1954), the Forgery Law (1961), the Bribery Law (1962), the Mining Code (1963), the Labor and Workmen Law (1970), the Social Insurance Law (1970), and the Civil Service Law (1971), among others. The purpose of these regulations is not to detract from the *sharia* but to supplement it by providing norms to deal with conditions not expressly covered in it. In areas of ambiguity, they might even present the official interpretation. For instance, the Social Insurance Law departs from the traditional pattern and follows an Ottoman precedent of 1911 by failing to make provision for male agnates and to distinguish among collaterals as legitimate claimants on a deceased's insurance.[41]

The Saudi rulers have also exercised their prerogative to change the structures of the legal order. There were reforms in 1927, 1931, 1936, and 1952, and, consequently, there is now a three-tiered system providing for appeal above the ordinary *sharia* courts. In extra-*sharia* areas, there was the creation in 1955 of a Board of Grievances *(diwan al-mazalim),* which finds its inspiration in Abbasid history. Faced with the growth of decrees outside the law, the Saudi leadership deemed it advisable to set up an administrative tribunal to hear complaints against government officials. As one example, the Foreign Capital Investments Regulation (1964) empowers the Board to be the final arbiter when a businessman believes the government has wronged him.[42] The *diwan* has proven to be an effective approach to modern problems and, more importantly, it has proven to be consonant with, not a deviation from, the nation's tradition. Less historically sanctioned but equally valid developments are the tribunals empowered by the new decrees to dispose of relevant disputes. Noteworthy is their nimble balancing of primary reliance on their codes with deference to the general guidance of the *sharia.*

The reasons combine to provide adaptation without crisis. It is a process the Ministry of Justice finds so natural it would have us believe that it is automatic: "As regards the regulations of nationality, administrative decisions, and the government setup, the Kingdom of Saudi Arabia has adopted the system prevalent in the modern world, a fact that requires no elaboration."[43]

Legitimation

There is a final, fourth, role Islam plays: it provides a continuing source of legitimation of the Saudi regime. It is a particularly important function at a time when monarchy is clearly an endangered species, and for a monarchy, like the Saudi, which has a history of prior limited success. Without the aura of the Wahhabi movement in the first place, the Sauds would have had little chance to lay claim to a tribally diverse and broad peninsula. In this century, active concern over the *ikhwan,* the self-appointed obligation to guard the holy cities, and a desire for a reputation of devotion have testified to the family's recognition of its dependence on Islam for its larger than Najdi claim.

Abd al-Aziz was particularly careful about securing formal approval from the religious authorities even when his might alone could have settled the matter — and, to a large extent, he probably received the former because of their recognition of the reality of the latter. One example will suffice. In 1944 an old Brother, much committed still to the starkest values of the *muwahhidun,* had been publicly denouncing the King for his impiety in selling good Muslim land to the unbelieving Americans. Summoning the *shaykh* to a gathering of the *ulama* and royal court in al-Riyad, Abd al-Aziz invited him to make his charge for all to hear. Uncowered, Abu Bahz insisted that the duty of a Muslim ruler is to resist the blandishments of non-Muslims, not to help them profit from them.

> Then the King left his throne seat and stood beside Abu Bahz and said, "I am now not the King, but only a Muslim, like you a servant of the Prophet, Abdul Aziz, appealing for judgment to the 'ulama', the judges of the Islamic law which binds us both equally." . . . Showing a thorough knowledge of the Prophet's life and traditions, the King cited several well-attested cases when the Prophet employed non-Muslims individually and in groups. "Am I right or wrong?" The judges replied unanimously that he was right. "Am I breaking the Sharii law, therefore, when I follow in the footsteps of the Prophet, and employ foreign experts to work for me? The Americans at El Kharj, and the other foreigners who operate machines, are brought here by me and work for me under my direction to increase the material resources of the land, and to extract for our benefit the metals, oil, and water placed by Allah beneath our land and intended for our use. In so doing, am I violating any Muslim law?" The judges returned a verdict of not-guilty.[44]

Less dramatically, perhaps, but equally effectively Faysal relied on Islam to legitimate his rule. The early years of that rule were a particularly inauspicious time for a traditional monarchy. Everywhere in the Middle East the Voice of the Arabs, the Egyptian radio, penetrated national borders, and everywhere it carried Nasser's denunciation of feudal rulers for retarding the development of their people and plotting with the imperialist giants of the West to preserve their own power. The deposition of King Saud in 1964 played into the Egyptian leader's hands and exacerbated Faysal's efforts to put his dynastic house in order. In late 1965 he moved to blunt the pan-Arabist attacks from Cairo and elsewhere by advancing the cause of pan-Islam, by encouraging the development of Islamic institutions and the holding of summits of Muslim leaders. Undoubtedly he made his appeal to the fraternity partly for its own merits, yet it is indisputable that his goal as well was to improve the image and thus acceptability of his regime. While the plan for an Islamic movement never progressed very far in international politics, it probably helped to quiet some domestic discord by reassuring the citizenry of its rulers' commitment to the faith.

King Khalid and Prince Fahd also were careful to rely on the *ulama* to validate their actions in ending the occupation of the Grand Mosque in late 1979. The several hundred who took this action, for reasons that remain clouded, presented both a direct political challenge to the government in the example of open-armed rebellion and an indirect but no less real political challenge by suggesting that the Sauds might not be so dependable after all as protectors of the holy places. In turning to the religious authorities for a *fatwa,* the governors sought not permission but pretext for doing what had to be done. The opinion served them well, for it was neatly structured, leaving no ambiguity or doubt as to the required course of action. It was the learneds' belief, in accordance with Quranic verse and Prophetic saying, that the authorities should, first, invite the attackers to surrender, then try to arrest them if they refused, and, finally, slay them if they resisted seizure. Officials could use "all means" to regain control, and, in the remainder of the injunction to behead dividers of the community, they also found a rationale for the eventual punishment of the captured.[45]

Since the affront to Islam was so egregious and the crime so heinous to Muslims everywhere, it is likely that the government could have acted to restore order without benefit of *fatwa.* While it is possible that such unblessed action would have brought short-term vindication of the Sauds' reputation, it is probable that asking for guidance cost them nothing and gained them a great deal in the long run. Precisely because the *fatwa* made clear, in its first paragraph, the King's immediate interest in having the support of the *ulama* and because it made explicit the Islamic teaching on the need to defend the *haram,* it helped the Saudis to address some of the speculation on the value of their guardianship and, hence, their stability. By calling on them to rescue the holiest place of Islam, the *fatwa* gave renewed life to their primary claim to legitimacy. But it did not remove the causes of the revolt, and, as a result, the longevity of that claim remains in doubt.

THE IMPACT OF ISLAM

It thus seems clear that Islam is an abiding, if not also central, reality in Saudi Arabia because the Sauds have relied on it to help unify a disparate peninsula, structure the polity itself, inform their decisions, frame their innovations, and legitimate their role. It would be a mistake to obscure this dynamic in accepting two equally misleading stereotypes. One, stressing the fundamentalist character of faith in the holy peninsula and the conservatism of a traditional dynasty, distorts the facts that modernization does occur and that the royal family can be innovative even when there is, and probably *because* there is, deference to the ancient store of values. The second stereotype dismisses the religious sincerity of Saudi Arabia's leadership and people by focusing on celebrated and indisputable circumventions of Islamic law. There is an error, however, in failing to distinguish between the marginal and core areas of Islam. Whatever the intent of Allah, the modern Muslim in Saudi Arabia distinguishes the significance of prohibitions on the consumption of alcohol from that of obligations to protect the person and dignity of women, to provide financially for one's family, to tithe for the poor, and to combat atheism. There probably is an evolving conceptualization of what values are central and how they relate to each other, yet we must avoid concluding that Islamic devotion is merely superficial when we witness weaknesses of the flesh.

This is not to imply any form of Islamic determinism, for it is indisputable that the faith is but one element, albeit a magnetic one, in the life of the believer. Just as importantly, it would be wrong to leave the suggestion that Islam has no role to play in political opposition—as might appear from this discussion. The problem of an analysis concentrating on the contribution of Islam to Saudi political development is that in trying to dispel one false impession—Islam and a modernizing monarchy are necessarily incompatible—it leaves another, conservative, one—Islam is inevitably the servant of monarchy. Islam has buttressed the regime for half a century, but the future is not surely as secure.

Most observers of the Kingdom have looked on its history and seen, not remarkable resilience and acceptable compromise, but internal contradictions and the steady wearing down of old ways. They believe that soon enough the tricky business of innovation and holding the *ulama* in check will become an impossible task even for the limberest Muslim mind and the most patient of technocratic characters. Islam will loom then as a barrier to later stages of modernization, as a retarding influence, say, in manpower development because of the inhibitions precluding a full economic role for women. To the view that "enough compromises have already been made to suggest that the future is not wholly secure from Secularist corrosion,"[46] these observers would object that the corrosive future is apparent already, as is the anachronism of a royal family tied to an Islamic ideology.

Since the downfall of the Shah, another group of observers stresses that modernization has left Saudis, if not disquietingly giddy, then profoundly confused. The common, sobering, result, they say, is likely to be the rise of militant fundamentalist Muslims who, like the *ikhwan* of an earlier period, will strike at fiendish innovations and their perfidious agents—in this case, the Al Saud. They cite the blunt criticisms of Khomeini, the Shiite riots in the Eastern province, and the Makka incident to suggest that Abd al-Aziz's descendents now suffer the same sword of Islamic righteousness he wielded against the Hashimites.

But these are long-term processes of which they speak, and it is hard for any of us to detect which, if either, will prevail. No clear political oppositional movement, fulfilling the assumptions of one process or the other, is apparent yet. From time to time an anti-monarchist group, Nasserist or otherwise, does appear on the scene, such as the Union of the People of the Arabian Peninsula. They seem not to have enjoyed much popular support to date, but it is possible that the urban-rural imbalance, the acute housing shortage, the maldistribution of wealth, and inflation will redound to the disadvantage of the royal family and to the benefit of a republican secularist alternative. No matter how irritating the disparity between modernization's ideal and practice, there are increasing signs that the people are finding their rulers wanting by the old yardstick of Islamic integrity. The problems of corruption and concentrated wealth seem particularly galling in light of the Sauds' pretensions to wear orthodoxy's mantle. And there is a widespread feeling that the attackers in Makka, while erring in their choice of target, gave expression to an entirely appropriate, though somewhat too ardent, sentiment of protest.

There are signs that the governors are beginning to fear more organized objection. Rare now are the public statements, such as that made by *al-Riyad*'s editor, that rapid development is the guarantee of Islam's vitality.[47] They are even showing that they are capable of seeing and perhaps learning the hard lessons; they are starting to prosecute corrupt officials and to penalize businesses that bribe. The haram seizure has given them a reprieve. Yet unless they aggressively follow the trail of corruption, no matter to which palace it leads, they run the risk of having Islam become a delegitimating force, gradually undermining their claim to rule and leaving them vulnerable to the *alim,* the engineer, or the colonel with a stronger and, if lucky, more popular idea.

There may yet be irony, then, in the Sauds' reliance on Islam. Until recently, appreciating the goals of the modernist thinkers but objecting to the solution of the secularists, they have struck largely a prudent balance in the dilemma of modernizing a traditional society. Change has been possible, but the types of change and the pace of change have had constantly to be calibrated with Islam. The faith has had this social and political relevance because it is part of the cultural and national heritages, intrinsic to the life and values of the common man, and, for all that, the stoutest pillar of the regime. The Sauds have shown themselves to have understood that a society when modernizing cannot move too far ahead of the ancient values of its people. The future is not as certain to reveal their added understanding that those values pace especially those who would be kings.

Pakistan: Quest for Islamic Identity

John L. Esposito

*D*URING THE 1970s Islam has re-emerged as a key factor in the politics of Pakistan. Calls for a more Islamic system (Nizam-i-Islam) of government began during the rule of Zulfikar Ali Bhutto (1971–77) and have continued as a central theme in the current martial law administration of General M. Zia-ul-Haq.

This study examines the role of Islam in the political development of Pakistan, focusing on her quest to determine and implement her Islamic identity and thus to articulate and realize what most Pakistanis have viewed as their *raison d'etre*. Focus will be given to those key events and issues during the first decades of Pakistan's existence which reflect her accomplishments and failings in ideological self-realization. Special emphasis will be placed upon the re-emergence of Islam in the contemporary period through an analysis of the use of Islam as a major force in the process of mass politicization as well as the ways in which Islamization has occurred through political, legal, and socioeconomic proposals and reforms during the Bhutto (1971–77) and Zia-ul-Haq (1977–) regimes.

MUSLIM PRESENCE IN THE INDO-PAKISTAN SUBCONTINENT

Muslims first made contact with the Indian subcontinent as early as the eighth century (A.D. 711) with Arab raids into the Sind under Muhammad ibn Qasim. Muslim settlement and rule actually began as a result of the tenth century invasion and conquest by the Central Asian Ghaznavids who established their capitol in Lahore in 1021. Further Muslim expansion eastward led to the establishment of the Delhi sultanate in the early thirteenth century and Muslim dominance of North India. Successive centuries witnessed the continued expansion of Muslim rule in India, and a cultural flourishing that culminated with the Mughal Dynasty (1526–1857).[1]

From the eleventh century onwards, a Muslim minority (never more than one-quarter of the total population in the Indo-Pakistan subcontinent) ruled the indigenous Hindu majority. Despite many points of contact and exchange, political, social, and religious, cultural co-existence did not lead to cultural assimilation. Thus, there remained throughout the ages—beyond differences of language, region, and class—two basically different and distinct Muslim and Hindu communities. This reality was to have a profound effect on the future political development of the subcontinent.

THE COLONIAL PERIOD: Mughal Decline and Foreign Dominance

The seventeenth century brought still another major turning point in the history of the subcontinent. European trade companies—French, Dutch, Portuguese, and British—began to establish settlements. The ensuing centuries of colonialism may best be characterized as the decline of Mughal Muslim rule and the rise of the British Empire in India. From the early eighteenth century onwards, although a Mughal ruler remained on the throne, in fact, the British were increasingly the dominant political and economic force. This process culminated in 1857 with the so-called Sepoy Mutiny (or what Indian Nationalists came to call the First War of Independence). The Mughal dynasty, and thus centuries long Muslim rule of India, was terminated and formal British rule established.

ISLAM AND THE INDEPENDENCE MOVEMENT

The independence movement in the subcontinent flowered in the twentieth century during the period between World War I and World War II. Hindu and Muslim leaders of the Indian Nationalist Movement had desired a united front. However, as religion was an integral part of the two great traditional cultures—a source of strength which inspired and assured as well as preserved their identity and way of life—Hindu and Muslim communal fears ultimately undermined any union. Specifically, Muslims were concerned about their rights in a vastly Hindu albeit secular state. Thus, although Muhammad Ali Jinnah and the Muslim League had sought at first to work with the Congress party and its leaders (Nehru and Gandhi), by 1940 Jinnah was speaking of the two nations of India—Muslim and Hindu:

> It is extremely difficult to appreciate why our Hindu friends fail to understand the real nature of Islam and Hinduism. They are not religious in the strict sense of the word, but are, in fact, different and distinct social orders, and it is a dream that the Hindus and Muslims can ever evolve a common nationality, and this misconception of one Indian nation has gone far beyond the limits. . . . The Hindus and Muslims belong to two different religious philosophies, social customs, literatures. They neither intermarry nor interdine together and, indeed, they belong to two different civilizations which are based mainly on conflicting ideas and conceptions. Their aspects on life and of life are different. It is quite clear that Hindus and Musalmans derive their inspiration from different sources of history. . . . To yoke together two such nations under a single state, one as a numerical minority and the other as a majority, must lead to growing discontent and final destruction of any fabric that may be so built up for the government of such a state.[2]

Jinnah and the Muslim League harnessed Islamic symbols and slogans to forge a mass movement whose goal was a separate nation—a Muslim homeland wherein Muslims might be free to pursue their way of life. Their goal was realized in August 1947 when the Indian subcontinent was partitioned into two separate nation states—India and Pakistan.

NATION BUILDING: Obstacles and Constraints

While most nations are based primarily on a common territory, ethnic background, or language, Pakistan was founded as a homeland for a people who shared a common socioreligious heritage—it was to be a Muslim nation. However, though juridically one nation, Pakistan was in fact a composite of people who were divided by many spoken languages (five major linguistic families with 32 distinct spoken languages),[3] strong regional sentiments, and distance (her two major provinces of West and East Pakistan were separated by over 1,000 miles of Indian territory).

Questions of national identity and ideology were overshadowed by basic issues of national survival. The process of nation building was severely constrained by the harsh practical realities of the post-partition period: settlement of vast numbers of Muslim refugees who had migrated from India, conflict with India over Kashmir, Muslim-Hindu communal rioting in the Punjab and, as a result, mass migrations of Hindus from West Pakistan to India—a complex of political and social upheavals which caused vast carnage, destruction and a breakdown of law and order. Such events rendered the situation of the new state precarious at best. Thus it is not surprising that the energies of the first years were devoted not to a realization of Islamic identity but rather to practical concerns assuring the survival of the state.[4]

Early attempts at the consolidation of political power and establishment of a viable political and economic system were further frustrated by the untimely death of the founder-architect of Pakistan, M. Ali Jinnah in 1948 (barely one year after independence) and the assassination of his protege and Pakistan's first Prime Minister, Liaquat Ali Khan in October, 1951—events which intensified the fragile condition of the new state.

ISLAMIC IDENTITY: Early Conflicts

Although religious ideology and symbols had been utilized to mobilize and unite Muslims during the independence movement, there was no clear understanding or consensus about the positive content of its ideology and its application in the new state's structure, programs, and policies. Put quite simply, the ideological questions the new nation faced were: What does it mean to say that Pakistan is a modern Islamic or Muslim state? How is its Islamic character to be reflected in the ideology and institutions of the state?

Two major events (the drafting of the Constitution of 1956 and the Anti-Ahmadiya Disturbances) during the first decade of Pakistan's existence provide insight into the problems and issues associated with the quest to articulate her Islamic identity. The process of framing the first constitution lasted for nine years. The constitutional debate provided the arena for a protracted battle between conservative traditionist and modernist factions—the former more inclined to revival of the past, the latter to modernization and reform.[5]

The two general directions represented by the ideals or models available were: (1) a traditional Islamic state in which the organic connection of religion and the state is exemplified by the *shariah,* a comprehensive Islamic law governing all aspects of life—private and public, sacred and profane, religious and secular or (2) a modern nation-state based upon Western codes of law with its secular presuppositions. On the other hand, there were neither modern Islamic states nor well-developed models of such a state(s) to which one could refer. The crux of the problem was that unless one was prepared to simply opt for a revivalism that called for a classical Islamic state or to advocate the adoption of a modern secular state, Pakistani Muslims faced a formidable task. Theirs would not be the path of simple adoption of one model but adaptation, not a mere following or imitation of a past Islamic ideal or a present secular reality but a breaking of new ground—a creative construction of a blueprint for a modern state and society which incorporated and realized the Islamic sentiments, ideals, and values upon which mass support for Pakistan's independence was based.

What complicated matters further was the fact that the leadership was ill-equipped by virtue of their inadequate training and orientation for this task. The political leadership was Western educated or oriented while the religious leadership, the *ulama,* were the products of a traditional religious education and world view. Thus the former lacked training in and understanding of their Islamic past, especially as it might be brought to bear upon the problem of defining Pakistan as an Islamic state; the latter, though they might be well trained according to traditional Islamic standards, had little appreciation for the demands of modernity and the disciplines required to provide effective reforms.

The Constitution of 1956 reflected the long years of debate and the differences between traditionalists and modernists. Its final form underscored the lack of any clear idea or consensus regarding an Islamic ideology and how to translate it into programs and policies. The document represented an eclectic compromise which embodied many of those aspects associated with a secular state while injecting several Islamic provisions. Perhaps the clearest indication of the forced nature of the compromise occurs in the Preamble in which, bowing to traditionist sensibilities, the assertion of popular sovereignty was qualified by subordinating it to that of Allah. "Sovereignty over the entire universe belongs to Allah Almighty alone, and the authority to be exercised by the people of Pakistan within the limits prescribed by Him is a sacred trust."[6]

The chief Islamic provisions of the Constitution of 1956 were: the title of the state was the Islamic Republic of Pakistan;[7] she was a democratic state based upon Islamic principles;[8] the head of the state (president) must be a Muslim;[9] a research center would assist in the "reconstruction of Muslim society on a truly Islamic basis";[10] finally, the so-called "repugnancy clause" stipulated that no law contrary to the Quran and *Sunnah* of the Prophet could be enacted.[11] Implementation of the latter provision was to be enhanced by a presidential commission which would recommend how existing law might be brought into conformity with Islam and which would provide within five years a compilation of those Islamic injunctions which might be the subject of future legislation.

The Constitution of 1956 clearly reflected Pakistan's ideological difficulties for it lacked any systematic statement and implementation of a clear Islamic rationale.[12] The relationship of many facets of this modern document (the principles of democracy, popular sovereignty, parliamentary political party system, equality of all citizens) to Islamic principles was never clearly delineated. While traditionists had advocated an Islamic state based upon full implementation of the *shariah,* they settled for a legal system in which no law was repugnant to Islam. Modernists had a document whose Islamic provisions would cause a minimum of inconvenience. However, the unresolved Constitutional questions and inconsistencies illustrate the roots of an ideological quandary that continues to surface in present-day concerns. This identity problem would continue to haunt Pakistan. Moreover, as will be seen later, it has re-emerged today in the total requestioning of the Islamic nature of Pakistan's political and economic system of government.

A second event which occurred during Pakistan's formative period and which also concerned her Islamic identity and character was the 1953 anti-Ahmadiyah disturbances in the Punjab province. During the constitutional debates religious leaders had sought to have the Ahmadiyah, a modern Islamic sect, declared a non-Muslim minority maintaining that their founder, Mirza Ghulam Ahmad (1835–1908), had claimed the mantle of prophethood and had thus denied an essential Islamic belief — that Muhammad was the final or seal of the prophets *khatm al-nubbuwat*). Furthermore, these religious leaders demanded that Zafrullah Khan, Pakistan's Foreign Minister, and other Ahmadi government officials be dismissed from office. They argued that a non-Muslim minority could not be fully committed to the state's Islamic ideology, and so non-Muslims should not hold key policy-making positions. The unfortunate result of this agitation was widespread rioting and murder of Admadis. A national court of inquiry was established to investigate the causes of these disturbances, and it issued a report commonly referred to as the Munir Report, named after Justice Muhammad Munir, President of the Commission. This report is significant because it provides insight into several problems which have been and continue to be central to Pakistan's quest for its Islamic identity: (1) the lack of any clear understanding or consensus regarding Islamic belief and ideology as well as the absence of a centralized teaching authority; and (2) the necessity for a bold reorientation (through a process of reinterpretation and reform of Islam) to meet modern needs and demands. While the *ulama* could join in declaring the Ahmadis non-Muslims, the *ulama* interviewed by the commission were unable to agree on the most fundamental questions, e.g., What is Islam? and Who is a Muslim? (What constitutes a believer?) As in the past, agreement could be reached in resisting a perceived deviation or threat to Islam, but consensus about the positive content of Pakistan's Islamic ideology (even the most fundamental questions of Islamic belief) seemed to be beyond even those who were the strongest advocates of an Islamic state. The Commission addressed itself to the inherent danger of this situation for Pakistan in the future and the need for reinterpretation and reform in its concluding statement:

> Nothing but a bold orientation of Islam to separate the vital from the lifeless can preserve it as a World Idea and convert the Musalman into a citizen of the present and the future world from the archaic incongruity that he is today. It is this lack of bold and clear thinking, the inability to understand and make decisions which has brought about in Pakistan a confusion which will persist and repeatedly create situations of the kind we have been inquiring into until our leaders have a clear conception of the goal and of the means to reach it.[13]

AYUB KHAN (1958-69)

In October 1958 Muhammad Ayub Khan led a military *coup d'etat*. While Ayub's government sought primarily to rebuild a strong centralized national government and to foster rapid socio-economic reforms, Islam continued to be a factor in Pakistan's political development. Ayub was himself a modernist Muslim in understanding and approach. He stressed the need to "liberate the spirit of religion from the cobwebs of superstition and stagnation which surround it and move forward under the forces of modern science and knowledge."[14] Ayub's modernist outlook was reflected quite clearly in the new Constitution of 1962, the establishment of the Advisory Council on Islamic Ideology and the Islamic Research Institute as well as the reforms embodied in the Muslim Family Laws Ordinance (1961). However, once again the struggle between modernist and traditionist factions resulted in minimizing the potential of these mechanisms of reform.

While the new Constitution of 1962 generally adopted the Islamic provisions of the 1956 constitution, there were some significant changes.[15] The new document omitted "Islamic" from the official name of the republic and the divine sovereignty phrase "within the limits prescribed by Him." However, under strong public pressure, these Islamic provisions were again restored by the first Amendment Bill of 1963.

Perhaps the most notable Islamic provisions of the new constitution occurred in "Part X Islamic Institutions" which, following the lead of the Constitution of 1956, called for the establishment of an Advisory Council of Islamic Ideology and an Islamic Research Institute, the former concerned with legislation and the latter with research, especially as regards Islam in the modern world.

The functions of the Advisory Council of Islamic Ideology were: (1) to make recommendations to the government regarding provisions that may better enable Muslims to lead their lives in conformity with the tenets of Islam; (2) to advise the government as to whether proposed legislation is repugnant to Islam.

The Central Institute of Islamic Research had been mandated by Art. 197 of the Constitution of 1956 "to assist in the reconstruction of Muslim society on a truly Islamic basis." Its Charter reflects the modernist approach to this objective emphasizing its role as defining Islamic fundamentals in a "rational and liberal manner" so as to "bring out the dynamic character in the context of the intellectual and scientific progress of the modern world."[16]

A connection between the Research Institute and the Advisory Council of Islamic Ideology existed since the Council could request the Research Institute to gather materials and submit an opinion on a particular legislative proposal.

However, the effectiveness of these Islamic institutions was compromised by their status as strictly advisory bodies. For example, in addition to the fact that the legislature could ignore a recommendation from the Ideology Council, it could even pass new legislation prior to consulting the Council. Furthermore, both the Ideology Council and the Research Institute were government-sponsored and supported, and their directors and members served at the pleasure of the executive.

Resistance to Ayub Khan's attempts to define Pakistan's Islamic identity in liberal modernist terms can be quite forcefully seen in two events: the agitational politics which forced the Director of the Central Institute of Islamic Research from office, and the bitter debate surrounding passage of the *Muslim Family Laws Ordinance*.

Dr. Fazlur Rahman, a scholar educated in Pakistan and at Cambridge University, was appointed Director of the Central Institute of Islamic Research in 1962. In addition, he served as a member of the Advisory Council on Islamic Ideology. The research conducted under his leadership and many of the publications in the Institute's journal, *Islamic Studies,* reflected modernist, reconstructive themes that alarmed many traditionists. Opposition intensified with the publication of Rahman's book, *Islam,* which contained several modernist interpretations objectionable to traditional religious leaders who seized this opportunity to rally their forces. The *ulama* and *mullahs* (local religious leaders) directed mass demonstrations against Rahman throughout Pakistan. These eventually led to his resignation. Their struggle, however, was as much with Ayub Khan as with his appointee, Dr. Rahman.

Traditionists took strong exception not only to Ayub Khan's modernist positions but also to his methods. Since Ayub viewed the *ulama* as chiefly responsible for the retrograde state of Islam and as generally ill-prepared to meet the demands of modernity, he tended to limit their powers and participation in government. Although the *ulama* were, according to tradition, the protectors of the new law (*shariah*) and therefore advisors to the government, Ayub did not acknowledge their status and responsibility within the Ideology Council, the Research Institute or the Commission for the Reform of Muslim Family Laws, which were all dominated by lay people.

The tension between Ayub Khan and traditionist religious leaders was especially evident in the debate surrounding the reform of Muslim Family Law. In many ways it crystallized two major questions associated with the long struggle to articulate Pakistan's Islamic identity: "Who shall have primacy in this process?" and "How shall change be brought about?"

The Commission on Marriage and Family Laws was established in 1955 and issued its report in 1956 with recommendations for reforms in the laws governing marriage, divorce, and inheritance. From that time until passage of the *Muslim Family Laws Ordinance* of 1961, a protracted debate between modernists and traditionists occurred. Traditionists objected to the lay dominance of the committee—one member of the *ulama* plus three laymen and three women—and questioned the lay members' knowledge and expertise in religious matters. In addition to this encroachment on the traditional province of the *ulama,* the Commission did not simply follow *(taqlid)* the family laws of the medieval law books *(fiqh)* but rather advocated substantive reforms through the exercise of individual reasoning *(ijtihad).* Thus, objections were raised not only to the proposed reforms but also to the methodology employed *(ijtihad)* and the qualifications of the Commission's lay members who did not satisfy the traditional criteria for a *mujtahid* (one qualified to exercise *ijtihad*). However, strong support from the Ayub government and women's groups, led by the All Pakistan Women's Organization (APWA), led to the enactment of the *Muslim Family Laws Ordinance* of 1961. The final version was weakened due to omissions and qualifications necessitated by conservative opposition.

SUMMARY

As one reviews the first two decades of Pakistan's existence and her quest to give shape to that Islamic aspiration which provided her *raison d'etre*, several conclusions emerge. First, while there was general agreement regarding the need for a Muslim homeland, what that meant was far from clear. Second, profound differences in education, outlook, and approach between modernists and traditionists presented formidable obstacles – as witnessed in the drafting of the 1956 Constitution and the *Muslim Family Laws Reform Ordinance* of 1961. Third, as a consequence of unresolved differences, *ad hoc*, piecemeal approaches were taken to reach an acceptable compromise. No systematic attempt to define Pakistan's Islamic ideology and then to consistently apply it had been made. The net result of this approach is exemplified by constitutions for an Islamic state whose Islamicity was established by the inclusion of a few Islamic provisions; by Islamic institutions (the Advisory Council on Islamic Ideology and the Central Islamic Research Institute) whose independence and effectiveness were seriously hampered by their excessive dependence upon the executive and whose power was at best advisory; and finally by a major piece of family law reform legislation whose passage was surrounded by controversy and whose final form was compromised both in its substantive provisions and its legal methodology.[17]

THE RE-EMERGENCE OF ISLAM
IN CONTEMPORARY PAKISTAN'S POLITICS

Zulfikar Ali Bhutto (1971–77)

While Islamic sentiment, however unclear and ill-defined, was viewed by most observers of Pakistan as a sensibility to be respected, successive governments had not considered it to be a major factor in Pakistan's political development. Primacy was given to political and social modernization and Islamic reform was surely tangential to this process.

When Zulfikar Ali Bhutto came to power in 1971, there was little to suggest any change in priorities. Bhutto was a modern secular politician with an ideological bent toward socialism. However, events in Pakistan gradually caused Bhutto to progressively increase his appeal to Islam and then, out of political expediency, to advocate Islamization (the process of rendering the political and socioeconomic system of government more Islamic).

Zulfikar Ali Bhutto had built his Pakistan Peoples Party (PPP) on the failure of the Ayub government to effect the significant socioeconomic reforms so necessary in Pakistan. His approach to the redistribution of wealth through nationalization and land reform were part of his socialist platform with its populist slogan: food, clothes, housing (*roti, kapre, makan*). Although influenced primarily by Western forms of socialism, the political realities of Pakistan—the opposition of the majority of *ulama* and especially Maulana Maududi's Jamaat-i-Islami[18]—moved Bhutto not only to maintain that he would never advocate policies contrary to Islam, but also to align increasingly his socialism with Islamic beliefs and values, most notably Islamic egalitarianism and social justice. Thus, despite the fact that the PPP had a broad following with differing viewpoints, from 1968 onwards, its socialism was increasingly identified with "Islamic socialism"[19] This process was helped substantially by Haneef Ramay and his monthly *Nusrat.* Through subsequent issues of *Nusrat* and later *Musawat,* the socialism of Bhutto and the PPP was increasingly presented as an Islamic socialism and identified more with normative Islamic belief and practice than with Western socialism. Attempts were made to root their policies in the great "ideal" historic period of Muhammad and the early righteous caliphs (*Khulafah-i-Rashidin*) with its sense of Islamic solidarity and equality (*musawat*). Toward this end such slogans as *Musawat-i-Muhammadi* (Equality of Muhammad) and *Islami Musawat* (Islamic Equality) were adopted. However, while such moves might allay the fears of some and make the socialist platform of the PPP more Islamically palatable, strong resistance to the PPP and to its socialism, despite its alleged Islamic character, remained, as was evident in the 1970 elections.

During the elections two major parties and ideologies were dominant: the Pakistan Peoples Party (PPP) and the Jamaat-i-Islami (J.I.) of Maulana Maududi. Talk of Islamic socialism was strongly resisted by the religious right—the *ulama* through their political organization Jamiyat-i-

Ulama-i-Islam (JUI) and the Jamiyat-i-Ulama-i-Pakistan (JUP) and especially Maududi's Jamaat-i-Islami which provided the most organized and forceful opposition. In March 1970, 113 *ulama* issued a *fatwa* (formal legal opinion) that condemned socialism as *kufr* (unbelief) and anyone who advocated, supported, or voted for it as outside the pale of Islam.[20] Maulana Maududi charged that the PPP's Islamic socialism was an illegitimate and superficial attempt to make that (socialism) which was against Islam acceptable: "They found out that their socialism cannot dance naked. . . . After realizing this they started calling socialism "Islamic". . . . If it is really based on the *Quran* and the *Sunnah* then what is the need for calling it socialism? . . . Now when they can see that this too does not work they have started calling it Islamic equality *(musawat)* and *Muhammadi musawat*. The object is the same — pure socialism."[21]

Despite this opposition, Bhutto and his PPP scored an impressive victory in the 1970 elections. However, though a minority, the religious parties, (J.I., J.U.I., J.U.P.) did have their impact. In 1973 the term "Islamic" socialism was omitted from the new constitution. More importantly, the Ahmadiyah question was raised once more by the traditionists. Finally, in 1975 President Bhutto yielded to renewed agitation against the Ahmadis which was sparked both for religious reasons as well as political concerns that Ahmadis occupied important positions in the government, especially the Armed Forces. Bhutto declared the Ahmadis a non-Muslim minority. In addition, the wording of the oath of office for the President and Prime Minister was changed to clearly require belief in the finality of the prophethood of Muhammad, i.e. that he was the last divinely sent messenger of God.[22] However, the criticism of Bhutto and his policies as fundamentally un-Islamic did not disappear. As we shall see, it was to have dramatic ramifications for his government in later years.

Three other political realities contributed to the reemergence of Islam during the Bhutto period: (1) the post-Bangladesh civil war period with its re-examination and renewed quest for the source(s) or roots of Pakistan's national identity; (2) the emergence of Arab oil economic power and Bhutto's attempt to align Pakistan more closely with the Arab world, and (3) most importantly, the March 1977 elections.[23]

As a result of the 1971 Civil War, Pakistan lost more than half of her territory and population as East Pakistan became the sovereign state of Bangladesh. Relations between West and East Pakistan had been strained throughout the post-partition period. With the loss of her eastern wing, Pakistan's unresolved identity problems surfaced once more as the question was raised: "Why Pakistan?" Amidst its regionalism, tribalism, vast linguistic differences, what made Pakistan a nation? What was the source of her national unity and identity? Such questioning quite naturally led to a re-examination of the events, motives, and reasons which influenced the formation of Pakistan. The level of concern and self-scrutiny was clearly reflected in the press and quite forcefully at the meeting of the First Congress on the History and Culture of Pakistan in April 1973 where a substantial portion of the program was devoted to this question.[24]

At the practical political level, Bhutto sought during the post-Bangladesh period to align Pakistan more closely with her Southwest Asian neighbors, in particular the Arab oil-producing states. He emphasized both their regional and, more importantly, Islamic ties. These were reinforced by constant shuttling to the oil-producing states, speeches which emphasized their common Islamic brotherhood and the holding of an Islamic Summit Conference in Lahore with representatives from all parts of the Muslim world (February 1974). Bhutto further underscored the importance of Islamic solidarity by accepting Anwar Sadat's mediation and call for reconciliation between Pakistan and Bangladesh in the name of Islam. Islam had become a prominent part of the Bhutto government's approach to foreign policy.

Despite Bhutto's appeals to Islam, opposition to his government and its policies continued to grow. His use of Islam was viewed as exploitation of religion by one whom traditional religious leaders judged as singularly un-Islamic in personal behavior and attitudes. This criticism played a pivotal role in the March 1977 elections. Nine opposition parties joined together under the umbrella of Islam to form the Pakistan National Alliance (PNA) whose leadership was controlled by three religious parties (J.I., J.U.I. and J.U.P). This "religious" dominance as well as the proven power of Islam in mass politicization strengthened the PNA tendency to cast its criticisms in Islamic terms. As PNA strength grew, Bhutto felt equally compelled to respond in kind. Religion, therefore, became a focal point as both sides espoused and committed themselves to a more Islamic system of government (*Nizam-i-Islam*).

The situation was not resolved by the March, 1977 elections. The PNA charged massive poll violations and demanded new national elections. In the agitational politics that followed, Islam continued as the principal political weapon wielded by both sides. Bhutto and his government were characterized as corrupt — un-Islamic — no better than *kafirs* (unbelievers). Mullahs and their mosques increasingly played a central role in mass politics. Demonstrations often originated at the mosque following the Friday congregational prayer and political exhortations from religious leaders. Slogans of "Islam in Danger" and *"Nizam-i-Islam"* summarized the battle cry and slogan of the PNA opposition parties.

In addition to imposing martial law and curfews, Bhutto introduced Islamic measures to counter his detractors' criticisms. In April 1977, he outlawed drinking, gambling and night clubs and declared that within six months *shariah* law would be established and enforced.[25] In July, fulfilling his promise in the PPP Election Manifesto, Friday, the traditional Islamic holiday, replaced the Sunday sabbath.

Nevertheless, these overtures were generally perceived as insincere stopgap measures and so did little to alleviate Mr. Bhutto's situation. They did, however, contribute to the momentum for an Islamic system of government — a sentiment which was to be used by General Zia-ul-Haq to justify his *coup d'etat* on July 5, 1977. In addressing the nation on the eve of the coup, Zia declared: "Pakistan, which was created in the name of Islam, will continue to survive only if it sticks to Islam. That is why I consider the introduction of an Islamic system as an essential prerequisite for the country."[26]

Zia-ul-Haq (1977–): Nizam-i-Islam

Zia-ul-Haq, Chief Martial Law Administrator (CMLA), is a practicing Muslim, and from the beginning of his rule, due to personal conviction as well as political expediency, committed his government to the introduction of the *Nizam-i-Islam*. During the first months of his tenure in office, legitimation for his government was clearly based upon the growing "discovery" and repudiation of the political excesses of the Bhutto government, and in sharp contrast to this "un-Islamic" behavior, an ever-increasing stream of appeals to Islam. Concrete steps were taken early to demonstrate the beginning of a new Islamic order. First, the Advisory Council on Islamic Ideology was reorganized and reinstituted. Second, Islamic penal reforms were introduced, i.e. the application of classical *shariah* punishments (*hudud,* penalties prescribed by the *Quran*) for crimes of theft, adultery, and decoity (highway robbery). Third, persons long known for their strong commitment to an Islamic order and associated with religious political parties — among them A.K. Brohi (Minister of Law and of Religious Affairs), Khurshid Ahmad (Deputy Chairman of the Planning Commission), Mahmud Azam Faruqi (Minister of Information) and Ghafoor Ahmad (Minister of Commerce) — were appointed to key government positions. The latter three are prominent members of Maulana Maududi's Jama at-i-Islami Party.

During the following year further steps were taken on the path of Islamization. These were announced in December 1978 in a presidential address entitled *Measures to Enforce Nizam-i-Islam*.[27] Zia maintained that despite Pakistan's Islamic purpose and destiny, during the three decades since independence little progress had been made. Symbolically, he took the occasion of the Islamic New Year in December to formally announce another new beginning—the enforcement of the Islamic system in Pakistan. This Islamic system, in an expanded and revised version, became law in February 1979 when on the occasion of the celebration of the Prophet Muhammad's birthday, Zia-ul-Haq formally promulgated the *Introduction of Islamic Laws*.[28] Zia's approach affirmed the traditional Islamic belief that Islam is a total way of life, encompassing "individual and collective life."[29] This wholistic approach was reflected in the reforms contained in both presidential addresses which not only affected prayer or worship but the educational, economic, and judicial systems as well.

Regulations governing the observance of daily and Friday community prayers were introduced. The first concerned the offering of *namaz* (i.e. the five times daily prayer/worship, *salat*) which constitutes one of the five pillars or essential practices of Islam. Since the government and its officials should set an example, all government departments were required to make arrangements for the offering of prayers during working hours. Moreover, the heads of departments were expected to lead the prayer or at least offer them with their workers.[30]

As noted above, Zulfikar Ali Bhutto had replaced Sunday with observance of Friday as the weekly holiday. While Zia continued this practice for all government offices, businesses remain free to choose their weekly holiday. However, the new regulations require that all business establishments close during the noon prayer period to permit mosque attendance for the Friday congregational *(juma)* prayer.

The second area of reform involved Islamic ideology and education. Zia affirmed Pakistan's commitment to a double-faceted ideology—Pakistan and Islam. Awareness of this national ideology was to be encouraged and reinforced through a revision of textbooks and curricula, the production of new textbooks which emphasized Pakistan's national Islamic ideology, an emphasis on Urdu as the national language through its replacement of English as the medium of instruction, and the greater use of Urdu in mass communications, especially T.V. and radio.[31]

The third area of reform concerned Islamic economic measures—the introduction of Islamic forms of taxation (*zakat* and *ushr*) and the abolition of banking interest *(riba)*. *Zakat* (almsgiving) is a Quranically prescribed almsgiving (2.5 percent computed on the net wealth (not simply on the income) of an individual, the proceeds of which are to be distributed to the less fortunate members of the Islamic community.[32] It is a pious act which reinforces the idea of an Islamic brotherhood whose members have a duty to provide for those in need.

Ushr is a form of *zakat*, a tithe due on productive land. While the term *ushr* is not used in the *Quran*, a specific verse (Quran VI: 141) was taken by later legal authorities as referring to *ushr*: "It is He who produceth gardens with trellises . . . with produce of all kinds . . . similar (in kind) and different (in variety): eat of their fruit in their season but render the dues that are proper on the day that the harvest is gathered."

Zia's first decree had little of substance to say about the enforcement of *zakat* and *ushr* other than to indicate that introduction of these "pillars of the Islamic economic system" presented formidable obstacles, among them: a determination of the income that these Islamic taxes would generate, what percentage of the nation's needs this would meet, and what other taxes might be required. With regard to *ushr* in particular "the existing revenue system will have to be revolutionized in order to introduce the system."[33]

In February 1979, the Zakat Fund was created with financial assistance from Saudi Arabia and the United Arab Emirates and a system established for the collection and distribution of *zakat* and *ushr* at the local, provincial, and federal levels. Although the collection of *zakat* was scheduled to begin July 1, 1979, and that of *ushr* in October 1979, as of May 1980 this has yet to occur.

Some headway has been made regarding abolition of the "curse of interest."[34] Although Zia has committed his government to an interest-free banking system, he has also made it clear that this will be a gradual process. Among the limited measures introduced thus far are: (1) certain loans from the government's House Building Finance Corporation are interest free and instead the Corporation functions as a shareholder in proportion to its investment (loan); (2) the N.I.T. (National Investment Trust) also operates completely on equity participation and the I.C.P. (Investment Corporation of Pakistan) is to do so with regard to its mutual funds.[35]

As of July 1, 1979, in addition to the N.I.T. (National Investment Trust), the I.C.P. (Investment Corporation of Pakistan) has moved in this direction, i.e. its 12 mutual funds issued since 1966 have been cleared of interest-bearing funds (bonds) by replacing these bonds with additional common stock. By July 1, 1980, all other activities of the I.C.P. will be interest-free. Furthermore, projected plans call for commercial banks to be rendered interest-free by 1982.[36]

The final area of Islamic reform occurred in the judicial system with the introduction of *shariah* laws governing crime and punishment and the creation of *shariah* courts. As noted previously, Zia had introduced the *hudud* system, i.e. unalterable punishments stipulated by the *shariah* for specific crimes. In Zia's *Introduction of Islamic Laws* of 1979, this system was set forth more fully and in greater detail. Drinking, adultery, false accusation of adultery, and certain forms of theft were declared subject to their respective *shariah* punishments of flogging, stoning, and amputation.[37]

The promulgation of the *Shariah* Benches Order of 1978 and its amendment in 1979 established a Bench in the High Court (*Shariah* Bench) and an Appeals Bench in the Supreme Court (*Shariah* Appellate Bench) in every province. Each *Shariah* Bench shall consist of three justices. Judicial review may be based upon petitions of appeal from individuals, or from the Federal or Provincial governments. Their purpose is to decide whether a current law is fully or partially repugnant to Islam, i.e. contrary to the injunctions of Islam as found in the *Quran* and *Sunnah* of the Prophet. All laws or provisions which are judged un-Islamic are to be amended by appropriate legislative action.

Implementation of the *Nizam* measures has been stymied by significant difficulties. First as indicated above, introduction of the Islamic economic measures (*zakat, ushr,* and banning of interest) require careful planning regarding their impact on Pakistan's economic development. Second, many Muslims have come to view *zakat* as a private obligation between themselves and Allah. Furthermore, they are accustomed to determining to whom they shall distribute it, usually family members, friends and neighbors. Thus, they question the government's right to enforce collection and are skeptical that politics and corruption will affect the proper distribution of these funds. Third, talk of the *Nizam* has brought to the forefront sectarian differences, especially those of the Sunni majority vs. the Shii minority. For example, the Shii legal school (Jafari) differs from the Sunni law schools—of the four schools, the Hanafi is the official school of law followed in Pakistan—in several respects regarding the *hudud* (Quranically-prescribed punishments) and *zakat*. For the Shii, unlike the Sunni, *zakat* is not compulsory on capital or trading money. Also, Shii differ from Sunni regarding the application of the *hudud* punishment of amputation. In an attempt to resolve this impasse, the Islamic Ideology Council has appointed a standing subcommittee consisting of three Sunni and three Shii *ulama*. Though some have tried to say that these differences are minor, the need to appoint the subcommittee, its somewhat stormy history, and its failure thus far to achieve any resolution, would seem to indicate otherwise.

Fourth and finally, the introduction of *shariah* Benches (Courts) to determine whether or not a law is repugnant to Islam, creates several difficulties: first, the judiciary in general is ill-prepared for such a task since the vast majority of judges and lawyers, though perhaps well-trained in Western law, have little training in or knowledge of *shariah* law. Recognition of this difficulty can be seen in the recent inauguration (Oct. 8, 1979) of a *shariah* faculty of law at Quaid-i-Azam University in Islamabad whose purpose it is to provide post-graduate training for lawyers and, in turn, Pakistan's future judges. The lack of current expertise is further attested to by the fact that both in the planning of the curriculum for the *shariah* faculty and in its staffing, Pakistan has had to look outside the country.[38] Second, the present system may well lead to a judge's nightmare; *shariah* courts may be inundated with requests for judicial review of virtually every law since not only the Federal and Provincial governments but every citizen may file a case without any court fee. More importantly, instead of the Constitution serving as the criterion, the Constitution itself is subject to the *shariah*. Given the richness and complexity of Islamic law, obtaining a single agreed-upon interpretation on *shariah* doctrine may prove quite difficult.

Perhaps the best example of the potentially radical and sweeping nature of this review system is the case filed before the Lahore High Court *Shariah* Bench in September 1979, by Justice B. Z. Kaikaus, retired Supreme Court Justice and sometime advisor to Zia-ul-Haq. Justice Kaikaus argued that Pakistan's present political system (popular representative democracy) was not Islamic, i.e. it has no Quranic basis. Moreover, he maintained that the traditional Islamic system of government which consisted of a ruler (*amir*) and a consultative council (*shura*) did not necessarily constitute a representative form of government. The failure of Pakistan to define its Islamic ideology – in particular to establish clearly the relationship of its government to its Islamic heritage in successive constitutions – means that, with the exception of the limited number of Islamic provisions discussed above, Pakistan's entire form of government is subject to judicial review.

Zia-ul-Haq has sought to legitimize his rule and policies through appeal to his commitment to realize Pakistan's original purpose and ideal – the establishment of an Islamic system or way of life *(Nizam)*. His personal piety and cordial relations with religious leaders and parties and his cabinet-level appointment of their protegés reinforced the expectation that Pakistan would indeed increasingly become a more demonstrable example of an Islamic order – politically, economically, and legally. However, the internal political climate today is far from optimistic.[39] What has caused the skepticism and pessimism regarding the introduction and enforcement of the *Nizam* among many of those who, in principle, advocate an Islamic state? Why do many privately, if not publicly, wonder whether the present regime may not also fall within Zia's judgment regarding Pakistan's past history that "Many a politician exploited the name of Islam and many a ruler did what they pleased in the name of Islam"?[40]

The most common statement used to summarize general criticism of the government is that it has only introduced a "negative" Islam and that, as has often occurred in the past, Islam is used or manipulated by the government to justify its policies. Many critics maintain that despite several years of rule, the major substantive Islamic reforms have consisted of prohibitions (gambling, alcohol, banking interest), Quranic punishments *(hudud)*, and taxation (*zakat* and *ushr*) without a comparable emphasis on more positive Islamic reforms. The economic measures (*zakat, ushr,* and limited prohibition on interest) are viewed by many as *ad hoc* measures whose place in and effect upon the economy of a modern state like Pakistan have not been sufficiently determined. At the other end of the spectrum are traditionist criticisms that the government is moving too slowly and should implement and enforce the *Nizam* immediately.

Politically, Zia-ul-Haq has used Islam to legitimize his coup and martial law administration. Postponement (originally elections were promised for within 90 days of the coup in 1977) and finally the cancellation of elections scheduled for November 1979, the disbanding of political parties, and the execution of Zulfikar Ali Bhutto have reinforced the sense that the Islam espoused by the government is negative, restrictive and manipulative. After cancellation of the elections, the formation of a special commission of experts to determine whether Pakistan's political system is Islamic contributes to the suspicion that Islam is being used as a *post-factum* justification of Zia's actions. This same question was on the agenda of the Advisory Council on Islamic Ideology. The President's decision to act prior to any formal finding by the Council and to extend his martial law administration, has further undermined his credibility.

SUMMARY

More than three decades have elapsed since Pakistan was founded as a Muslim homeland. Despite its avowed ideological commitment, the quest to articulate its Islamic identity has yielded limited results: constitution-

ally, Islam is the state religion of Pakistan; its president and prime minister must be Muslim; no law is permitted which is repugnant to Islam; the
hudud punishments have been introduced; and two specific agencies —
the Advisory Council on Islamic Ideology and the Islamic Research Institute have been established to assist the government.

In the socioeconomic sphere, Islamic measures may be seen principally in the limited banning of usury, the announcement of the yet-to-
be-implemented *zakat* and *ushr* revenue system and the establishment of
the *shariah* Benches to determine whether or not current laws are un-
Islamic.

What are the problems which emerge from Pakistan's path of Islamization? First, while appeals to Islam have proven effective in times of
crisis (e.g., independence movement and the PNA struggle with the Bhutto
government) for mass politicization, subsequent attempts to define and
effectively implement reforms which would bring about a more Islamic
political and economic system have been far less effective. The reasons
are many. Among the more important are: (1) the parties who rally under
the banner of Islam in times of crisis vary widely as to their ultimate political goals and agendas. A broad spectrum of visions regarding the ultimate nature of the state have existed. They range from Jinnah's idea of a
homeland where Muslims might be free to live their lives to a conception
of a religious state which is formally Islamic in its ideology and institutions. Failure to define terminology more carefully has compounded the
situation. The terms "Muslim homeland," "Muslim state" and "Islamic
state" have been used freely and, at times, interchangeably with little sense
of a need to draw clear distinctions regarding their meanings and consequent effect upon Pakistan's ideology and political, social, and economic
institutions. Thus, while the state's official title is the Islamic Republic of
Pakistan, nowhere is the particular significance or meaning of "Islamic
Republic" stated clearly and systematically. Although Pakistan is spoken
of as an "Islamic State," it bears little resemblance to a classical Islamic
state nor has it produced an agreed-upon formula by which it might be regarded as a modern Islamic state. Rather, it resembles most nations in the
Muslim world whose official designation as "Muslim" is based upon their
Muslim majority and a very limited number of Islamic provisions in an
otherwise Western secularly inspired model of government.[41]

The second major problem affecting the process of self-statement
in Pakistan has been the "actors" — individuals or groups equipped to provide leadership. The Western-oriented secular elites who comprise much
of Pakistan's bureaucracy (civil and military) have provided the continuity of leadership, governance, and law throughout Pakistan's tumultuous

history. These elites have for the most part neither appreciated nor been equipped to provide a political system sensitive to Pakistan's avowed Islamic *raison d'etre* and thus capable of meeting her spiritual ideological as well as material needs. Their approach to sociopolitical development has too often been one of uncritical adoption (of Western models) rather than adaptation to the history and values of their country. Modernist Muslim intellectuals or reformers, i.e. those who desire substantive reinterpretation and Islamic reform, have had a limited impact.[42] They have been few in number, have had limited access to positions of influence, and have received little support. The traditionists (Maudud and the majority of the *ulama*) reflect the more conservative religious character of the majority of Pakistan's population and have been effective in agitational politics. However, with the exception of Maulana Maududi's Jama at-i-Islami, they have not been able to set forth their own explicit models for Pakistan's Islamic state. Instead they, on the one hand, call for introduction of the *shariah* and, on the other, have often been content to simply accept a legal system in which no law is repugnant to Islam.

This compromise raises an important question. Classically, an Islamic state is one which is governed by the *shariah*. The crux of the problem then is reflected in this question: Is this classical criterion met by simply stating that no law may be repugnant to Islam i.e. the Quran and *Sunnah* of the Prophet? Or is it essential for *shariah* rule that the laws of a modern Islamic state be *derived* from the *shariah* whether by simple appropriation of the past or reinterpretation and reform?

The most basic political problem for traditionists has been their inability to attain a sufficient degree of agreement and cooperation among themselves to work constructively toward their common Islamic goal. This has undermined their credibility and effectiveness in Pakistan's political development.

The organizational problems among religious leaders point up a crucial difference between Sunni and Shii Islam. Whereas, Shii Islam, as evidenced in modern Iran, has a limited religious hierarchy—a handful of popularly-acknowledged religious leaders (*ayatollah*s) who have a position of leadership and teaching authority—the Sunni Islam of Pakistan lacks any effective religious organization or hierarchy and teaching authority.

At the heart of Pakistan's ideological difficulties has been a failure to move beyond the use of Islam in an *ad hoc* piecemeal fashion. For example, Fazlur Rahman in analyzing the process of constitution making in Pakistan has called this phenomenon an "Islamic fetish": "a mere *ad hoc* and mechanical application of the term 'Islamic' to certain concepts to the exclusion of others. 'Islamic justice and tolerance' . . . [but] Why are not human rights Islamic? What about education and health?"[43]

The fact that Pakistan's leaders have been unable to provide a more systematic approach in setting forth and implementing her Islamic ideology has had profound consequences. While an *ad hoc* approach may seem the most expedient and least troublesome path in the short run, long term it does not provide a clear substantive ideology upon which to base a sense of national identity and some sense of unity amidst Pakistan's significant linguistic and regional differences. Failure to face head on and to resolve fundamental differences of interpretation has perpetuated the still present problem that beneath Pakistan's Islamic and nationalist rhetoric and terminology is a vacuum, an unresolved identity crisis which promises to be a source of continued unrest. Furthermore, this will mean the continued danger that Islam will be manipulated for political purposes whether by secularist, liberal modernist, or traditionist. Even sincere efforts are open to the question, indeed accusation, "Whose Islam is this?" and the sense that interpretations of a single individual or group are being imposed from above.

Current attempts to introduce a more Islamic system of government, although ostensibly meant to remedy the ideological failures of the past, suffer from the same underlying problems — they are also *ad hoc*, selective, lack any formal consensus and means of legitimation. Given the reality of martial law administration, its regulations may be viewed as imposed by the Chief Martial Law Administrator, Zia-ul-Haq, rather than legislated by the national assembly or approved by a recognized Islamic council.

Attempts by Zia-ul-Haq to question the Islamic character of Pakistan's political system as well as a similar challenge before the *Shariah* Bench by Justice Kaikaus strike at the heart of the problem. Motives aside, such fundamental questioning is possible as long as Pakistan's Islamic identity remains unresolved.

The cyclical reappearance of this problem is strikingly reflected by the fact that the issues raised today were emphasized in the Munir Report of 1954. The responses of the *ulama* questioned by the commission clearly showed that western political notions of democracy, popular sovereignty, parliamentary legislation, equal rights and opportunities for minorities were contrary to their beliefs regarding the principles of an Islamic state.[44] Awareness of this dichotomy between traditionist and modernist had motivated the commission's recommendation that a bold reinterpretation and reform be carried out.

The Islamic measures introduced by Zia clearly raise many questions which Pakistan, and other Muslim countries that may choose to follow more Islamic systems of government, must face: What constitutes a modern Islamic state? Are there essential political, legal, and economic institutions and practices which must be present? Are modern political notions such as democracy, representational government, political party system, etc. admissable? If so, how and why? What is the status and role of minorities; given the ideological commitment of the state, are minorities to be excluded from policy-making positions?

Pakistan has established two vehicles—the Advisory Council on Islamic Ideology and the Islamic Research Institute—for addressing questions of ideology and institutional development. However, they have lacked the status, support, political independence, and sufficient resources (monetary and staff) necessary to make substantive headway towards the resolution of these questions.

Moreover, the most important *lacunae* remains that of education. Pakistan, as well as other Muslim countries that seek to provide a more Islamic political and social order, will require the work of experts who have not only mastered their own disciplines (politics, economics, etc.) but are grounded in their Islamic heritage. At present, their numbers are very limited, and so cooperative efforts between Muslim countries will continue to be not only useful but absolutely necessary.

It is especially imperative that general educational reforms, primarily aimed at eliminating illiteracy, be accompanied by a commitment to provide quality Islamic religious education (*Islamiyyat*) in state-run schools and a well-rounded curriculum in religious schools (i.e. modern as well as traditional disciplines) to overcome the educational dichotomy (secular vs. religious) which has been so prevalent. This divergence in orientation and outlook, as indicated earlier in this study, has caused long-standing tension between the political and religious leadership and has had serious consequences. Effective and lasting change requires the cooperation of both groups in drafting reforms and obtaining mass support for them so that change will not simply be legislated but internalized.

W. C. Smith has written: "It is an observable fact that in the first decade of Pakistan's history the leadership failed to (that is, did not) lead the Pakistani aspiration towards an Islamic quality for the state. . . . Pakistan's coming into being was such that an Islamic failure has tended to become an ideological failure, a moral failure, and a political failure."[45] While the political leadership possessed a "unique fitness in the realm of making the new state viable," they also displayed an "ineptness for the task of rendering it Islamic."[46] These observations written some twenty-three years ago continued to be true for subsequent decades. An educational system that will provide a political leadership which possesses both the administrative skills and an informed appreciation for its Islamic heritage remains a desideratum.

The education and training of religious leaders is of equal importance due to their influence on the religious education and outlook of the vast majority of the population as well as their proven ability to play an effective role in mass mobilization. A well-educated class of religious leaders i.e. trained both in traditional religious and modern disciplines will go far in bridging the gap between tradition and modernity. As a class, they will no longer be seen as either obstacles to needed change or as lacking adequate training to speak sufficiently to contemporary problems; they will be better prepared to contribute to constructive reform. Moreover, since religious leaders can provide an air of legitimacy that even the best lay Islamic experts lack, their support is essential.

More than three decades have passed since Pakistan was established as a Muslim homeland. She has endured serious political instability (three martial law regimes, wars with India, and a civil war with Bangladesh) and has faced massive socioeconomic problems. At the same time her original purpose and aspiration have often been either overlooked or selectively used both by the political leadership and its opposition. The 1970s saw a re-emergence of emphasis on Islamic identity and ideology in the politics of Pakistan. It became a dominant theme in the PNA opposition to the Bhutto government. Under Zia-ul-Haq, government commitment to establishing the *Nizam-i-Islam* has meant a strong emphasis on Islam in the language of politics and in political and economic reforms. Whatever the fate of the Zia-ul-Haq's government and its interpretation and implementation of the *Nizam*, the re-emergence of Islam as a central theme in Pakistan's politics has resulted in a focusing on questions and issues of Islamic identity and ideology which will not easily disappear.

Islamic Resurgence in Malaysia

Fred R. von der Mehden

CONTEMPORARY NEWS MEDIA, popular literature, and now scholarly works have "suddenly" become aware of a resurgent Islamic self-identity spreading through the Muslim world. Often superficial reports have commented upon changes in the Middle East, ranging from the increased wearing of traditional attire among middle and upper class women in Cairo to the more dramatic events surrounding the fall of the Shah, moves toward an Islamic state in Pakistan and Iran, and the rebellion in Afghanistan. Meanwhile, changes which have been taking place among Southeast Asia's approximately 135 million Muslims have been largely ignored, with the possible exception of the Moro uprising in the Southern Philippines. This paper addresses the role of a resurgent Islam in one of the two Islamically oriented countries of Southeast Asia, Malaysia. We have not seen the high drama of Iran there, but a new Islamic self-awareness is leading to a political and social environment different from previous decades. In this analysis four factors will be considered: (1) the traditional roles of Islam in Malaysia; (2) the religious resurgence; (3) reactions of political organizations; and (4) possible future trends.

TRADITIONAL ROLES OF ISLAM IN MALAYSIA

The central political and social characteristic of Malaysia is its multi-communal population.[1] Very little of any political importance that goes on in that country is not influenced by the ethnic (Malaysians call it racial) and religious diversity that is to be found among its almost 13 million people. Within that population approximately fifty percent are Muslim, and the vast majority of these are Malays living on Peninsula Malaysia. To the Malay it is almost unthinkable to be anything but a Muslim, and the constitutional and legal structure is established to protect that link. Not only is it illegal to attempt to convert a Muslim, but the Malay Sultans are the chief protectors of that religion on the peninsula. Within Malay society there is an integrated perception of religion, traditional values, and village and family life. It is difficult for the Malay to disentangle Islam from this whole.

While half the country is Muslim and largely Malay, the rest is composed of ethnic groups considered foreign to the country by the dominant community. The largest of these minorities, the Chinese, compose approximately 38 percent of the population of the Peninsula and reflect varying degrees of acceptance of traditional Chinese religious patterns.[2] The rest of the population is largely Indian and Hindu, although Pakistanis and Arabs who follow the Muslim faith are generally granted the same privileges as Malays. This very diversity leads to tensions and conflicts and tends to reinforce the identity of the Malays, particularly given the fact that the more urbanized Chinese maintain a higher economic and educational level than do the more rural Malay Muslims.

Thus, the first political and social fact of life of Malaysia is and has been the relationship of religion and ethnicity; the second religious point of reference must be the ritualistic and somewhat traditional attitude toward Islam that is to be found within the Malay community. Observers have noted the limited interest in contemporary modern trends of Islam among religious and political leaders. Others have commented upon the ritualistic emphasis given that religion by Malays and the great interest shown in specifics of Islamic law. This traditional theological pattern when combined with the integrated social concept of the Malay Muslim has helped to develop a somewhat homogeneous religious pattern among Malay Muslims. There is comparatively little of the divisiveness that has been found in Indonesia since the entrance of modernism, and variations in practice that are to be found in Indonesia are also more limited in Malaysia.[3]

A third and somewhat ambiguous element in Malaysia has been the relationship of Islam to the state and to politics. While we find on the one hand a political and constitutional system protecting Islam, on the other the more intolerant elements within the Muslim community have never dominated Malay politics. This situation needs greater explanation for it tends to interpret the present role that a resurgent Islam plays in Malaysia. Early Malayan* politics was not without its more intransigent religious nationalists and, in fact, the present Prime Minister Dato Onn resigned from the now dominant Malay party, the United Malay National Organization (UMNO), because it would not allow non-Malays to become associate members.[4] There were also other smaller political parties that reflected Malay Islamic chauvinism, and the chief opposition to the government since its inception has been an organization characterized by such attitudes, the Pan-Malayan Islamic Party (PMIP, now known as Partie Islam Sc Malaysia, or PAS). Yet, the very size of the non-Malay population demanded a politics of accommodation, and by the time of the first municipal elections of 1952 UMNO found it necessary to cooperate with other communal organizations. Out of this was formed the Alliance, a multi-ethnic organization composed of three political parties — the Malay UMNO, the Chinese Malayan-Chinese Association (MCA), and the Malayan-Indian Congress (MIC).[5] In the 1970s this group was further expanded into the National Front incorporating other smaller parties.

The multi-communal composition of the dominant political organization did not end religious-ethnic tensions both within and without that organization. Since its formation the Alliance has been faced with divisions in its own organization as Chinese members of the MCA considered themselves junior partners and more traditional Malay-Muslim elements of UMNO demanded a greater role for Malays and Islam within the state and society. As well, the Alliance faced opposition from the outside from dissatisfied Chinese on the one side and traditional Malay-Muslims on the other. Points of contestation related to education, language, and particularly the special rights granted Malays who were considered sons of the soil and therefore deserving special subsidies, quotas, and other favorable legislation.[6]

However, against this backdrop of communal accommodation and conflict, there developed until the late 1960s a constitutional pattern which provided for a state favoring Islam but guaranteeing religious freedom to others. In a somewhat ambiguous set of provisions Islam became the official religion of the new state while at the same time guaranteeing that every religious group had the right to manage its own affairs, establish and maintain institutions for religious purposes, acquire property, and establish and maintain institutions for the education of their children in their own religion. If constitutionally and legally non-Muslims are protected, Muslims are under Islamic law and, as previously stated, Sultans

---

*The country was known as Malaya until 1963 when Sabah and Sarawak joined the federation and it became Malaysia.

are to see to their needs. With regard to Muslim law religious courts are employed to see that the rules are followed among those of that religion. The text for the provision of that law is as follows:

> Muslim Law and personal and family law of persons professing the Muslim religion, including the Muslim Law relating to succession, testate and intestate, betrothal, marriage, divorce, dower, maintenance, legitimacy, guardianship, gifts, partitions and noncharitable trusts; Muslim Wakfs and the definition and regulation of charitable and religious trusts, the appointment of trustees and the incorporation of persons in respect of Muslim religious and charitable institutions operating wholly within the State; Malay custom; Zakat, Fitrah and Bait-ul-Mal or similar Muslim revenue; mosques or any Muslim public place of worship, creation and punishment of offences by persons professing the Muslim religion against precepts of that religion, except in regard to matters included in the Federal List; the constitution, organization and procedure of Muslim courts, which shall have jurisdiction only over persons professing the Muslim religion and in respect only of any of the matters included in this paragraph, but shall not have jurisdiction in respect of offences except in so far as conferred by federal law: the control of propagating doctrines and beliefs among persons professing the Muslim religion; the determination of matters of Muslim Law and doctrine and Malay custom.[7]

Thus, the situation has been one in which Islam is the state religion and Islamic law governs the acts of believers, but constitutionally other religious groups are to be allowed freedom to practice as they wish. In actuality there have been infrequent difficulties for Christians in terms of advertisement of church services, visas for missionaries, etc., in part due to the fear of efforts to convert Malay-Muslims. There were also reports, particularly in Sabah under previous state leadership, of forced conversions to Islam[8] and more recently there have been efforts to convert Chinese, but in this case without the previous high levels of pressure. Yet, Malaysia has an Islamic state religion which until recently operated within a political structure which emphasized the politics of accommodation. In fact, the very necessity of the ruling UMNO party to cooperate with non-Muslims made this compromise necessary.

RESURGENT ISLAM

A number of events have occurred in this past decade which have challenged this postwar religious-political pattern. First, in May of 1969 a series of bloody riots between Chinese and Malays led to a period of emergency rule and stronger efforts by the government to raise the level of Malay economic and political power.[9] These riots resulted in considerable reflection among Malay politicians and demands that greater efforts be made to meet previous goals of communal equality.

This was the beginning of a major "tilt" toward the Malays in governmental policy. Whereas traditionally Malay-Muslims had held almost all the major positions in the Cabinet, this pattern was extended even further. Secondly, UMNO, while continuing in partnership with its Chinese and Indian co-members of the Alliance and even expanding it into the larger National Front, now displayed its power more aggressively. It became obvious that the senior partner desired to dominate the political scene to an even greater extent than it had previously. The centerpiece of government policy became the National Economic Policy (NEP) which was formulated to redress dramatically the economic imbalance between the Malays and other communities. Through special subsidies to Malay firms, quota systems at all levels of the work force in industry, economic programs to raise the Malays' ability to compete in the marketplace, and a variety of other methods, it was hoped that by 1990 there could be a major change in the economic position of the Malay-Muslim community. While this was to be done through growth and thus not at the expense of the other communities, many Chinese and Indians felt that they would be penalized by these new policies.

Finally, the government began to become even more active in advancing the Islamic cause. Under the first Prime Minister of Malaysia, Tenkgu Abdul Rahman (1957–70), the government had practiced a policy of accommodation to the extent of downplaying the role of Islam except during election periods when it was in competition with PMIP.[10] In fact, during this period considerable tension often developed within UMNO as more traditional members of parliament and local party leaders felt that the government was not sufficiently attentive to Malay-Islamic needs. It was during this time that government officials stated the desirability of staying open on Friday because of international tin markets, and the necessity to pattern attitudes more after the "Protestant work ethic," and one government minister even extolled the usefulness of alcohol.[11] This was an era of ambiguity in Alliance politics as government leaders on the one hand attempted to accommodate their Chinese and Indian co-workers, while on the other they sought to appease the Islamic traditionalists both within and without the party. This politics of ambiguity became particularly apparent during elections and other times of stress.[12] In the 1970s there was an obvious increase in support for Islamic causes. While still attempting to maintain the politics of accommodation, the government moved toward aiding new missionary groups financially and rhetorically, developing more extensive contacts with international Islamic activities, and expanding the role of Islam in radio and television, as well as during public appearances by politicians. Much of this appeared symbolic and ritualistic, particularly to the new more fundamentalist Muslims who were demanding more forceful policies leading toward an expanded role for Islam.

A second factor aiding the resurgence of Islam in Malaysia during the decade was the 1973 OPEC oil embargo and increased cooperation and activity among Muslims in the Middle East. Some cynics have argued that the expanded interest in Islam among Malaysian politicians reflects a desire to obtain economic aid from the Arabs or to guarantee continued oil during future embargoes (there is strong support for the belief that Malaysia would join in a future OPEC boycott). Certainly, there has been a tilt toward the Arab cause in the Middle East although there always has been a degree of sympathy for the Palestinians. The plight of the Palestinians has provided emotional support for the world-wide Islamic cause. This sympathy and empathy has increased and anti-Israeli attitudes have been expressed in the media and by political leaders. Manifestations of these changed attitudes have been press comments by political and religious leaders and mass demonstrations during the 1973 Arab-Israeli War.

A third force lending strength to a resurgent Islam has been the movement of Malays to urban areas and of students to the universities at home and abroad. During this decade there has been an increased number of Malays, particularly youth, moving into the cities of Peninsular Malaysia. Many have come to participate in expanded governmental activities, but others have been involved in the increased interest in industry and commerce which has been developing in recent years. In part, this immigration is a result of the New Economic Policy which seeks to bring more Malays into the modern economic setting. One estimate is that by 1980 32 percent of urban Malaysia would be Malay.[13] The implications of this to rising Malay-Muslim awareness are not difficult to see. As one perceptive Malaysian scholar has commented:

> In a society where ethnic consciousness is pervasive, Malays who have not just become part of a largely non-Malay milieu are bound to develop an awareness of their ethnic background which may not have been there when they were amongst their own ethnic kind in the rural areas. One can argue that even in societies where ethnic consciousness is not as pervasive, a first generation community in a somewhat alien setting is expected to manifest a similar psychological response. A sense of

insecurity, a feeling of suspicion, of distrust, are some of the accompanying elements of this increased ethnic awareness. Islam provides a useful channel for the expression of this awareness since it touches the life of an ordinary Malay in a thousand different ways. No other cultural symbol of the Malay community can be as effective.[14]

It should also be noted that missionary and party leaders have declared that this concentration of Malays in urban areas makes political and religious proselyting considerably easier. It has been argued that these contacts which the Malay Muslims have with urban life may increase their desire to emphasize Islamic traditions, in part because of interaction with the Chinese who are more prepared to compete in urban life and secondly due to reactions to the "yellow culture" elements of modern society. Certainly, there is considerable discussion among Malay religious leaders and popular writers regarding the problems and dangers of contemporary society as it relates to Islam.[15]

The large-scale movement of Malay youth into the secondary schools and universities of the country has also had its impact. In large part due to government subsidies and quotas the number of Malay youth in secondary and tertiary education has increased dramatically. These young men and women often come from rural areas and towns to urban universities where they also find it necessary to compete in a new environment. As well, they come in contact with faculty members embued with Muslim fundamentalist beliefs. Government officials have complained about the type of indoctrination which these students have gained from faculty members who have rejected some of the elements of the politics of accommodation.

Even more influential have been the students and faculty who have been abroad, particularly those educated in England who have become the forefront of Muslim fundamentalism as it is now developing in Malaysia. Students educated in London, Manchester, Birmingham, and other English cities have formed groups attempting to expand their knowledge of and interest in Islam, and politicians and religious leaders of all stripes have remarked upon the strength of fundamentalist Islamic thought in these areas.[16] The Prime Minister has spoken adversely about these people although his own daughter returned reflecting these views. (After he had criticized young women returning wearing "curtains", his own daughter stepped off the plane in traditional dress.)[17] Many of these students are even more strict in their adherence to traditional Islamic views than are orthodox spokesmen in Malaysia. It is interesting to note that, in part due to students returning from the universities at home and abroad to teach in Malay secondary schools, cooperation between urbanized Muslim fundamentalism and traditional religious groups in rural areas is increasing.

Finally, events in Iran and Pakistan helped to increase Islamic self-awareness in Malaysia. The examples of Iranian Muslims who were displacing the Shah and the development of the Pakistani Islamic state have not gone unnoticed on the Peninsula. In fact, Muslim activists in Malaysia have used these events to excite their membership, attract new adherents, and force the government to consider more carefully their cause. Islamic leaders from Malaysia have visited these countries, returning to report the successes of a resurgent Islam in the Middle East. In fact, these spokesmen have complained that a government-controlled press has not properly reported events in Iran and Pakistan and that the achievements of Islam in these states have been hidden in order to diminish the strength of the traditional Islamic forces in Malaysia.[18]

In recent years numerous external manifestations of the Islamic resurgence have appeared in Malaysia. Some of these have been seemingly superficial, while others appear to have major significance for the country's political future. Among the apparently superficial aspects of this resurgence have been changes in attire and increases in rhetoric supporting Islam. Many observers have noted the increased wearing of conservative Muslim garb by women in particular.[19] The growth of this attire has been seen primarily in rural areas where even young children have participated. However, young women at the university as well as many returning students from abroad have taken up traditional dress as a means of symbolically displaying their support for Islamic fundamentalism and their rejection of some of the "undesirable" elements of modernization.

There has also been an increased expression of Islamic rhetoric on a variety of issues, although this was always part of the political debate in Malaysia. Thus, we see an acceleration of a past trend, not an entirely new development. Among the points of discussion are the need for increased support for Muslim goals for the Malaysian society, demands for greater adherence to Islamic law, and warnings regarding dangers to Islam in Malaysia. Some of these statements seem unimportant, such as reports that Australian sausage has pork in it as a means of destroying Islamic purity, or that television is destructive of religious piety with tales of television sets being thrown into the water. While the rhetoric itself reflects changing views of the role that Islam should play in Malaysia, there are deeper and more important demands.

An example of this changing situation is the increased call for stricter adherence to Islamic law and the implementation of the Islamic state. In the latter case religious and political leaders, including the head of PAS, have demanded a constitutional amendment which would prohibit any act of government that was contrary to Islamic law and principles. Admittedly, when pressed many of these leaders are somewhat vague as to what that Islamic state would be like, at times referring to Pakistani and Iranian examples. However, there have been demands for specific Islamic conditions. For example, recently there has been considerable debate as to whether insurance is proper for Muslims, and Malays have long questioned the proper role of interest. In the latter case new experiments in Pakistan have been looked upon with some favor by a few Islamic leaders.

An issue which illustrates best the old yet changing patterns related to Islamic law can be seen in the issue of Khalwat, or close proximity between the sexes.[20] Khalwat has long been outlawed by religious authorities and different Malaysian states have various punishments for those found guilty, usually amounting to an approximately U.S. $100 fine or one month in jail. As early as the 1950s the then PMIP was demanding stricter control of Khalwat and more severe penalties. More recently, there have been continuous demands from religious and oppositional leaders for increased penalties, in some cases calling for the whipping of those convicted. It should here be noted that a few religious leaders have attacked this anti-Khalwat crusade as leading to both undesirable fears among non-Muslims and, most particularly, diverting the minds of the Islamic population from more central issues of their faith. However, during the past year the issue has become even more serious in terms of intercommunal relations as demands have been made for the conviction of non-Muslims for Khalwat if practiced with a Muslim with both falling under Islamic law. This type of case came before the high court in 1962 at which time it was stated that Islamic law was not binding on non-Muslims. However, several states are considering the issue, as is the National Council for Islamic Affairs. This effort is looked upon by many non-Muslims as a sign of increased Islamic chauvinism and a danger to the previous politics of accommodation (a view presently supported by National Front leaders).

The most dramatic and one of the most well-publicized manifestations of Islamic resurgency has related to desecration of Hindu religious shrines during the past two years.[21] There had been some signs of anti-Christian views among Muslim missionary groups, but violence had not taken place against other religions until 1978. At that time there began a series of attacks on Hindu temples in Peninsula Malaysia. By 1979 there had been more than two dozen such attacks, one of them leading to several deaths and the arrest of a number of Muslims from a fanatical element of the missionary movement. These members of the so-called Army of Allah were apparently almost entirely Indian and Pakistani and were part of a very small organization. However, their desecrations led to charges by the government that religious extremism could easily lead to the kind of violence that took place. This group, like the small organization allegedly involved in extremist activities in Indonesia, is not very important in itself. However, like the issue of Khalwat, it has made more difficult the politics of compromise exemplified in the early years of Malaysia's independence.

Finally, one of the most significant aspects of the Islamic revivalism in Malaysia has been the development of numerous active Moslem missionary groups in the country. Unlike the extremist Army of God, these organizations seek the peaceful development of Islam. However, they differ in terms of target groups and general philosophy. In 1979 there were seven major missionary or Dakwah groups active in Peninsula Malaysia plus a variety of small organizations. The six were: (1) Institute Dakwah Islam—sponsored by the prime minister's department; (2) Yayasan Dakwah Islam—sponsored by Islamic Foundation in Malaysia and overseas; (3) ABIM (Islamic Muslim Youth Movement)—a private organization receiving financial aid from the Middle East; (4) PERKIM (Muslim Convert Association)—sponsored and led by Tengku Abdul Rahman and receiving funding from the government and overseas; (5) Darul Arkam—religious intellectual group oriented toward commune-type living; (6) Jamaiya Tabligh Islamiah—a religious intellectual group; (7) Jamaatul Tabligh—radical Indian Muslim.

The Dakwah groups in Malaysia can be divided into three broad groups.[22] The first and least important in terms of numbers is composed of various extremist organizations including those involved in activities such as desecration of Hindu temples. Not all of these groups have been caught up in violent acts, but they remain on the fringes of the Dakwah movement. Aside from the Army of God (Tentera Sabillullah) there is a splinter of Darul Arkam which was apparently involved in temple desecrations. Both have been proscribed by the government. The aforementioned Jamaatul Tabligh is also radical but more in an intellectual sense than the others. The Islamic teachings of this organization are considered improper by the government and its teachers have found their activities limited by officials.

The second category is composed of traditional missionary organizations emphasizing the conversion of non-Muslims. Primarily responsible for conversion attempts in Peninsula Malaysia is PERKIM, with similar groups in Sabah and Sarawak being the United Sabah Islamic Association and Islamic Association of Sarawak. These organizations obtain their funding from various sources including government aid, some foreign and private donations, and in the case of PERKIM and USIA economic enterprises. Dakwah activities of this nature are not new to Malaysia, but gained impetus in the latter 1960s and the early 1970s as Malay consciousness rose. Dakwah movements of the traditional missionary type have not been involved directly in political activities. However, they have raised Islamic consciousness within the Malay population, and some observers believe that some 80 percent of the Malay university students are part of one of the many Dakwah organizations. The efforts to convert Chinese, in particular, have led to some degree of uneasiness within that community, especially given somewhat fanatic statements by a few missionary leaders.

The third type of Dakwah organization seeks as its primary objective the instillation of a firmer belief in Islam among the Muslim population itself. Thus, rather than emphasizing the conversion of nonbelievers, these groups attempt to foster fundamentalist attitudes within the Malay population. (It is important to differentiate these fundamentalists from government-supported Dakwah activities such as the Institute Dakwah Islam.) One such organization (Darul Arkam) claims some 50,000 members and has considerable support from religious and educational leaders. It has attempted to develop commune-type systems of self-reliance and emphasizes moderation and puritanism. Adherents have been known to have refused to own television sets or to see foreign films because of the improper morality of such purveyors of "yellow culture."

However, the Dakwah organization which has become the dominant one in the media and among discussions of religious and political leaders is the Malaysian Youth Islamic Movement (ABIM). This is purportedly a youth movement led by a young charismatic activist named Anwar Ibrahim. It is difficult to know the exact numbers within the organization, although some reports give it 30,000 members and mass meetings have often drawn very large crowds. Ibrahim himself is a product of the University of Malaya and was detained in the mid-70s for his student activities. He is now president of ABIM as well as Asia and Pacific representative to the World Association of Islamic Youth (WAMY). Ibrahim has been deeply involved in international Islamic developments and has traveled widely to observe and participate in Muslim activities. Given the importance of Ibrahim in the movement it is useful to comment upon his thinking at this time.

Anwar Ibrahim says that his main desire is to inculcate a greater depth of Islamic thinking into the hearts of Malays, stating that the main challenge now is to sow the seeds of Islamic understanding in the society and particularly among the youth. He also comments that he is not particularly interested in efforts to formulate new laws regarding Khalwat and other minor infractions of Islamic teachings, arguing that these only detract from consideration of the more important issues facing Islam in Malaysia. When asked as to what he meant by the need for emphasizing more Islam in the country, he commented upon this as related to communal relations, politics, and economics.[23] With regard to intracommunal relations, Ibrahim states that he favors a multi-racial society and that efforts to enforce minor elements of Islamic law only hurt relations among the races. In an interview with a local Malaysian newspaper he commented:

> Islamic leadership is multi-racial because Islam is a universal religion which rises above regional or communal limitations.
> Left-wing leadership, i.e., whether it be Communist or Socialist will create conflict of classes. Communal leadership which is narrow, will definitely strengthen communal discords.
> However, Islamic leadership will be based on moral and humanitarian leadership, and one that implements Islamic laws, a just and equitable economy which will be planned carefully. Islamic leadership is not chauvinistic and should not be chauvinistic, and does not try to belie the importance of the aid and support of other groups and minorities.

As to politics he states that his main interests are in the maintenance of a democratic system, and that if a truly Islamic state were established then present efforts by the government to restrict freedom would be eliminated. In the same interview he argued that:

> The future society should be more committed and have a better understanding of the Islamic struggle, with the aim of creating a fair society, one that respects human rights.
> As for the future politics in the country—whether it be based on Islam or not, should be one that chooses one philosophy of life, and a national policy which guarantees real justice for all. Since this is the basis of Islam, then I am sure that man will choose the Islamic way.
> This is especially so when Islam places high regard for the rights of minority groups, the freedom of worship, the opposition to corruption, and the suppression of cruelty, with a just economic program which will abolish class distinctions, and wipe out narrow communal feelings.[24]

In terms of economics he has been defined as a Muslim socialist but states that he is not. He does want greater equity in the society, favors the takeover by the state of primary industries such as palm oil and tin, but argues that the government already is officially controlling petroleum so this does not necessitate further change. While declaring his nonsocialist leanings, he obviously fits the pattern of Islamic socialism seen in other societies. He has used the events in Iran and Pakistan as weapons against government, but in private states that neither of these experiments quite fits what is needed for Malaysia.

ABIM's opportunity and danger comes from the increasing number of young fundamentalists among the youth of Malaysia, and particularly from those returning from the United Kingdom. These more intense young adherents to Islam have at times accused Ibrahim of being insufficiently supportive of Muslim causes and too much of a reformist. However, he has developed considerable contact with the international Muslim community and has maintained close relations with the Islamic movement in the United Kingdom. Whether he is able to stay out of a direct role in politics remains a central issue for him and Malaysian politics, but there is little reason to believe that he cannot further develop his influence at home and abroad.

REACTIONS OF POLITICAL ORGANIZATIONS

The resurgence of Islam has further complicated an already tense political situation. As has been noted, non-Malays have become increasingly wary regarding what they perceive to be a growing intolerance within the Islamic community. Spokesmen for the Chinese and Indian population are particularly worried about the extent to which the intensity of Islamic self-awareness might draw Malay parties into a stronger support for religious fundamentalism. The two political organizations that receive the greatest attention in this regard are the ruling UMNO and its major Malay rival, PAS.

When anyone speaks of government policies of Malaysia as they relate to Islam, it is really the views of the Malay section of the National Front, UMNO, that are being discussed. UMNO has always been faced with divisions within the party between those more interested in economic and political modernization accompanied by accommodation with other races and those who have expressed more strongly their Malay and Islamic beliefs.[25] In the years when former Prime Minister Tengku Abdul

Rahman was attacking the "narrow nationalism and the Koran in order to win a few seats" local UMNO organizations were pressuring the government to promote more purely Islamic policies. For example, in this period local elements of the party were demanding a change in the Red Cross symbol, a ban on pork and lard in hospitals, increased Islamic education, banning of intoxicating liquor, the closing of all government offices and businesses on Friday, and withdrawal of recognition from Israel. These views, plus the added pressure from the principal Malay challenger, the PMIP, led to a somewhat ambiguous series of statements from the government as it attempted both to accommodate other communities and maintain the support of the more traditional Muslims in the party. The then Deputy Prime Minister Razak argued that "We have done all that we could within our power to maintain the Islamic religion,"[26] and in the post-independence years UMNO attempted to re-enforce its religious support by way of establishing *ulama* sections and co-opting members of the religious community. At the same time the Prime Minister stated that "Our country has many races and unless we are prepared to drown every non-Malay, we can never think of an Islamic Administration."

In the 1970s UMNO has found it increasingly necesssary to deal with the resurgence of Islamic fundamentalism in its effort to support the politics of accommodation while sustaining the support of traditional Islamic membership. Publicly and privately UMNO leaders have given an optimistic view of their capabilities in this matter while at the same time following a strategy combining attack and co-option.[27] In the first instance Muslim fundamentalism has been characterized as extremist and "un-Islamic" and one spokesman declared that the three main dangers to Malaysian society were drugs, communism, and religious extremism. As well, efforts have been made to taint Islamic fundamentalism with the violence of the extremists who desecrated religious shrines. Other weapons have also been available to the Malaysian government to curb possible opponents although these have been employed to a limited extent. The Sultans in the respective states, as protectors of Islam, have considerable power available to them including the ability to control the movement of religious teachers. The government can detain possible "subversives," and there are laws against activities and speeches that could lead to communal disturbances. One example of the employment of government power was the ruling that university professors and lecturers can no longer participate in political activities. One factor that may have been involved in this decision was the active support by some faculty members of fundamentalist organizations.

At the same time UMNO has attempted to establish itself as the chief supporter of Islam in Malaysia. It has presented itself as the moderate middle-ground group between Islamic extremism on one hand and "left-wing materialism" on the other. A variety of methods have been developed to co-opt elements of the Islamic resurgency including the employment of the Islamic center in Kuala Lumpur, the development of a Dakwah month, renewed efforts to take the forefront in the international Islamic movement and attempts to influence overseas students. For example, the head of the UMNO youth, Haji Suhaimi Kamaruddin, attended the WAMY conference in March, 1979, stating that his organization would contribute whatever it could to aid Muslim youth, and Malaysia has been host to international Muslim gatherings. There has also been an increase in symbolic support for Islam as illustrated by the growing employment of Islamic references in political speeches and the increased appearance of religious programs on radio and television.

The reasons for this mounting effort by the government to play upon Islamic opinion is not difficult to see, given the twin necessities of maintaining the support of traditional elements of UMNO and the possible use of Islam by members of the opposition. However, other factors may also be involved including the traditional view that Islam could act as a device for uniting Muslims against Marxism and the possible attraction of Arabic economic support to a fellow Islamic country.

Traditional Malay opposition to UMNO has been presented by PAS, a Muslim-oriented organization based primarily in rural areas and the East Coast of Malaysia which has been variously characterized as conservative, traditional, populist, and chauvinist.[28] Although the party was soundly defeated at the national level during the last parliamentary elections, it still obtained 35 to 38 percent of the Malay vote in several states. PAS has always declared itself to be the true supporter of both the Malay and Islamic principles. It has attacked UMNO for being unwilling to give its full support to Islam and has criticized such government policies as maintaining office hours on Friday, using lottery funds to build and maintain religious edifices, allowing the sale of liquor, and has long called for an Islamic state in which all Malays could "adopt Islamic principles in the life of the individual, society, and the state.[29]

In recent years PAS leadership has continued its strong support of the Islamic state, particularly since the ending of its brief partnership with UMNO and the National Front. The leadership has argued that the government has a narrow view of Islam which looks upon the religion as a barrier to progress and incapable of meeting the needs of modern society. While arguing the desirability of the multiracial society, PAS has from time to time stated that the politics of accommodation has been tilted toward aiding the other races rather than the Malay. To meet contemporary problems PAS leadership states that a major effort must be made to educate Malays to follow Islam even more closely and that once Malays have seen how their religion fits into their way of life, they will accept the necessary new laws required to develop a truly Islamic state. The president of the party, Datuk Asri, has declared that major changes are needed in the legal, economic, and educational systems of Malaysia.[30] All of these must be molded to fit the Islamic pattern athough he has been somewhat vague in defining how this is to be implemented. In the past he and other PAS leaders have attacked the parliamentary system as it now operates with its strong executive and weak parliament. PAS leaders argue for an Islamic Council to interpret how laws ought to be formulated according to the dominant Malaysian Islamic sect. Asri has regularly spoken in favor of the greater use of Islamic law and a constitutional amendment to assure that all government policies follow its precepts. In recent years spokesmen have specifically commented on the need for adhering to Islamic law to meet problems in land, insurance, loans, Khalwat, etc.

The new Islamic self-awareness provides PAS with both an opportunity to bring new members into the party and the danger of being outpaced by organizations such as those involved in the Dakwah movement. The entrance of Malays into the city is considered by some PAS officials as an opportunity to proselytize among them and growing fundamentalism fits traditional PAS principles. At the same time the young foreign and university-trained fundamentalists are from a different background than the locally led PAS leadership. There are already signs of new blood from the Dakwah movement entering into PAS, perhaps to challenge the older politicians. Thus, PAS, like UMNO, looks upon Islamic resurgence as a not altogether desirable event.

ANOTHER IRAN?

In conclusion note should be taken of one possible result of the Islamic resurgence in Malaysia. The Iranian revolution of 1979 and its possible replication in Southeast Asia has been a major point of discussion among foreign observers including embassies, visiting journalists, and multinationals. In each case central offices in the United States and Europe have requested information on possible similarities. Within Malaysia the employment for political purposes of the Iranian revolution as well as the Pakistani Islamic constitution by the opposition has fanned an already major interest in the events in the Middle East. Spokesmen for both Dakwah movements, such as Anwar Ibrahim, and PAS, such as Datuk Asri, have returned from the Middle East extolling the virtues of the changes taking place in both Iran and Pakistan. As noted in previous pages, there has been an acceleration of interest in Islam and Muslim fundamentalism. Demands of Muslims in Iran and Pakistan for more conservative dress, an end to the "Yellow Culture" of the West, the implementation of an Islamic state, the need to restructure the economy to fit Islamic principles, etc., have all been echoed in Malaysia. Nor does it appear that the drive toward expanding the role of Islam in Malaysian society is transitory. Yet, there are fundamental aspects to Malaysian politics in religion that make the possibility of a Malaysian Islamic revolution improbable. We can note three primary reasons for this assertion:

1. Malaysian Muslims are not Shiite and there has not developed within Islam in Malaysia the type of religious-political hierarchy that can provide the leadership for such a revolution. To the extent that this exists it is in the hands of the state in terms of the role of the Sultans. These somewhat symbolic rulers at this point provide a bridge between the government and people but are part of the traditional Malay establishment. Certainly, they are not at the forefront of any ideological crusade to foster fundamental changes in the political or religious fabric of the country.

2. The political and religious opposition to the government is badly fractured and often poorly led. The rival political party on the Malay side, PAS, has long been accused of continuing to accept a leadership ill-equipped to compete effectively with UMNO. There has been little modernization of either the party's elite or organization and at this time it does not offer a serious challenge to the continued dominance of UMNO. The Chinese and Indian opposition, both with and without the National Front, has a long history of internal dissension over policy and leadership. The non-National Front rivals are further limited by constitutional controls on discussion of centrally important communal issues and fears on all sides of another 1969 riot situation.

Religious organizations also do not afford a serious competitor to the Malay political establishment at this time. As previously noted, they vary markedly in terms of goals and generally eschew public political stands. There are possibilities for an increased role for ABIM both within the Dakwah movement and opposition party politics, but considerable caution is being displayed by Anwar Ibrahim and his colleagues. There is no question that some of ABIM's membership is beginning to infiltrate into the leadership of PAS and that Ibrahim's charisma is having some effect on the general populace, but at this time it is difficult to assess the long-term impact of ABIM and its leader.

3. The government and particularly UMNO does not provide the vulnerable target that the Shah and his cohorts presented in Iran. UMNO has successfully dominated the center stage of the Islamic and Malay cause in Malaysia. Many Malays apparently fear that if it lost this role their own controlling position in Malaysian politics would be seriously diminished, and UMNO has played upon that fear. It should also be noted that Malays have developed a strong loyalty to the feudal establishment of the Sultans and other elements of the Malay elite which lend their support to the UMNO leadership. Finally, the party has shown the capability of defeating or co-opting dangerous opponents and issues. This combination of UMNO as symbolic leader of the Malay cause and astute gamesmanship tend to make the danger of a Malaysian Islamic revolution improbable.

While few if any outside observers see a replication of Iran or Pakistan in Malaysia, the next few years do present the possibility of a changed political environment due to the Islamic resurgence. Traditional Malaysian politics has operated on the basis of an often sensitive balance among the country's communities. This politics of accommodation may be sorely tried by increased Malay-Islamic self-awareness and demands for expansion of the role of Islam in Malaysian politics and society.

Islam and National Integration through Education in Nigeria

Akbar Muhammad

HISTORICAL AND POLITICAL OVERVIEW

*L*OCATED IN WEST CENTRAL AFRICA, Nigeria is the most populous country on the continent.[1] Its extensive oil wealth makes it one of the richest states of the Third World and an important member of the Organization of Petroleum Exporting Countries; after Saudi Arabia, it is the second largest exporter of oil to the United States. Politically, Nigeria is one of the most influential countries in international organizations, including the Organization of African Unity, the United Nations, and the Organization of Non-Aligned Countries. In view of the fact that among the three religions — Islam, Christianity, and Animism — most Nigerians are adherents of Islam, Muslim leaders play a significant role in international Islamic conferences and congresses.

Nigeria is a country struggling to attain nationhood. The formidable obstacles to the achievement of national unity lie in her multiethnic composition and the different experiences of her peoples. The population of over eighty million people consists of more than 250 ethnic groups, the most important of which are the Hausa, Yoruba, and Ibo (Igbo). Statistically, the Hausa, with the ethnically related Fulani and Kanuri (of Bornu), form the largest cultural group in the country; traditionally, they claim Middle Eastern origin and are overwhelmingly Muslims.[2] There are small numbers of animists and Christians amongst them. The Yoruba, the second most numerous people, derive their ethnic origins from a heavenly figure who is said to have descended at Ife, their holy city. Today, Islam and Christianity claim a similar percentage of Yoruba adherents, and there remains a number of followers of Yoruba traditional religion or animists. Until about a century ago, the lesser known Ibo were almost wholly animists; now the larger part of them profess Christianity. These peoples are dominant in the northern, southwestern, and southeastern regions of Nigeria respectively. It must be emphasized that religion, as an important element of culture and ethnicity, has greatly contributed to the historical "sub-national" character of Nigeria. Many of Nigeria's pre-colonial polities were firmly based upon a religious foundation and political authority was vested in religious personages.

The bulk of Nigeria's approximately forty million Muslims live in the former "Northern Region" of which at least two-thirds are adherents of Islam. The largest group is the Hausa who are mainly farmers, merchants, and craftsmen, and number about 25 to 30 million. The approximately five to six million Muslim Yoruba of the southwest are basically urban. The Fulani are both pastoralists and semi-sedentaries who together number about five million. Lastly, the approximately three million Kanuri (including the Shuwa Arabs) of the northeast are occupationally varied — farmers, merchants, and transport and construction workers.

Islam was introduced into Bornu in the eleventh century, possibly by Fatimid missionaries/traders or their descendants from North Africa, and into the rest of the Northern Region during and after the fourteenth century by persons of similar occupational backgrounds from Sudanic western Africa. By the beginning of the nineteenth century the Northern Region had received "doses" of Islamic culture from several sources, including Egypt. Thereafter, it spread into northern Yorubaland and down to the present capital, Lagos. Under the cultural influence of northern and Sudanic Africa, the North was exposed to Arabic, Quranic studies and *sharia* (Islamic Law) of the Maliki rite (*madhhab*).[3] Muslim intellectuals, whether *mallam*s (Hausa, from the Arabic *muallim* teacher) or *alufa*s (Yoruba) were meticulous readers and transmitters of the classical Muslim texts. It was this group of scholarly élites who ultimately were to provide leadership for the country's Muslims.

No historical outline of Islam in Nigeria, however brief it is, can ignore the revivalist movement of the early nineteenth century and its most prominent leader and hero, Usuman dan Fodio (Uthman b. Fudi, d. 1817), often known as "the Shehu" (Arabic, Shaykh).[4] Ethnically, he was a Fulani born into a clerical clan which probably migrated from Senegal. One of the main influences on the Shehu was his teacher, Jibril b. Umar, who abhorred the religious syncretic tendencies of the "venal mallams" and the alleged Muslim rulers of Hausaland. The Shehu charged some of the most respected leaders of Hausaland with unbelief (*kufr*):

Among those syncretists who claim that they are Muslims and carry out the practices of Islam . . . are those who worship trees by sacrifices to them, make offerings, and daub them with dough. They are unbelievers. . . . There are others who claim that they possess knowledge of the Unseen through written magic or by sand-writing, from the positions of the stars, or the language of the birds and their movements . . . There are persons who place cotton and wool on stones, along the roads, under trees, or at a crossroads. . . . Those who practice black magic try to separate those who love each other, or husband and wife: all of that is unbelief.[5]

Usuman dan Fodio's criticisms of the rulers and their associates, the "venal mallams," eventually led to the Fulani *jihad*s which were undertaken between 1804 and 1820. By the latter year almost all of the Hausa states were subject to the Fulani and their Hausa followers. Thus, the Fulani Empire came into existence with a proclaimed purified Islam as its base. The heretofore relatively small and unimportant village of Sokoto became in 1809 the political and military capital of the realm ruled by the Shehu, now the Sarkin Musulmi or Amir al-Muminin (Commander of the Faithful).

Bornu and Yorubaland were never fully incorporated into the Fulani state, despite the several attempts by the Jihadists. Bornu remained, for the most part, independent, except for the period 1808 to c. 1820 when its capital (Birni Ngazargamu) was controlled by the Fulani. The northern section of Yorubaland was incorporated as a consequence of proselytization and the appeal of the secessionist commander of Ilorin in 1817 for aid against the animistic Yoruba Kingdom of Oyo. It was not until the middle of the present century that Islam began to make inroads amongst the Ibo.

In short, the Hausa-Fulani *jihad*s produced a multi-ethnic state, known as the Sokoto Caliphate, in which Islamic culture and the *sharia* were to be the binding force and the legal code of the state. In such circumstances Arabic was destined to become the language of the intelligentsia and all who aspired to high offices of state were automatically required to have a minimal working knowledge of it. As Islam took deeper root amongst the populace, the Hausa-Fulani realm became increasingly known in the wider Muslim world—through commercial relations, pilgrimage to Mecca, and the stream of itinerant teachers who moved up and down the caravan routes which connected it with other areas of western, central, and northern Africa.

The strong Islamic identity of northern Nigeria served as a bulwark against the encroachment of "the foreign." British colonialism, fully imposed by 1903, recognized the general political and cultural cohesion of the North and proceeded cautiously to incorporate it as the "Protectorate of Northern Nigeria." In applying the principle of indirect rule, most British administrators went to great lengths to obtain economic and political concessions with a minimum of interference in the internal affairs of the emirates. The dislike of several rulers for the "unbelievers" was made crystal clear. In 1902, the Caliph Abdurrahman of Sokoto declared his opposition in writing to then High Commissioner Frederick Lugard: "From us to you. I do not consent that any one from you should ever dwell with us. I will never agree with you. I will have nothing to do with you. Between us and you there are no dealings except as between Mussulmans and Unbelievers ("Kafiri") War, as God Almighty has enjoined on us. There is no power or strength save in God on high."[6] The impressive forces of the Fulani, however, were no match for the British maxim guns. The imposition of colonial rule went apace, but almost always careful not to unduly upset the internal political and religious status quo. This cautious approach was not only adopted in the case of the Hausa-Fulani emirates but also toward Bornu.

The overall effect of British administration in Northern Nigeria was the reenforcement of that region's sense of difference from other parts of the country. Indeed, here as elsewhere, the colonial power considered Muslims more "civilized" than their animist neighbors. Lugard's 1914 scheme of amalgamation united the country into two large units, the Northern Protectorate and the Southern Protectorate. But administratively, the Muslim emirates continued to be almost completely cut off from the animistic and Christian South. Thus, the majority of the Muslim population maintained their cultural exclusiveness, their educational, political, and legal institutions being largely preserved.

The story of the southern region is markedly different. By 1900, there were no large states in southern Nigeria; they had been destroyed by either the Atlantic slave trade or outright conquest. What remained was a conglomeration of small and dispersed polities increasingly penetrated by European commercial interests and missionary activity. The relative success of these efforts — and to a degree amongst Muslim Yoruba — exacerbated the already existing socio-cultural disparities between the two regions. It was not until the latter years of their administration that the British took serious measures toward the political integration of the country; those efforts continue to this day. National unity in Nigeria has been and is viewed as a goal which can be achieved only through educational, political, and legislative integration. Given the demands of modernization thrust upon the newly independent state, it is the Muslim Nigerians who were compelled to make the greatest compromise while attempting to retain as much of their culture as possible.

In many colonial territories, and definitely in almost all African countries, the road to independence was by way of multi-party politics. In multi-ethnic colonies that road seems *necessarily* to have been through multi-ethnic parties; that is, particular parties represented more than one ethnic group. As in most other colonized territories, early Nigerian political organization and protest began amongst those indigènes who were closest to the colonial structure and more involved in its institutions. The leaders were Western-educated and their appeals were primarily directed at those who shared a similar cultural and intellectual background. In the southern areas of the country it was the Creole, non-Muslim Yoruba and Ibo who initiated the drive toward internal self-rule in the 1920s and 1930s. Although party branches were established in some of the northern towns, it is clear that initially neither the "party bosses" nor the emirs took their activities in that region very seriously. Indeed, most of the political representatives and the members in the North were of southern and/ or non-Muslim origins. Subsequently, however, a positive consequence of this southern activity was the realization on the part of the Hausa and Fulani that their southern countrymen might prove to be a real threat to northern interests should the country gain independence.

The most important political party to emerge in the "Far North" was the Northern People's Congress (NPC) formed in October 1951. It was led by Alhaji Ahmadu Bello, a descendant of Usuman dan Fodio and the Sardauna of Sokoto, and Alhaji Mallam Abubakar Tafawa Balewa.[7] Clearly, the NPC was a reaction to the inroads made by the southerners and the perceived threat from dissident Muslim and non-Muslim northern political organizations — thus, the NPC motto "One North: One People Irrespective of Religion, Rank or Tribe." The separatist inclinations of the party were further shown in its stated objectives:

> To study and strive to preserve the traditions which bound culture to the past, while reforming these traditions to render them capable of meeting modern conditions . . . To educate the Northerners of their civic and political responsibilities, to organize them to accept the leadership of the Northern Peoples Congress, and to support its candidates for elections to the Regional and Central Legislatures and to Local Councils . . . To study the cultural, social, political and economic pastimes of the Northerners so that they can adjust themselves to the present changing world with a view to overcoming all the difficulties and barriers that are placed

before them . . . To inculcate in the minds of the Northerners a genuine love for the Northern Region and all that is northern, and a special reverence for Religion, Laws and Order and the preservation of good customs and traditions, and the feeling that the sorrow of one northerner shall be the sorrow of all and that the happiness of one is also the happiness of all . . . To make every possible effort in order to hasten the date of Self-Government for Nigeria and the consideration of introducing of a "Permanent Federal Constitution." . . . To seek for the assistance and co-operation of or to give aid to any organization or individual in or out of the Northern Region whose aims and aspirations coincide with those of the Party.[8]

While membership in the NPC was open to non-Muslims they were automatically excluded from the party's highest executive positions and thus were little more than tokens. The policy makers were northern élites who had been absorbed with the Islamic fundamentalism of past decades, and who had developed superior organizational skills through attachment to the bureaucracy of the colonial Native Authority. Most representatives of this group were emirs, teachers, and low-level civil servants. An earlier group formed in Kano in 1950, the Northern Elements Progressive Union (NEPU), under the leadership of Mallam Aminu Kano, became the opposition party and allied itself with the southern National Council of Nigeria and the Cameroons (NCNC) founded by the well-known American-educated Ibo, Dr. N. Azikiwe in 1944. However, while there were other smaller political and cultural groups in the North that agitated the Native Administration for various types of changes, undoubtedly the NPC was the major force in the region; it won resounding victories in future regional and federal elections.

Northern Nigerian separatism was forced to deal directly with southern nationalists from the date of the submission of the so-called Richards Constitution (the first of three) in March 1945 until independence on October 1, 1960. The constitutional proposals of the British governor Sir Arthur Richards sought "to promote the unity of Nigeria, to provide adequately within that unity for the diverse elements which make up the country and to secure greater participation by Africans in the discussion of their own affairs."[9] Knowing full well that the northern leaders were not eager for unification with the South, but that nothing less would be acceptable to the urban nationalist élite, the British administration proceeded to divide the country into three regions—North, West, and East. Each region had a legislative council and sent representatives to the colonial Legislative Council in Lagos. Most of the Council members were unofficial delegates from the regional legislatures. Southern nationalist protests, accusing the government of encouraging and fostering "tribalism," led to the 1951 constitution which required the appointment of regional and governmental ministers. One dominant party emerged in each region: the NPC in the North, the Action Group (AG, organized by a Yoruba, chief Obafemi Awolowo in 1951) in the West and the NCNC in the East. In accord with the 1954 constitution, which posed the model for a federal government, the party leaders became regional premiers; thus, Alhaji Sir Ahmadu Bello became Premier of the North. In the same year the NCNC won six of the ten seats in the Federal House of Representatives while the NPC won only three. Thereafter, an NCNC-NPC coalition government was formed. The revised constitution of 1957 provided for a federal prime minister. This post went to the former Minister of Transport, Vice President of the NPC and its leader in the House of Representatives, Alhaji Sir Abubakur Tafawa Balewa. In his speech to Parliament (September 1957) he said:

> To me the most important result of the constitutional changes in 1954 was the introduction of a federal form of government for Nigeria — a system which I had advocated as far back as 1948 in the old Legislative Council. I am pleased to see that we are now all agreed that the federal system is, under present conditions, the only sure basis on which Nigeria can remain united. We must recognize our diversity and the peculiar conditions under which the different tribal communities live in this country. To us in Nigeria therefore unity in diversity is a source of great strength, and we must do all in our power to see that this federal system of government is strengthened and maintained.[10]

It should be mentioned that the attainment of internal self-rule was not exactly a smooth transition. "Tribalism" was a common characteristic of Nigerian politics. Throughout the period of constitutional discussion and debate no sector of the country was devoid of this subnationalism. While the prevailing attitude in the East and West was for the early creation of a unitary state, the North held political leverage due to its greater population and Britain's determination to create a national state. Although there can be no doubt that the northerners desired independence from the British, they knew that the southerners were more politically, educationally, and administratively capable of governing themselves. Therefore, the NPC procrastinated in a bid for additional time to prepare themselves for modern internal rule. In the mid-1950s an official northern delegation was so harrassed during a visit to Lagos that some of its members determined never to participate in a government with southerners. In a subsequent conference in London, and before the federal system was established, the Sardauna of Sokoto stated unconditionally and uncompromisingly that the only form of national government in which the North would participate was "a loose, non-politicized union."[11] In view of the greater internal cultural diversity of the south, which did not go unnoticed by the North, inter- and extra-party conflicts over issues involving ethnicity were common — especially amongst the Yoruba and the Ibo. However, their leaders were able to cement themselves into an alliance strong enough to gain self-rule for the East and West in 1957. It was not until 1959 that the North attained the same. In the following year the British and the Nigerians felt that the latter could begin living together independently. The experience has been very painful.

The period 1960–66 witnessed what many viewed as the gradual breakdown of local and federal government, caused by rampant mismanagement, corruption, laborers' dissatisfaction, popular disappointment with and disrespect for government, census disputes, resurgent subnationalism, the conservative and pro-Western tendencies of Balewa, and the growing predominance of the North. The southern attitude toward Sokoto was not improved by the Sardauna's visits to African and Asian Muslim countries in the early 1960s and his subsequent relations with them. He was assassinated in early 1966 during a rebellion of part of the army in the North (at Kaduna); the mainly Ibo rebels intended a national coup. These factors *inter alia* led to the installment of a military government headed by the Ibo Major-General Aguiyi-Ironsi in 1966. Premier Tafawa Balewa had been murdered in Lagos, and Dr. Azikiwe, who had been president since 1961, acquiesced in the change. Between May and July, however, a series of riots occurred which claimed the lives of thousands of northerners and southerners. These events led to the second coup of July by northern soldiers (again in Kaduna), and apparently without agreement as to the successor of Aguiyi-Ironsi who was killed. Eventually, Lieutenant-Colonel Yakubu Gowan, Army Chief of Staff, emerged as Head of State. In May 1967, he declared the division of the country into twelve states: the North was divided into six states, thus placating southern fears of eventual northern domination. The East and West became three states each.

A serious crisis developed within less than a week: the Ibo Colonel Odumegwu Ojukwu announced the secession of the East under the name of the Republic of Biafra. It was not until January 1970 that the central government was able to re-establish control over the secessionists. (Ojukwu now lives in exile in the Ivory Coast.) Throughout the Biafran affair, tension remained high between Muslims and Ibo junior civil servants and businessmen in the North; some of the incidents led to the abandonment of the region by Ibos. However, Muslims in general were not seriously affected by the debacle. They generally supported the central government and were, indeed, influential in securing international support for it, especially in the Muslim countries of Africa and Asia.

But Nigeria's house was far from being in order, and yet another coup was required to put it on course. The administrative and governmental changes made by the Gowan government including the creation of new states, did not rid the country of its aforementioned ills; mismanagement of the now oil-based economy was another problem. Though somewhat lessened, ethnic fears continued to be apparent. And there was widespread apprehension about military rule. In 1970 Gowan promised to return the country to civilian administration by 1976. Popular and military distrust was manifested in the third coup (this time bloodless) that brought a Muslim northerner, General Murtala Mohammed to power. (Gowan pledged his loyalty to the new government and later went to Britain to study.) The new Head of State presented a five-stage plan to be completed in 1979 at which time the country would be returned to civilian rule. Those stages comprised the following: (1) the matter of creation of states was to be settled and a draft constitution presented by 1976; (2) the new states were to be firmly established and functioning, and a constituent assembly was to have approved a draft constitution by 1978; (3) the ban on political activity was to be removed in 1978 in preparation for the re-emergence of political parties; (4) election to the state; (5) election to federal legislatures and the installation of a democratically elected government by October 1, 1979. In its attack on administrative, governmental, and military corruption, the régime of Murtala Mohammed acted decidedly. The abortive coup of February 1976, staged by a small group of dissident officers took the life of Mohammed but did not affect his policies. His successor, Lieutenant-General Olusegun Obasanjo, a Yoruba Christian, implemented those policies with dedication and determination. After thirteen years of military rule, Nigeria returned to civilian administration on October 1, 1979. A national party and constitutional government was installed, headed by President Alhaji Shehu Shagari, a Fulani and former secretary of the NPC (1951–56).[12]

THE PROBLEM OF EDUCATIONAL DISPARITY

The greatest political problem for Nigerian Muslims, especially the northern majority, is the maintenance of their religious and ethnic distinctiveness in the face of growing internal and external challenges. These challenges emanate from the breakdown of the old political unity of the Northern Region, the threat that forces of political modernization pose to the traditional order, and the weakening grip of "conservative Islam" on the younger and more mundane generation. The present Sardauna of Sokoto, Alhaji Sir Siddiq Abubakar III, is reported to have said, "Nigerians of all faiths are too ready to abandon their traditions in favor of 'modernity'."[13] Obviously, this is an international phenomenon in religion-centered societies. But for traditional northerners it has a special connotation: the further separation of Islam and political authority and, by extension, the weakening of the religious and social foundations of their society. The somewhat modernized leaders, who have had considerable contact with the wider world of Lagos, Europe, and other African and Muslim countries, form a constant threat to traditional élites in their bid for political support. Although not restricted to the old northern leaders, another challenge comes from the Muslim Yoruba and others who have had sustained contact with other non-Muslim indigenous groups and western culture.

Thus, Nigerian Muslims, especially northerners, have been subject to continuous attack as being unsuited to a modern society. The main argument of the detractors has been the Muslims' lack of Western-type education, the implication being that it is the primary instrument for social and political integration in a pluralistic society. Therefore, it is important to consider the causes of the educational disparity between Muslims and non-Muslims, and what has been done to close the gap. The approach used here seeks to show points of educational similarity, divergence, and convergence.

Education in pre-colonial African societies was mainly "utilitarian."[14] Aimed at the acquisition and development of useful skills and crafts, it provided the essential preparation and training for the student to benefit himself and his community. Competency in a particular craft or trade was decided by pre-determined communal and/or family factors (for example, the need for additional carpenters). Abilities were acquired by observation, instruction, and practice.

Character training was another significant aspect of education. It involved learning proper manners, morals, etiquette, and discipline. This kind of instruction was imparted by older members of the household or the extended family. Religion was an integral part of such training, and some students went on to specialize in priestly activities and divination, especially in societies in which the performance of religious functions was not limited to particular families or clans. African emphasis on work and the practical side of life left a very small place in society for specialists in other-worldly matters. Boys and girls received much the same behavior training up to about age seven or ten. Then they were separated for instruction in the male and female roles they were expected to fill in adulthood.

There are points of confluence and diversion in indigenous African and Islamic education in Nigeria. To be sure, character training, etiquette, craftsmanship, selling and buying, agriculture, weaving, dyeing, and animal husbandry were aspects of the education of Muslims as well as animists. The oral literature of both groups is pregnant with symbols, parables, and tales which were transmitted and interpreted by the elders. But a significant basic difference between the two systems is the degree to which the Muslim child imbibes a kind of learning which originally was alien to his culture.

Islamic learning is based upon a corpus of Arabic *written* literature: the Quran, *Sunna* (sayings and deeds) of the Prophet Muhammad, exegesis and the *sharia,* or Islamic law.[15] Some knowledge of classical or literary Arabic is essential to the acquisition of an Islamic education. During the post-*jihad* period this corpus became more voluminous with the addition of hundreds of exegetical, administrative, legal and historical works in Arabic and Hausa. Parts of this literature were interwoven with indigenous tales to form the core of oral and written Hausa lore. And the pursuit of this kind of education caused many Muslims to travel to other Islamic centers in western and northern Africa and the Middle East. Pilgrimage to Mecca, *hajj,* became the fulfillment of a religious duty and a great stride in the quest for learning.

The seemingly simple fact that the Muslim child was trained in a literate tradition distinguished him from his non-Muslim neighbor or countryman. It did not encourage assimilation and integration; rather it inculcated a sense of belonging to a distant and wider world. In its more traditional and conservative form, Islamic learning instilled in some Muslims a feeling of superiority vis-à-vis their neighbors.

In principle, Islamic education was far less utilitarian than indigenous African education. It did not impart mundane skills with which the child could satisfy his economic needs; rather it stressed and regulated the relationship between God and man and man and man. Thus it encouraged character building, morality, and religiosity. As in the case of the non-Muslim child, the Muslim, too, was guided by communal and familial factors. The exception to the general lack of direct economic utility of an Islamic education was the possibility of a child becoming a *mallam,* teacher, of Islamic disciplines. Indeed, the teaching profession became not only respectable but also economically rewarding, especially when it was combined with the production of amulets and magical potions. Also, many *mallams* were successful traders.

The Christian missionary endeavor in Nigeria began in the 1840s with the establishment of schools and missions by the Church Missionary Society (CMS), the Wesleyan Methodist Missionary Society, the Roman Catholic Mission and the United Free Church of Scotland.[16] Following the waterways and land routes, they moved into the main Yoruba and Ibo towns throughout the nineteenth century. As harbingers of Western civilization, the Christian proselytizers introduced their religion, the rudiments of the English language and certain Western agricultural and craft techniques. By the time they seriously turned their attention to the north, the British forces were burdened with the tasks of subjugation and pacification. The end of Hausa-British hostilities was accompanied by Lugard's promise to recognize the then status quo and not to interfere with northern Islamic institutions. Although a few missionaries were eventually allowed into the area, their activities were almost restricted to non-Muslim communities. Generally their impact on the Muslims of Kano, Katsina, and Zaria was negligible; but the training given to a few sons of traditional rulers in language, geography, health, sanitation, and arithmetic was to prove useful.

The colonial government's assumption of responsibility for education contributed little toward a useful educational balance and national integration. The system which it introduced into the North was aimed at the maintenance of the traditional status quo, emphasis being on character and behaviour training, producing a skeletal cadre of low-level administrative assistants from amongst the traditional élites and the *mallams*, and imparting such minimal technical and craft skills as would ensure the smooth operation of government. Learning of English, the only hope for a truly national medium of communication, was not encouraged; Hausa, now written in Roman characters, largely remained the language of instruction. The smallness of the English-speaking class in the North resulted in the arrival of sufficiently trained southerners and others who were settled in stranger-quarters (*sabon garis*) outside the walled cities. From the administrative point of view, the situation was so acute that Lugard's successor, Governor Sir Hugh Clifford (1919–25), stated in 1920:

> In the northern provinces there has been until recently a certain tendency to regard education of the local population with some uneasiness and suspicion, as a process likely to exert a disintegrating and demoralizing effect upon the characters of those who are subjected to it; and where this feeling has been overcome, a further tendency is observable to regard education too exclusively as a handmaid to administration. . . .

> After two decades of British occupation, the northern provinces have not yet produced a single native . . . who is sufficiently educated to enable him to fill the most minor clerical post in the office of any government department. . . . . The African staff of these offices throughout the northern provinces are therefore manned by men from the Gold Coast, Sierra Leone, and from the southern provinces of Nigeria. . . . Education in the north has been practically confined to the vernacular and to Arabic, has been allowed to become the almost exclusive perquisite of the children of the local ruling classes. . . . In the southern provinces the position is very different.[17]

While Clifford severely criticized the state of Western education in both provinces, the colonial government did not implement measures to correct the imbalance. One year after the end of his term Southern Nigeria (eastern and western regions) could boast of having 3,828 primary (138,249 pupils) and 18 secondary schools (518 pupils) compared to the North's 125 primary schools (5,210 pupils). At about the same time, there were over 20,000 Quranic schools in the Northern Protectorate alone and no secondary schools.[18] Most scholars attribute the disparity to the Lugardian administration and Muslim fears of the possible consequences of Western education. The latter reason is of paramount importance as it bears upon the range of questions relevant to the formerly wide-spread internal image of the northerner, the political and social development of the country and, indeed, the stereotype of Muslims elsewhere under colonial administrations.

Muslims were (and are) protective of their Islamic cultural heritage; thus, they have paid a high price for their educational inadequacies in developing countries. From their perspective Western education was a direct threat to Islam, and therefore to their basic and cherished traditions and ideals. Their fears were intimately connected with religious beliefs and moral behaviour: exposure to Christian and Western education probably would result in conversion to Christianity. The situation is forcefully stated by the prominent Nigerian Muslim educationist, Professor Aliu B. Fafunwa, himself a product of CMS and American educational institutions:

> Muslim education in Nigeria was retarded not because the Muslims were unprogressive or because their religion was opposed to formal education but because 'education' in those days tended to mean Bible knowledge, Christian ethics, Christian moral instruction, Christian literature, some arithmetic, language and crafts — all geared to produce Christians who could read the Bible . . . Christian clerks, Christian artisans, Christian

carpenters, Christian farmers, Christian husbands and wives and Christian Nigerians. When the Christian missions started converting animists and a few Muslims, the majority of Muslim parents barred their children from attending the 'free Christian schools' for fear of conversion.[19]

According to the noted Christian Nigerian historian, Professor Emmanuel A. Ayandele: "This fanatical religious concept of schools by Christian missions was central to the development of education in the period [1842–1914] . . . it emphasized their view of the proper Nigerian citizen, the Christian, and explains why they wished forcible conversion of "pagans" and elimination of Islam."[20] Therefore, Western-style education in the north was severely limited. With respect to Nigeria as a whole and the influence of missionaries on Western primary education down to the period of decolonization [1945–60], Coleman remarks: "As late as 1942 they controlled 99 per cent of the schools, and more than 97 per cent of the students in Nigeria were enrolled in mission schools. By 1945 there were comparatively few literate Nigerians who had not received all or part of their education in mission schools.[21]

In the face of the spread of non-indigenous education and its cultural and economic opportunities, Muslims were confronted with a dilemma. The challenge was not restricted to the heavily populated Muslim areas of the North, but was also present in the *sabon garis* which produced an increasingly competitive commercial and clerical class who served in various northern administrations. Moreover, southern Muslims (mainly Yoruba), being more vulnerable to European influence, were particularly hard-pressed to implement measures to reduce the attraction of Western education and to prevent conversion to Christianity.

The three decades between 1930 and 1960 witnessed a considerable upsurge in Muslim-sponsored educational institutions. Throughout the period much progress was made in Western-type education. Within the national Muslim context, the stimuli for the somewhat momentous change came from several directions: the British administration, the aristocratic political élite, Indo-Pakistani reformist activity and the consequent competition with orthodox Muslim organizations. Direct British influence and aid was at its fullest in the North where, during Clifford's governorship, Katsina College (a secondary school) was established in 1922. One of its most prominent graduates (1930) was Alhaji Sir Ahmadu Bello who realized that the demands for Western training had "increased far beyond supply" and that Muslims were "suffering severely from lack of sufficient educated people to fill the available posts, whether in Government or in Native Administration or in commerce."[22] Amongst the other institutions inaugurated in the northern cities was the Northern Provinces Law School in Kano which was founded by the Emir Alhaji Abdullahi Bayero (d. 1953)[23] after his 1934 pilgrimage to Mecca. Established to train *sharia* judges, it was partly run along Western lines and included English and arithmetic in its curriculum. Subsequently, the school underwent changes which modernized its curriculum and administration: in 1947, it became the government-administered School for Arabic studies; from the mid-1950s it was the major primary teacher-training college in the North; finally, converted into the Abdullah Bayero College, in 1962 it became an extension of the modern Ahmadu Bello University at Zaria (the second oldest university in Nigeria). Thus, the major thrust toward Western-style educational development was undertaken jointly by the British administration and Muslim political leaders.

In Southern Nigeria, however, the real stimulus for Western education was British-Muslim cooperation aided by foreign Muslim elements. Having witnessed the Christianizing effects of missionary and government schools on their children, the Muslims, while desiring the non-religious aspects of Western education, persisted in their refusal to enroll their offspring. In Lagos, a *modus vivendi* was reached following the arrival in 1894 of the Sierra Leonean Arabic specialist, al-Hajj Harun al-Rashid, who had been educated at the University of Fez (Morrocco), and a Muslim convert and representative of the Sultan of Turkey, Abdullah Quillam. (It is noteworthy that the Lagos Muslims initiated the contact with the Sultan which prompted his written reply.) In 1895 the West Indian missionary-diplomatist and Pan-Africanist, Dr. Edward W. Blyden, arrived and was appointed Agent for Native Affairs. While the first two urged upon the Muslims the necessity and benefits of Western education, the latter played the role of a sensitive advocate of the Administration. An agreement was reached by which the Western-style Government Muslim School was opened in 1896 followed by two others located nearby. Apart from Arabic and Islam, the curriculum included English and arithmetic. These primary schools attracted some Muslim pupils from missionary schools as well as hundreds of others.[24]

From the 1920s onwards the primary agents of Western educational influence amongst the southern Muslims were Islamic organizations and societies, especially the then India-based Ahmadiyyah movement[25] and the Yoruba-led Ansar-ud-Din Society. The Ahmadiyyah emphasized educational modernization, as they had done in India, as a weapon against Christianity and secularization. Despite their heretical theological views, until recently they were very successful in winning converts and increasing the number of their schools in southern Nigeria. Given the favorable disposition of the government toward their efforts, they very well may have inspired orthodox Muslims to found Westernized and competitive institutions. The Ansar-ud-Din was inaugurated in 1923; in 1929, seven years after the Ahmadiyya opened their first school, the Ansar-ud-Din inaugurated their own in Lagos, and later became the foremost Muslim educational society in the southern region. According to one of its pamphlets, prior to its founding "only two or three Muslim schools were being run. The Christian missionaries, on the other hand, dominated the educational life of the country, and pressure was being exerted on some of the Muslim pupils attending the Christian schools to convert to Christianity."[26] By 1963, the Society had "over 200 primary schools and nineteen post-primary."[27]

In 1955 the Premier of the Western Region Chief Obafemi Awolowo, introduced Universal Primary Education (UPE), thus becoming a pace-setter for future governments. A similar scheme was implemented in Lagos in 1957. This political act, supported by 50 percent of the region's budget, had far-reaching effects on the number of southern Muslims receiving Western-type education. In 1960, he could boast that 90 percent of the region's school-age children (1.1 million) were receiving primary education. Undoubtedly, a number of them were southern Muslims registered in either regional institutions or supported schools of organizations like the Ahmadiyyah or the Ansar-ud-Din.[28] A similar plan was not launched in the Northern Region "principally for financial reasons compounded by the enormity of the number of children of school age . . . (at least half of Nigeria's children of school age live in the north). . . . While some Northern political and religious leaders were keen to expose the child to the modern educational system, most . . . were reticent about the blessings of Western education. Consequently the thought of universal free primary education hardly crossed the minds of most leaders in this area. . . . The Northern government at this time was concerned more with the development of education in rural areas and the promotion of adult literacy. . . ."[29] In 1962, however, the Northern Ministry of Education did form a sort of partnership with "voluntary agencies" to develop and promote modern primary education, but with strong Islamic cultural tendencies.

Therefore, a significant assimilational effect took hold amongst Yoruba Muslims: those who retained their Islamic affiliations in spite of studying in missionary schools together with others who were trained by the Ahmadiyyah, the Ansar-ud-Din, and similar associations, became English speakers and models of a "new Muslim élite" in sharp contrast to the traditional *mallam*s. And in view of "the restraint imposed by Yoruba culture, which not only discountenances extremism but smugly allows what can be called religious co-fraternity," social integration and development were facilitated greatly.[30]

The importance of this aspect of socialization should not be underestimated. It provided a basis for a three-way cooperation between indigenous Muslims, non-Muslims and Europeans. Whatever one may think, it allows for the coexistence in one household of adherents of Islam, Christianity and animism — a situation which is not very uncommon in southern Nigeria today. The situation in the North was quite different. Recalling his years at Katsina College, Alhaji Ahmadu Bello lamented in 1961: "There were no people from non-Muslim areas among us. I see now that this was perhaps a fault; it might have been better to have had more varieties of men in the College. Anyhow, a similar College should have been established for non-Muslims, but that was not part of Sir Hugh Clifford's plan. He had in mind the special colleges for princes, I think, which they had in India."[31] But even at that time the obdurate attitude of the north toward European education and its die-hard protectionalism yet continued to widen the gap between the two Muslim communities.[32] Contact between northern students and foreign Muslims was limited to a few Sudanese employed to teach Islamic law and some Indo-Pakistanis; the overwhelming majority of the teachers were northern aristocratic graduates and British expatriates. The non-Muslim northerners — Hausa, and later Ibo and others — were targets of missionary educational activity and were thus "modernized" at an earlier period and were able to relate on certain levels with southern Muslims and non-Muslims. This facility was clearly demonstrated in their political organization in the 1940s and 1950s. Lastly, a significant by-product of southern religious tolerance was the aid it gave to the spread of Islam amongst the Yoruba and Ibo peoples (a subject well-deserving of further research). This characteristic of southern Nigerian Islam manifestly facilitated the sociopolitical integration and development of the region. (My discussions with southern Yoruba Muslims in Egypt, the United Kingdom, and the United States during the 1960s and 1970s clearly indicated that they viewed Western education as the best aid to Islamic proselytization and political integration in Nigeria.)

The last two decades have witnessed great strides toward educational unification in Nigeria, and influential persons and Muslim organizations have played no small role in the process. It is interesting to note that the majority of the northern Muslim leaders who rose to high political office in independent Nigeria were generally sons of or associated with the northern political élite, exponents of traditional Islamic elementary schools, and members of the Qadiri (Khadiriyya) Sufi Brotherhood. Most of them received their post-primary education at Katsina or Kaduna College, and themselves became teachers in Westernized northern government or Native Administration schools; some received further educational training in the United Kingdom. The leaders of the associations generally were and are graduates of missionary schools and received their higher education in Europe, the United States, or at one of the Western-influenced Nigerian institutions.

What then became the place of the Quranic schools and the traditional *mallams*? They continued to exist and enjoyed considerable prosperity. As protectors of Islamic culture — not just the religion — their position was not seriously threatened. Many of those employed in public schools to teach religion and Arabic maintained their own schools, teaching students whose parents desired for them more exposure to Islamic learning than was provided by public schools; *mallams* also taught adults.[33] In 1964 there were 27,600 Quranic and 2,777 Ilm (secondary) schools in the north serving 422,954 and 36,419 students respectively.[34] As one would expect, however, serious disagreements between *mallams* and Western-educated Muslim intellectuals have arisen in recent years. Apart from the Western-derived institutions' infringement upon the economic livelihood of the *mallams*, they complained that such 'the new education' was turning the Muslim youth away from Islam, and indirectly served its non-Muslim detractors. The modern intellectuals reminded them of Prophet Muhammad's saying, "Seek education even to China," but to no avail.

Certain Islamic societies, apart from those already mentioned, have influenced educational and social change. Owing to the paucity of relevant published information it is not possible to assess their total impact on the Muslim community. The earliest known associations appeared in the southern part of the country amongst the Yoruba. In 1954 the Muslim Students' Society of Nigeria (MSSN) was founded by southern Yoruba with a view to organizing Muslim students in a national organization and to shield them from un-Islamic influences. During the 1960s the MSSN opened branches on the northern campuses of Ahmadu Bello University (Zaria) and Abdullahi Bayero College (Kano). By the beginning of the 1970s it had 400 branches at post-primary and secondary (Muslim and Christian) schools, universities, and teachers colleges with some of its own members employed to teach Islam and Arabic in a Western fashion. It has received patronage from some of the highest northern officials, including the Sultan of Sokoto, despite its Ahmadiyyah proclivities; it also encourages Muslim-Christian "tolerance and understanding."[35] An associated organization of intellectuals, the Muslim Lecturers,

Administrative and Technical Staff, was inaugurated in 1968 "with an initial membership of seventy-four representing four of the [then] five Nigerian Universities." In his "Appeal for Funds" its president, Professor Aliu Babatunde Fafunwa, stated the organization aims:

> to promote higher education and offer scholarships to needy Muslim students in the Nigerian Universities; . . . to publish a regular journal which will take its place among the religious and secular literatures of the world . . . [and which] will promote Islamic scholarship and . . . welcome healthy dialogue between Muslims and non-Muslims . . . [and to] serve as a messenger of truth by giving the lie to the tons of ill-conceived literature . . . published in learned non-Muslim circles around the world . . . and to promote Islam at the five Nigerian Universities and raise funds for building of Mosques and educational centres in Nigerian institutions of higher learning.[36]

The northern associations seem to have stressed proselytization and Islamic preservation more than support for Western-type education. The most influential has been the Society for the Victory of Islam (Jama atu Nasril Islam) founded in 1961 by the Sultan of Sokoto as "a trans-brotherhood religious organization" to serve Alhaji Ahmadu Bello's political aims in the North.[37] With its center in Kaduna the Society is known to have built only one school which presumably was operated along Western lines, given his own educational background. After the 1967 dispersal of the Northern Region the Society continued to work for Muslim unity, locally and internationally, but its educational endeavors seem to have been minimal. In a recent attempt to organize the activities of "preachers," the Society issued a public warning to the effect "that all Muslim scholars should henceforth preach the teachings of Islam from the context of the Holy Koran and the Hadith," and that violators "should be handed over to the police for disaffection and breach of public peace." The directive had the support of the present Sardauna, Alhaji Siddiq Abubakar III.[38]

In 1963–64, an association variously known as the Youth of Islam, the Society of Young Muslims in Nigeria and the Society of the Overflowing of Islam, emerged from the ranks of the Reformed Tijaniyya of Kano. While the Society's leaders were sons of prominent Muslim personages, its major concern throughout the North was the reform of "Islamic education and society."[39]

Other organizations with seemingly similar aims are The Helpers of Islam Society (Ansarul-Islam founded in 1944), and The Light of the

Religion (Nur-ud-Din) Society. Although the greater part of their activities seems to be directed toward the construction of mosques and administrative complexes, primary schools and classrooms are often attached. They also add mosques and prayer rooms to existing schools and universities.[40] These organizations are supported by public subscriptions, businessmen (and probably business women for which Nigeria is known), and traditional political leaders.

An important source of external support for Muslims in Nigeria, educationally and organizationally, has been Muslim countries. This is not a new phenomenon, for traditionally Muslim governments and educational institutions have allotted places for African Muslim students in technical, scientific, and Islamic universities. Foremost amongst these have been Egypt, the Sudan, Saudi Arabia, and Pakistan. Egypt's famous Al-Azhar University and its affiliated institutes have been particularly attractive to Nigerian students since independence. Its Colleges of Islamic Law (*sharia*), Arabic Language (Lugha Arabiyya), and Religion (Usul ad-Din), all of which are modernized and offer non-Islamic required courses, have graduated a relatively large number of Nigerians. In 1963 the Ansarul Islam Society's Mahad Deeny (Institute of School of Religion in Ilorin) became associated with Al-Azhar.[41] Also, foreign Muslim teachers and professors have been employed in Nigerian schools and universities. Lastly, the annual pilgrimage to Mecca continues to be a source of modernization for Nigerians, as thousands of pilgrims tend to spend years in Saudi Arabia, the Sudan, or Egypt on their return journey to Nigeria. While most of them habitually seek regular employment in Saudi Arabia and the Sudan, some have gained scholarships. In view of the fact that pilgrimage and education abroad are sources of prestige, undoubtedly such returnees have had a considerable impact on educational modernization; the exact roles which they and foreign Muslim educators have played in national integration and modernization deserves further research.

Thus far, we have emphasized internal factors which have aided Muslim educational development. But what has been the role of the Federal Government vis-à-vis national education and its developmental influence on the education of Muslims? It appears that the greatest governmental effort to redress the educational imbalance between Muslims and non-Muslims was the introduction of the Universal Primary Education Scheme (UPE) in October 1976. The plan is financed by the Federal Government and administered by the nineteen state governments. Under its provisions, all children from age six were to exercise their "right" to enter primary school in 1976, and by 1980 all children up to age eleven were to be enrolled. Primary education is to become compulsory in 1980. With a standardized curriculum and further impetus given to "Nigerianization" ("indigenization") pupils are to gain a general education similar to that of American and British children. In view of the fact that education is the primary way of "Nigerianizing" the young, Nigerian cultures, religions and history are emphasized in the program. It is hoped that the psychological effects of the daily saluting of the flag, the reiteration of the new "pledge of loyalty" and the singing of the national anthem will increase the pace of national integration. Following is the "pledge of loyalty":

> I pledge to Nigeria, my country
> To be faithful, loyal and honest,
> To serve Nigeria with all my strength,
> To defend her unity
> And to uphold her honour and glory
> So help me God.[42]

The text of the new national anthem is:

> Arise, O Compatriots, Nigeria's call obey
> To serve our Fatherland
> With love and strength and Faith
> The labour of our heroes past
> Shall never be in vain
> To serve with heart and might
> One nation bound in freedom, faith and unity.
>
> O God of Creation, direct our noble cause
> Guide our leaders right
> Help our youth and truth to know
> In love and honesty to grow
> And living just and pure
> Great lofty heights attain
> To build a nation where peace and justice shall reign.[43]

The themes of unity, honesty, religious faith, internal peace, and social justice are clear and indicative of the main sources of past social and civil conflicts. The supplication for God's help for the youth of Nigeria is not only an expression of the former Federal Military Government's hope that they will build a better society; it is also reflective of popular concern for social and religious deviance of youth, many of whom are alleged to be Muslims.[44]

It should be borne in mind that no federal legislation affecting the whole of Nigeria, including that on education, can be passed without the agreement or acquiescence of Muslim political élites. It is necessary, therefore, to consider the 1977 National Policy on Education as the most significant indicator of the general Muslim attitude toward Western-type education. The document establishes four levels of training: pre-primary (roughly age 2–5), primary (5–11), junior and senior secondary (11–14 and 14–17 respectively) and higher (17–21 and above). The first paragraph of the Introduction emphatically states that "Education in Nigeria is no more a private enterprise, but a high Government venture that has witnessed a progressive evolution of Government's complete and dynamic intervention and active participation." And significantly "The Federal Government of Nigeria has adopted education as an instrument par excellence for effecting national development."[45]

The government considers education a "lifelong" endeavor the foundation of which is the first nine years of basic learning. Recognizing the importance of ethnic culture, private schools, and the use of a child's mother tongue is encouraged at the pre-primary level; also, all children are urged to learn either Hausa, Yoruba, or Ibo. English, the official language, is introduced "at a later stage" of the primary educational experience (normally between ages five and eleven). Religious instruction, under the rubric Religious Knowledge, will be taught, and "No child will be forced to accept any religious instruction which is contrary to the wishes of his parents." Using all available means of communication, parents are to be made "education-conscious," and "a burning zeal for education for their children" is to be instilled in them. The provision of teachers for the subject is the joint responsibility of the federal and state ministries of education. With specific reference to traditional Muslim schools, the *National Policy on Education* states: "as a means of accelerating development in primary education in certain areas, the State Governments are already considering measures by which suitable Koranic Schools and Islamiyya Schools, with necessary adjustment of curricula, could be absorbed into the primary school system. . . ."[46] With regard to secondary schools, they are to be administered by the government upon the graduation of the first group of UPE students. However, "the take-over will be without prejudice to community involvement and participation"; by 1977 some state education authorities had begun the process. Secondary schools are urged to become "unity" schools, admitting students of various ethnic origins and from all parts of the federation. The government is to "set an example by a programme of Federal Government Colleges which admit students on equal quota basis from all the states." At this stage "moral and

religious instruction will be taught . . . through . . . studies and practices of religion. The mere memorizing of creeds and facts from the holy
books is not enough. . . ."⁴⁷

A student of Islamic institutions will recognize Muslim influence
on the *National Policy on Education*; that is not to say that other factors
were not considered. The longevity of the learning experience is reminiscent of the famous command of Prophet Muhammad, "Seek knowledge
from the cradle to the grave." Such a pursuit is often and understandably
interrupted by the necessity to seek employment, study being resumed at a
later time—even in the closing years of one's life. Certainly, the inter-
religious character of the educational system would not be repulsed by
most Nigerian Muslims. Suffice it to say that rote learning has been dis-
couraged for centuries by scholars of stature, though it continues in some
of the heartlands of Islam. A notable aspect of the UPE Scheme and the
National Policy on Education is that they are acceptable to the vast majority of the Muslim leadership, especially those in the "Far North" and
many traditional *mallams*. It should be made clear that the hitherto
patron-client relationship between the two groups has reinforced their respective positions in society. The deference shown to the traditional political élite is sustained by the *mallams'* inculcation of respect (both spiritual
and temporal, in the Western sense) for them in their students. Therefore,
the new educational policy further threatens to downgrade the social status of the traditional aristocracy as often has happened in other Muslim
societies in recent decades. In view of the fact that the military in post-
colonial countries is an agent of Westernization (and sometimes a stabi-
lizing force), much of the credit for the emerging change in Nigeria must
be due to the Muslim military leadership and their generally good relationship with Westernized Muslim intellectuals. (Significantly, for most
of the thirteen years of military rule the governors and some lower-
ranking officials in heavily-populated Muslim states were ethnically the
same as the citizenry.)

What has been the reaction of the traditional élite? Intense hostility to change has been tempered by the gradualness of its institutional-
ization. The experiences of the past sixty years have been instructive to
those who would oppose educational change. Early attempts at succession, whether in the North or the South, were met with firmness and reso-
luteness; the political boundaries are not likely to be changed. The first
group of Western-educated Muslims are still present in the country and
by and large hold professional, academic, or administrative posts in regional or federal employment areas. The examples of early proponents of
Western-type education who have occupied some of the highest state and

federal posts, including *inter alia* Alhaji Mallam Aminu Kano, Alhaji Maitama Sule and President Alhaji Shehu Shagari, have not gone unnoticed.[48] The breakup of the old regions into states, the temporary abolishment of political parties, the forced decline in the political role of the traditional leaders, and the government take-over of universities (presently thirteen, mostly in the North), all of these factors support educational and political development. If traditions die hard, then their advocates die harder. Some *mallams* and their associates proposed the inclusion of Arabic in the primary curriculum, arguing that it is a prerequisite to an understanding of the Quran and the hadith; others pointed out that it is an important international language. Their efforts will have been in vain unless Arabic can be taught as a component of Religious Knowledge in some states.

With regard to UPE, Sultan Siddiq Abubakar III is helping to ensure *mallams* a place in the scheme by encouraging refresher courses in Islamic studies and personally presiding at degree-granting ceremonies for successful candidates. On the occasion of his being awarded an honorary doctorate degree by the University of Nigeria at Nsukka, the Sultan informed his audience that Islam does not "neglect the important obligation of earning a living through hard work," and that Usuman dan Fodio was a precursor of UPE having urged widespread literacy. In his remarks, considered by some as rather pungent, he indicated a degree of personal apprehension about the effects of UPE. "It may well be that if the Universal Primary Education Scheme produces God-fearing, honest, patriotic and dutiful citizens, there may be a place in the mercies of Allah for those who have had the wisdom to formulate and implement it. . . ."[49] Let me pray to Almighty Allah that our newer species of intellectuals who have travelled so far from home will turn their attention to indigenous traditions a little more. Only if they do so can the products of the Universal Primary Education Scheme inherit a better and greater Nigeria."[50]

In sum, the UPE Scheme provides a framework for the convergence of Islamic and Western education. The graphic point at which the two systems meet vary according to the states. Given the greater intensity of Islamic traditionalism in the northern states, one can hardly expect the new policy to be applied evenly in the near future—if ever. The probability is that certified or accredited Muslim schools will continue to emphasize aspects of Islamic culture, even in non-religious courses (as is done in Catholic schools in the West). Such schools will meet the educational criteria of the government, the Sardauna, and many of the Muslim intellectual élites. In the secular institutions, courses in Religious Knowledge preserve, in some measure, the Islamic character of Muslim students.

While the *National Policy* does not reinforce Islam, one should not conclude that Islamic culture will diminish greatly. The government's commitment to the Nigerianization of education implies an eagerness to retain the indigenous cultures of which Islam is one. The retention of Nigerian languages in the early primary school years ensures a degree of cultural continuity. Indigenous languages will continue to be spoken in homes and used in mosques, and English will continue to be a second language for most Nigerians. The emphasis on Nigerian cultures will serve as a reminder to Muslim students of their great intellectual and historical past and encourage national Muslim unity.

Apart from the formal educational process, there are other means to facilitate cultural retention. Muslim student organizations and cultural associations, which are accommodating responses to modernization, promote Islamic adherence by constructing mosques and prayer-places on school-grounds and campuses, and organizing informal seminars and other extra-curricular activities. The MSSN is a participating member in the World Organization of Muslim Youth (based in Saudi Arabia) which is dedicated to combatting un-Islamic influences on young Muslims. Similarly, the Nigerian mass media fosters cultural continuity through articles, talk-shows, and competitions relevant to the Islamic heritage.

Islam is a significant part of the basic design of the Nigerian cultural tapestry. Unfortunately, too many Western Islamists — and Muslim traditionalists — tend to ignore this fact. Indeed, it is debatable whether Islam in northern Africa is more intense than Nigerian Islam. Those who would contend that the Sufi aspect, often considered a reinforcer of Islam in northern Africa, seem to forget the indigenization of Sufism in that region. The same phenomenon occurred in western Africa: the brotherhoods and the indigenous "secret societies" merged under the hierarchical spiritual leadership of the *shaykh*s, *marabout*s and *mallam*s (elsewhere, *ayatollah*s and *mullah*s) who became the custodians of the Islamic tradition. As a group, their function is not limited to teaching and preaching; their influence is felt in many areas of the private and public domains of Muslims (and sometimes non-Muslim) society. Nigerian man, like many of his Third World brothers, is a very spiritual man; the degree of his Westernization — or his secularization — is exaggerated too often by Western observers. Whatever nourished Islam in other parts of the Muslim world will sustain it in Nigeria: modifications in the secondary forms should not be seen as necessary aberrations in the basic content. The merger of Nigeria's cultural traditions will produce the *Nigerian nation.* At that point Islam will have demonstrated its often unperceived flexibility.

∾ 11 ∾

Religion and Modernization in Senegal

Lucy E. Creevey

*A*s MODERNIZATION OCCURS, religion in a given society should also change. According to much of the literature on the subject, development in social, political, and economic spheres should be paralleled by changes in religious attitudes. During the process of modernization individuals supposedly break away from the all-encompassing hold of traditional associations and institutions such as the church, family, or kin groups. Although still related to his family and other traditional associations, the nature of an individual's contacts apparently changes. The more modernized individual is assumed to be in relation with and influenced by, many more groups of people. The roles he and others in his society play are typically more differentiated. The factors which shape the way he thinks and acts become themselves more varied and diverse. He supposedly becomes more willing to adopt new ways of doing things and accepts standards of performance based on achievement-oriented and universalistic criteria.[1]

In the sphere of religion this change of attitude has been called secularization. This is said to involve limiting the authority of religious institutions, rationalizing morality, and decreasing emphasis on the mystical or supernatural. Thus, for an individual to accept the so-called modern, universalistic style of life he should act out of rational, pragmatic calculation of the known costs and benefits of the actions, rather than out of fear of other-worldly reprisals or simple observance of custom and tradition. This does not mean that he should reject all association with a religion but it should mean that the religion he chooses will be "modern," that is will emphasize rationality and social concerns and play down the importance of ritual, the notion of punishment or rewards in Heaven, and the necessity of obedience to the religious hierarchy.[2]

The various dimensions to the concept of modernization cited above include diverse facts of human life. Not surprisingly, change does not occur uniformly — individuals may "modernize" more rapidly in one area than in another. Thus Schnaiberg tested the unidimensionality of modernism measured by indices relating to mass media exposure, extended family ties, nuclear family role structure, religiosity, environmental orientation, and production/consumption behavior to prove that the evidence for a unidimensional modernism phenomenon was not strong.[3] Further, measuring change becomes extremely complex because the meaning of an individual measure may itself change. Thus being baptized, married in church, and even attending church may not be an indicator of strong religious affiliation in a society in which middle class social norms pressure the upwardly mobile individual to conform to such rituals. In Chile (during the period before the leftist Allende government and the right wing coup of 1973) exactly such a situation prevailed — although no longer seeing the church and its priests as having authority over their daily lives (as they had done at an earlier stage in Chile) workers, even Communist ones, generally observed church rituals.[4]

Yet to admit that modernization in general — and secularization in particular — are complex processes should not eliminate the possibility of studying the subject. Enough has been written to make a careful scholar wary of falling into the ethnocentric Western bias of some earlier studies; still the trend or direction of change found in current work remains the same as that discovered by some of the first studies on development.[5] There should, then, be adequate material from other cases to hypothesize the following: as Senegal grows economically and becomes more industrialized and more urbanized, and as mass education spreads, and the service network is extended, and as the political system develops, religion and religious attitudes and behavior should also modernize.

The object of this paper is to test this hypothesis from data collected in 1960, 1965–66, 1976, and 1978. The data is not uniform in kind or quality. A survey of religious and political attitudes in the Medina (one of the oldest and poorest African housing districts in Dakar) is available from 1976 but no earlier survey exists. Extensive research on historical and current documents in Arabic and French concerning the role of religion in Senegal was done in 1966 but not repeated. Major Muslim leaders were systematically interviewed in 1965–66 but only a selected sub-group (or their successors) were re-interviewed in 1976. Newspapers and journals from 1960 to the present, both those from Senegal and other relevant foreign ones (like *Jeune Afrique* and *Le Monde*) have been canvassed. Government statistics have been collected for the entire period. Government leaders and their assistants, students, Muslim disciples, and opposition political activists have been interviewed on each of the research trips mentioned, although the same people were not, of course, in the same posts on each visit given the long span of time. In the end, however, the validity of the conclusions reached here depends on the familiarity of the writer with Senegal and the fact that each source reinforced — cross-checked — information from other sources.

Senegal, the site of this study, is a small country, a former French colony on the coast in West Africa, which became independent in 1960. Secularization is especially interesting in Senegal because religious groups and religious leaders have had a significant role in politics since the colonial period. The decreasing or changing role of religion, then, should have a clear impact on all facets of life. Before discussing religion, however, social, political, and economic background statistics will be presented. Then the position of Islam in Senegal — the beliefs and practices of its adherents, and the role of its leaders — will be examined.

ECONOMIC AND SOCIAL CHANGE

Senegal has a small population — only 4 million people in 1974. Relative to most other West African countries, Senegal is quite urbanized — 28 percent living in cities over 20,000 in 1971[6] — but the bulk of the population still lives outside the towns and cities and still depends on agriculture for their livelihood. The rate of population growth and of urbanization, however, is also a salient fact to consider: Senegal's population more than tripled since the beginning of the century and at an ever-increasing speed of growth. Urban concentration increased similarly, focused particularly in Dakar, which had 64 percent of the urban population in 1974.

While the population of Senegal grew (in 1972–74) at a rate of 2 percent *per annum,* the economy was also growing. However the economic growth rate was much slower. Between 1960 (the year of independence) and 1974 the industrial sector grew by only 9 percent.[8] The most striking factor change in this growth was in the extraction and export of phosphates which expanded markedly relative to other industrial products. In the early seventies phosphates began to be a notable part of Senegalese imports where formerly peanuts had dominated. Indeed, the production of peanuts actually declined between 1960 and 1974.

For the individual Senegalese the high rate of urbanization and the economic growth pattern indicate an ever higher probability of involvement in a money economy and exposure to Western material goods and Western ways of thought. However, the fact that few Senegalese are employed in the industrial sector (or in mining) and most in agriculture means that this change is a slow process. The rural sector is more resistant to change because the pattern of traditional life is less altered by the imposition of cash-crop production than when individuals or groups move to the city. There diversity of customs, competition for jobs and a variety of other factors accelerate the adaptation to modernization process. Even in the urban sector, though, many traditional customs persist. Family relationships and modes of living resemble closely those in the rural area. Although adapted to the necessarily cramped housing conditions of a densely populated area, the extended family reassembles itself as much as it can.[9] Furthermore, only a small number of people actually are employed for wages. In 1972 in the Dakar region, only 18,218 people out of a population of 714,149 held wage-paying jobs.[10] The rest were jobless or engaged in the "informal" sector. The latter is that portion of the economy not reported in official statistics including many activities from vending hot cakes for pennies to large-scale trading. Most individuals in the informal sector receive very small returns and, more significantly for this study, this entire class of employment is more adaptable to traditional life styles, thus does not force individuals into the competitive, achievement-oriented mode as quickly as do wage-paid jobs generally.[11]

Education and political development also reflect individual adjustment to change. By 1974 26 percent of school-age girls and 45 percent of school-age boys were in school.[12] It is difficult, however, to find parallel statistics for political development. Senegal has been independent for nineteen years (as of this writing) but the same party which took over at independence is in office, and the president who dominated politics then is by far the most powerful person now. Although the law now permits a multi-party system, electoral returns are a very poor indicator of political participation.[13] Except in the very early years of party formation, after World War II, when Leopold Sedar Senghor, the president, was organizing his political following, there has been little effort to politicize the Senegalese masses. Even then Senghor constructed his political machine by winning the support of rural traditional leaders through whom he gained the vote and allegiance of the peasants.[14]

RELIGION IN SENEGAL: BACKGROUND

The importance or meaning of religion for the individual Senegalese within this social context must be very carefully studied. In this area, most of the available information relates to national (or regional) structures rather than individual preferences or behavior patterns. Senegal is a predominantly Muslim country (80 percent), although the government is secular—and the president is Catholic. Virtually all the Muslims belong to a brotherhood, organizations which are controlled by leaders called marabouts. The brotherhoods—*tariqa* or Sufi orders—were introduced from North Africa to Senegal during the late eighteenth and early nineteenth centuries. The major brotherhoods established in Senegal were the Qadriyya, the Tijaniyya and the Muridiyya. The latter is an offshoot of the Qadriyya (founded in the nineteenth century) and its membership is almost entirely inside Senegal and largely among the dominant Wolof tribe. It is second in size to the Tijaniyya which has followers all over North and West Africa and, in Senegal, among the northern Tukulor, the Wolof and other ethnic groups. The Qadriyya is much smaller with followers mainly in the area near the Mauretanian border and among Maures living in Senegal.

The brotherhoods became politically important in Senegal because conversion to them was part of a revitalization process for Senegal. That is, by the middle and end of the nineteenth century the traditional social order in Senegal had been severely shaken by exposure to the French. The French broke the power of traditional leaders militarily and simultaneously introduced new values and habits. The brotherhoods offered to the Senegalese an order of life that was more able to adjust to the new influences of the French and the insecurity they produced. Brotherhood leaders, then, took on many of the temporal roles of traditional chiefs including military leadership. In Senegal, however, the marabouts quickly abandoned outright military opposition and consolidated their power by acting as intermediaries between the foreign colonialists and the rural inhabitants. The marabouts themselves were Senegalese. Originally some were of lower caste than the former chiefs but shortly after conversion the marabouts were virtually all of upper caste families. Thus the traditional order had broken down and reformed incorporating into its structure the brotherhoods.[15]

Because conversion occurred fairly recently nineteenth and twentieth century pre-independence observers in Senegal often commented on the shallowness of the religious practices they witnessed. Only a handful of religious leaders knew any Arabic and, of these, most knew only enough to read the Quran. The majority of the Muslims in Senegal knew a few verses of the Quran. Many did not regularly pray five times a day nor observe Ramadan strictly. Muslim family codes were mixed with pre-existing practices. Although Islamic law took precedence where the earlier practices openly violated it, often what resulted was a confused mixture—thus inheritance to leadership in the religious hierarchy appeared to follow conflicting patterns; the eldest son did not invariably inherit.[16]

In addition, there were few mosques and few centers of Islamic learning although many hundreds, indeed thousands, of Senegalese children learned snatches of the Quran by rote from ink-daubed wooden slates at Quranic schools run by the marabouts.[17] In fact, to many, the most outstanding characteristic of Islam in Senegal was not erudition but the contrary, superstition. Muslims in Senegal typically gave obedience to their leaders which crossed the lines from respect to religious devotion. Marabouts—at least the few most powerful ones—were believed to have every kind of power allowing them not only to intercede with Allah for his favors for faithful followers, but also to intervene directly in worldly problems. Thus, even educated followers of a modern leader, Al Hajj Ibrahim Niass (d. 1975) insisted that he had magically crippled one opponent Senegalese politician and caused another clan leader to be burned alive.[18] Such superstitious beliefs were typical of Islam as it first spread in its Sufi or brotherhood form in North Africa in the eighteenth century.[19] Nor are they currently unusual among uneducated peoples in other countries, including those where the religion is Christian. But they gave a shape to Senegalese Islam causing criticism from outside purists and also resulting in an unusual degree of political power for Muslim marabouts in Senegal.

In some parts of North Africa, orthodox Muslims objected to some of the excesses of Sufi brotherhoods. Opposition by well-educated Muslim students and intellectuals to the so-called "exploitation" of the credulous peasants was combined with condemnation of rural brotherhood leaders for collaborating with the French. In Senegal, however, the group concerned with reforming Islam has been small. Muslim leaders have sent their sons or protegees to be educated in North Africa and the Middle East. These students and other Senegalese who spent long periods in Muslim countries have at times protested against the laxity of religious observance in Senegal.[20] But to date they have had little influence. This fact, combined with the lack of a protracted anti-colonial war, prevented the undermining of maraboutic authority on the basis of the type of doctrine they either preached or condoned among their followers.

Senegalese Muslim brotherhoods, then, had a peculiar political advantage. Although the French initially distrusted Muslim brotherhoods as a threat to their hegemony, they eventually came to rely on their support for control of the peasant masses. The French, then, pursued a careful policy of interfering in internal brotherhood politics when any issue or leader threatened to disturb their political balance. Simultaneously, they provided money and other forms of support to brotherhood leaders to assure continued help in getting peasant co-operation for — or at least acquiescence to — French programs and policies.[21] Significantly, Muslim leaders in the central Wolof region and to a lesser extent among the Tukulor of the north pushed their followers to grow the cash crop, peanuts. They became major entrepreneurs thus reinforcing and expanding their political influence.

When Senegalese politicians began to organize the nationalist movement after World War II, they recognized the importance of Muslim leaders, especially in the countryside, and vied with each other to gain their support. The backing which the major marabouts gave the party of Leopold Sedar Senghor was a telling factor in his victory over his opponent, Lamine Gueye.[22] And the Muslim leaders continued to play an important role behind the scenes of modern political decisions during the post-1960 independence period.

The marabouts did not make policy, but their support was essential for the stability, and even viability of Senghor's government. Whenever a crisis occurred they emerged into the open with public announcements and demonstrations by their followers, such as those observed by this writer on the occasion of the break-up of the Mali Federation in 1960. Thus in 1963, during the major crisis surrounding the so-called attempted "coup" of Mamadou Dia (Senghor's second-in-command), the President openly underlined his government's need for Murid Brotherhood's support in a speech to the head of that brotherhood: "Eighteen years ago . . . I exposed . . . the objectives of my policy to you. . . . Immediately you understood me . . . you helped me. Since then you have all seemed compromised and the friends of yesterday abandoned me [reference to Mamadou Dia], I always found comfort, advice and support next to you."[23]

RELIGION AND POLITICS IN THE SEVENTIES

Over the period since independence changes have taken place. In the early sixties the political leaders were relatively young men in contrast to the marabouts who had served under the French for decades. In mid-seventies the leadership of the party and the government was notably an older group than had been in office in the earlier period. The most important Muslim leaders were not young men either. Age still gave them status value in the traditional world but the marabouts of the seventies were often not the men who had influenced politics ten years before and during the French colonial period and thus had less experience or prestige.

Of the hundreds of marabouts in Senegal, only a handful were significant in politics nationally. The others provided the lieutenants and sub-lieutenants who make up the factions and sub-factions of the various brotherhood hierarchies, all more or less subordinate to the khalif of whichever brotherhood in Senegal. The most powerful marabouts traditionally were found among the Mouride (Muridiyya) leaders because of the tight discipline of the order and its control of the central Wolof zone. The Tidjaniyya brotherhood, split into several factions and less disciplined, had less power as well, although some very influential Tidjani marabouts played their part in Senegalese politics from time to time.

Thus the most important changes in the seventies were to be looked for in the Mouride leadership. The most important change in leadership occurred in 1968 with the death of Falilou Mbacke, the khalif of the Mourides and a close supporter of Senghor. Earlier studies have documented tensions between the government and Mouride leaders, and demonstrated the "give-and-take" between the two sides. But the overall tenor was one of cooperation by Falilou who had the brotherhood tightly unified under his leadership, having defeated earlier attempts to challenge his authority when he took office. The heir apparent was his brother Bassirou, who died unexpectedly in 1966, so that Abdou Lahat, the next brother in line, in fact inherited, although he was relatively unknown in Senegalese politics. What is more important, the new khalif did not have the individual loyalty of his order.

The succession principle among the Muslim leaders, as mentioned, is somewhat flexible. The founder of the Mourides was succeeded by his son, and thereafter by his brother Falilou. He indicated — and it was widely assumed — that he would be succeeded by a brother, but there is enough uncertainty when a khalif dies for all powerful marabouts to become restive, particularly if their personal following is as extensive as that of the heir apparent, or even greater. When Falilou died, Cheikh Mbacke — son of the eldest son and heir of Ahmad Bamba, and one of the most powerful and wealthy Mouride leaders — explored the possibility of contending the succession himself, before deciding to become a major supporter of Abdou Lahat.

In contrast, the eldest son of Falilou did not openly seek his father's position — albeit retaining the loyalty of many of his subordinate leaders — and apparently remained somewhat aloof from the new khalif. The eldest son of Bassirou was named by Abdou Lahat as his delegate in governmental negotiations, although he also maintains a slightly separate power base. The importance of this tangle of claims and counter-claims was that the new khalif did not achieve the same solid front within his brotherhood that Falilou had. Consequently, his dealings with the government often reflected both his efforts to bind his order more tightly behind him and his dependence on Cheikh Mbacke, never an avid supporter of Senghor although too clever to appear an open enemy of the President. In 1977, however, Cheikh Mbacke died which lessened the threat of opposition to both Abdou Lahat and President Senghor.

The net result in 1978 in relations between Abdou Lahat and the government was that Senghor faced a more hostile, if somewhat less powerful, Mouride leadership. The game of "give-and-take" altered accordingly. For example, there was no longer any close personal communication between Senghor and the new khalif who made a point of appearing personally aloof from politics. Thus, Dakar was treated in March 1976 to the spectacle of a presidential audience for all the major Mouride leaders (including the khalif) and their entourages, apparently to emphasize their unity and Abdou Lahat's desire not to appear alone in political dealings.[24]

With consummate political skill, Senghor evolved a method of dealing with the new Mouride leaders. His chief agents were Abdou Diouf, the Prime Minister, and Ousmane Camara, the Minister of Higher Education, who developed extensive ties to various Mouride leaders, and to men in the Khalif's entourage. At every important ritual Muslim celebration the government was represented by these politicians, accompanied by the governor of Diourbel and a range of other officials. As in the past, at each public occasion mutual felicitations were ceremoniously exchanged. Thus *Le Soleil* reported that the governor of Diourbel spoke for the President at the 1975 Tabaski festival: "He then congratulated through Serigne Bassirou Mbacke the constant and remarkable support given by the religious authorities, particularly by the Khalif Abdou Lahat Mbacke, for the economic and social development of the nation."[25]

If there was a difference in these dealings it was that both the President and the Khalif were less likely to make direct requests to each other for assistance. It was still expected that important rural programs would be supported either by the Khalif or by his more powerful subordinates. Thus, at the same Tabaski festival the eldest son of Falilou accepted congratulations for Mouride cooperation, and assured government leaders that all his followers would pay off the loans they had incurred over the last harvest period.[26] Thus, too, the government made a substantial contribution to the improvement of the Khalif's personal "field" which almost doubled in size since the sixties, and included a substantial garden enterprise. As the main Dakar newspaper pointed out: "Without doubt with these new extensions, Touba-Belel is the biggest and best maintained field in Senegal.[27]

The government also agreed to give major technical and financial assistance for the development of Touba, the Mouride capital, a pet project of the Khalif. As an apparent *quid pro quo,* he agreed to allow the government to close the Occas market — which had long flourished as a center of black market and smuggling activities — despite the opposition of many influential Mourides who wished to retain this source of considerable income. However, the Prime Minister's powers of persuasion were evident: the Khalif was converted to the view that the market was a deterrent to the holiness of Touba.

Of course, matters did not always run smoothly because the Khalif was withdrawn and less favorably disposed to the government than his predecessor. On a number of occasions he openly marked his displeasure at some ministerial actions, for example at a major Mouride festival in 1976 when the nation was shocked by the Khalif's cold reply to the warm speech of the Prime Minister, both of which were broadcast. The explanations for this rebuff vary, but it is thought that Abdou Lahat was displeased by Diouf's open reference to his request for aid for Touba since the public image of the independence of the Khalif was thereby weakened.

But recurrent outbursts of hostility did not indicate real opposition to the government. Abdou Lahat and his associates continued to go along with Senghor and his policies. They did not side with the new political parties, probably because the opposition could not offer nearly as much as the established government. They tolerated schemes which they actively disliked, such as the Family Code (which in theory made polygamy more difficult), and the increasing spread of Western education.

Among the weaker brotherhoods no new leaders had emerged on the national scene in the seventies. The two non-Mouride leaders who had had a national role in the sixties were less important. One, Seydou Nourou Tall, had been widely known for his long collaboration with first the French and then the Senegalese government, but in 1978 was well over 100 years old. Although this outstanding Tidjani leader still appeared at public meetings, he had to be supported on each side, and his political acumen (understandably) had faded as age dulled his mind.

The other nationally influential marabout of the Tidjani order, Ibrahima Niasse, had played an active role in the Muslim world outside Senegal, and was often outspoken in internal politics. When he died in 1975, there was some confusion over the succession, but eventually his eldest son, Abdoulaye, took the leadership of his order. It was too early of course, to be sure what Abdoulaye could do with his position, but in 1978 he had nowhere near the reputation or power of his father.[28]

By mid-1978, Abdul Aziz Sy, the leader of the largest Tidjani group, appeared old, grey, and withdrawn, although he still intervened for his followers when they needed help from the government, as he did ten years ago. But he always avoided direct involvement in politics generally, and maintained a much lower temporal control of lesser marabouts and followers than did the Mouride leaders. The Prime Minister established good relations with Abdul Aziz Sy, symbolized, for example, by representing the government at major Tidjani festivals in the Sy capital at Tivaouane.[29] But this order is far less of a problem for the government, and also less of a potential support as well.

Non-Mouride marabouts in Senegal, then, in the mid-seventies, accept the programs set forth by the government. None saw fit to back opposition leaders, probably for the same reasons that the Mouride had not — viz. their lack of power. Occasionally, governmental actions called forth a flurry of protests. For example, the Family Code was unpopular with all of them. Thus the khalif of the Layenne order (centered near Dakar) announced at the major festival of his brotherhood that the section dealing with polygamy was contrary to the teachings of Islam. Simultaneously, however, his chief assistant thanked Senghor for bringing peace to the country, and "for the help which his Government has always given to the Layenne order."[30] This was a more or less typical reaction, because traditional Muslim authorities will advise their followers to ignore any rulings which are directly contrary to Islam. As the government avoided such a confrontation, however, this was not a crucial problem. The marabouts remained then, at one and the same time, major intermediaries who legitimized the government and traditional leaders who were suspicious of, if not actively opposed to, education and rural reform.

RELIGIOUS ATTITUDES AND BEHAVIOR PATTERNS IN THE SEVENTIES

At some point in the modernization process, according to the hypothesis advanced here, the role of the marabouts as intermediaries in politics should cease. What such a point is cannot be easily identified. Furthermore, marabouts could continue to have a significant role as advisors on temporal matters — as did Catholic priests in Chile at a much later stage in the urbanization and modernization process. Although no longer believed to have magical powers, and although the average Senegalese might recognize other, secular opinion leaders, marabouts might be influential in non-religious matters for a long time to come. The entire situation is more complicated because the current political leadership was trained — and obtained its political base — in the French colonial era. Senegalese leaders maintain the political patterns of the forties. This is certainly in part a necessity but it is also a reflection of habit and, ironically, may reinforce the power of Muslim leaders. To what extent that reinforcement creates an artificially strong Muslim hierarchy will only be seen if the Senegalese government is replaced with a radically different group — an eventuality which could occur if a coup succeeded.

The only evidence available on this point is a 1976 survey carried out in an old, poor African slum or tenement district of Dakar. Because there is no survey available from the sixties (or earlier) and because the sample is an urban one, it may fairly be said to prove nothing about the changing attitudes of the majority rural population. Yet urbanization increases rapidly in Senegal and, in addition, ties between the city and the countryside are close and constant. Many of the major marabouts, although based in the countryside, have town residences and, when there, lines of faithful followers may be seen waiting for an audience. Religious films sponsored by the brotherhoods or neo-brotherhood organizations (whose elected leadership is approved by the major marabouts) are shown regularly throughout the city and are well attended. City mosques — whose imamates are sometimes controlled from outside Dakar — regularly draw huge crowds on Fridays. The marabouts themselves, furthermore, have their hands into urban business concerns as well as agricultural investments. The late Cheikh Mbacke had a huge fleet of trucks (run by his followers) and was a major urban real estate owner. Thus, too, a devout Mouride of considerable importance owned one of the largest hotels — opened for the arrival of Secretary of State Henry Kissinger in 1976.

The brotherhoods are, then, influential in the city while the city population continuously interacts with rural peoples. Many urban dwellers visit their region of origin regularly and others stay for a brief time in the city, returning to the countryside for the peanut harvest season and then finding their way back to Dakar again. The attitudes and behavior patterns of city dwellers, thus, cannot be completely distinct from their rural counterparts and may indicate what types of changes will occur when modernization is further advanced into the countryside.

The 1976 sample of 2 percent of the Medina dwellers, or 205 men, was drawn from heads of households. This assured a relatively old sample which therefore under-represents the views of the young and perhaps better eduated.[31] The sample is further skewed because the Medina is a relatively stable area — not one made up of new migrants to the city. New migrants were there, often as members of the household, but their opinions were not solicited.

The major social characteristics of the group were the following. First, they were in plurality Wolof with the Lebou (a Dakar area ethnic group) second in size and the Tukulor, third. As such this was a relatively common ethnic distribution for Dakar.[32] As mentioned, the group was relatively old, more than half of them being above 50, and relatively uneducated, about half having no schooling and almost half of the rest having had only four years of primary school or less. The overwhelming majority of these men had been in Dakar more than ten years and intended to remain there. Very few were unemployed (although a few were retired) and they were mostly in low-paid workers' jobs: domestic service or waiters, construction, small shop or stall owners or vendor office boys. A tiny handful were nurses or teachers. Although they did not intend to return to the country, most of those surveyed visited the area in which their relatives lived often.

Ninety percent of the sample were Muslim and most of these men belonged to a brotherhood. The Tidjaniyya order had the largest number of adherents, followed by the Qadriyya with the Muridiyya third. This too is a not-surprising distribution for Dakar although the Mourides are under-represented for the country as a whole. It does (indirectly) reinforce the image of the Mourides as a rural, agricultural order centered in the peanut-growing zone.

The respondents clearly saw religion as important. Virtually all Muslims prayed five times a day every day and went to the mosque on Friday regularly. Over 80 percent sent their children to Quranic schools as well. Yet in regard to the marabouts they exhibited a rather tolerant or disengaged view. Almost all of them talked with marabouts but most of them talked only of religious matters. Many of the others may have talked of family problems in a general sense but most clearly did not rely on the marabouts for support in temporal matters. This was demonstrated by a series of questions on whom the respondents consulted when problems arose. For illness most consulted a doctor — an obvious choice but not historically so in Senegal. Twenty percent consulted family, friends, and others and perhaps a marabout as well but even this group did not name the marabout as *the* or *a* significant source of council. Only 2 percent did deliberately isolate the marabout as the primary aid in sickness. The same kind of response was given in regard to finding a job for oneself or one's children. Marabouts received even less of a vote of confidence in the financial domain. Most people went to worldly figures representing the area of concern such as banks for money, government officials for jobs, doctors for sickness. They also consulted ethnic group leaders and family and friends which was a pragmatic choice in Senegal where jobs, assistance, and privileges still come through extended family and ethnic ties.

Most of the respondents still thought marabouts were important to Senegal but stated that they were important because they were religious leaders, that is as "ministers" of the Muslim faith. This answer does not suggest that the respondents were ignorant of the immense political power marabouts have had and still have. Rather it shows their own priorities and their own distinction between matters of religion (belonging to a marabout) and worldly matters, belonging presumably to Caesar. Thus they gave money to marabouts, as did their rural counterparts, but their action may be seen as a religious donation, according to Islam an act of grace. Thus, too, 13 percent belonged to a religious organization—by which they mean a neo-religious association. Many more belonged to "modern" groups like trade unions or sports' associations. But those who did join religious groups apparently did so without letting the religious group organize the non-religious aspects of their lives.

CONCLUSION

Islam continues to spread in Senegal even as the country gradually develops socially and economically. Aid from North Africa has helped build impressive mosques, supported larger numbers of students to pursue college studies in Muslim countries and, even, provided teachers for primary and secondary level studies of Arabic and the Quran. So far such assistance, however, has had little impact on the average Senegalese—except that he can see, or worship in, the new mosques. But the old pattern of religious loyalties is gradually changing. The hypothesis advanced at the beginning of this paper is not, in some sense, proven by the results of this study. At a national level, the marabouts' influence is only slightly weaker in politics than it was ten or twenty years ago. However, the results of the survey in Dakar suggest that religious attitudes are changing. Among the respondents, the marabout was no longer the all-powerful figure who was the leader in all domains, but simply a man of religion, a teacher of the faith. This still gives an urban marabout potentially more authority than his secular peer, just as a priest has elsewhere. But it suggests a drastic role change is predictable in the foreseeable, if long-term future. Marabouts may use their present sources of power to become urban investors but in the long run their authority is likely to come more from the actual economic resources they have, than from their religious position.

The results here may also suggest that the theories of modernization and development are too broad to capture usefully the way change in religious attitudes and behavior occurs in a given place at a given time. In Senegal it may be more useful to look at the changing patron-client relationships between marabout and follower. It is far easier and more meaningful to document the changing role of the marabout as leader as time goes on than it is to demonstrate that the society is becoming more secular in the usual meaning of the word. It may, in fact, be more religious — the shallowness observed by early visitors to Senegal may be replaced by a depth of religion and a regularity of religious observances consistent with the longer period that Islam has been in Senegal.

NOTES

Chapter 1 — ISLAM AND POLITICAL DEVELOPMENT

1. For examples, see Willard G. Oxtoby, "Western Perspectives on Islam and the Arabs," Ch. 1 in *The American Media and the Arabs,* edited by Michael C. Hudson and Ronald G. Wolfe (Washington: Georgetown University Center for Contemporary Arab Studies, 1980).

2. This is the theme of Edward W. Said's important book, *Orientalism* (New York: Pantheon, 1978).

3. Maxime Rodinson, *Islam and Capitalism* (London: Penguin Books, 1966, 1977). To Rodinson, Islam (for better or worse) is not a primary factor either as a support or impediment to "development." Rather, it accommodates itself to deeper processes of social change and serves as an instrument in the hands of political and economic actors.

4. See, e.g., "An Interview with Khomeini," by Oriana Fallaci, *The New York Times Magazine* (October 7, 1979), pp. 29–31.

5. Gabriel Almond and G. Bingham Powell, *Comparative Politics: A Comparative Approach* (Boston: Little, Brown, 1966), Ch. 11, esp. p. 308.

6. Ibid., p. 34.

7. *The Quran* XVI: 90. In this and subsequent quotations I have used the translation by A. Yusuf Ali (Beirut: Dar Al-Arabia, 1968).

8. *The Quran* XLII: 38.

9. See E.I.J. Rosenthal, *Islam in the Modern National State* (Cambridge: Cambridge University Press, 1965), pp. 69–72.

10. So writes Altaf Gauhar, "What Chance Success for a Destiny Built on the Past?" *The Guardian* (Manchester) (February 25, 1979), p. 9.

11. *The Quran* II: 143 and XIII: 11.

12. For an introductory treatment and selections, see Ralph Lerner and Muhsin

223

Mahdi, eds., *Medieval Political Philosophy: A Sourcebook* (New York: The Free Press of Glencoe, 1963), Part I, "Political Philosophy in Islam," edited by Muhsin Mahdi.

13. Constantine K. Zurayk, "Tensions in Islamic Civilization," Papers in Contemporary Arab Studies, no. 3 (Washington, D.C.: Georgetown University Center for Contemporary Arab Studies, 1978), p. 16.

14. Albert Hourani, *Arabic Thought in the Liberal Age, 1798-1939* (London: Oxford University Press, 1962), p. 372.

15. R. Hrair Dekmejian, "The Anatomy of Islamic Revival," *The Middle East Journal* 34, 1 (Winter 1980): 1-12, p. 12.

16. Imam Ruholla Al-Khomeini, *Islamic Government* (*Al-Hukuma Al-Islamiyya*) (Cairo: n.p., 1979), with an introduction by Dr. Hassan Hanafi.

17. Oriana Fallaci, "An interview with Khomeini," *The New York Times Magazine* (October 7, 1979), pp. 29-31; *Islamic Government,* passim and pp. 13-14, 17-20, 34-35.

18. The phenomenon is drawn from the work of Karl. W. Deutsch, specifically his "Social Mobilization and Political Development," *American Political Science Review* 55, 3 (September 1961): 493-514.

19. Donald Eugene Smith, *Religion and Political Development* (Boston: Little, Brown, 1970), p. 244. He writes, "Once one has determined that the true meaning of 'Islamic society' is 'just society,' one can forget entirely the shariah and other historical embodiments of the idea of justice. In fact, if social justice is indeed the main idea, it is no longer necessary to speak of Islam at all. The purely cultural aspects of Islam may continue to be cherished, but its sociopolitical ideas are no longer relevant. Though secularization has condemned these *ideas* to oblivion, Islamic humanism has made its contribution to the universalization of *values.*" Ibid., pp. 244-45.

20. Among them, H. A. R. Gibb, *Mohammedanism* (New York: Oxford University Press, 1962), pp. 190-92.

21. Manfred Halpern, *The Politics of Social Change in the Middle East and North Africa* (Princeton, N.J.: Princeton University Press, 1963), Ch. 7.

22. Ibid., ch. 8, esp. p. 135.

23. Ibid., p. 153.

24. Hourani, *Arabic Thought in the Liberal Age, 1798-1939,* p. 144.

25. Richard P. Mitchell, *The Society of the Muslim Brothers* (London: Oxford University Press, 1969), pp. 225, 239.

26. Daniel Lerner, *The Passing of Traditional Society: Modernizing the Middle East* (Glencoe, Ill.: The Free Press, 1958), p. 73.

27. Michael C. Hudson, *Arab Politics: The Search for Legitimacy* (New Haven: Yale University Press, 1977).

28. Suad Joseph, "Muslim-Christian Conflicts: A Theoretical Perspective," in *Muslim-Christian Conflicts: Economic, Political, and Social Origins,* edited by Suad Joseph and Barbara L. K. Pillsbury (Boulder, Col.: Westview, 1978), pp. 5-7.

29. See, e.g., Joseph Schact, "Sharia," in the *Shorter Encyclopedia of Islam* (Leiden: Brill, 1953), pp. 524-29.

30. Hisham Sharabi, "Islam and Modernization in the Arab World," in *Modernization of the Arab World,* edited by J. H. Thompson and R. D. Reischauer (Princeton, N.J.: Van Nostrand, 1966), pp. 26–36, p. 26.

31. I am indebted to Dr. Asad Abdel-Rahman of Kuwait University for making this point in a lecture at the Center for Contemporary Arab Studies of Georgetown University in April 1980.

Chapter 2—ISLAM AND MODERN ECONOMIC CHANGE

1. See, for example, the discussion in Maxime Rodinson, *Islam and Capitalism,* translated by Brian Pearce (Austin: University of Texas Press, 1978).

2. That is, actual Marxism in the Islamic world has tended to be a fringe phenomenon, popular in theory (for example in universities or at political rallies), but not in practice—as in contemporary Iraq or Syria, or espoused with greater vigor only in isolated areas like southern Yemen.

3. The authors are currently undertaking a study of the Islamic economic system and its economic implications for such questions as income distribution, efficiency, and the operation of factor markets.

4. In practice, a third system has evolved which has applied to all citizens. In the past, as is indicated below, this has involved a blurring of the distinctions between the two groups, generally in favor of universalizing a particular tax and of increasing tax receipts. In the contemporary period, it has also included neutral taxes, often copied from the industrialized countries, that are by nature universal.

5. Tax, as the term is used today, is not altogether an appropriate term, since it implies a payment made under duress of legal penalty to a government entity; still the word *tax* serves as a convenient term where no other modern English word might be an improvement. As we shall indicate below, *zakat* includes alms given privately by one individual to another.

6. The specific interpretation of this and other taxes varies among the various orthodox legal schools—Hanafi, Shafi, Maliki, and Hanbali. For more detail, refer to Nicholas P. Aghnides, *Mohammedan Theories of Finance* (New York: Columbia University Press, 1916).

7. Against the latter came to be levied the *ushr,* or tithe, and many commentators then distinguished this as basically different from *zakat.*

8. *Zakat* plus the first three pillars listed above are *sine qua non,* absolutely required of all true Muslims. The obligation of the *hajj* is qualified; one must be financially able to undertake the pilgrimage.

9. *Sura* XIII, v. 22; a similar phrasing is found in *Sura* XXXV, v. 29. This and all following Quranic quotations are taken from the translation of A.J. Arberry, *The Koran Interpreted* (London: George Allen and Unwin, 1955). This translation follows the traditional Quranic ordering of the chapters, or *suras.*

10. *Sura* LXX, v. 24.

11. For example, this is the interpretation cited as primary by Joseph Schacht in the article on *zakat* in the *Encyclopedia of Islam* (Leyden: Brill, 1934).

12. According to Schacht in *Sura* XXIX, v. 31 and 55, and in *Sura* VII, v. 156, *Sura* XXI, v. 73, etc.

13. As, for example, in *Sura* XCII, v. 14 ff.: "Now I have warned you of a fire that flames . . . from which the most Godfearing shall be removed . . . he who gives his wealth to purify himself." The expiation connected with the payment of *zakat* is clearly connected with sins of economic origin; thus, it is particularly recommended to the rich.

14. Cf. Aghnides, *Mohammedan Theories of Finance,* p. 203.

15. However, transactions undertaken specifically to avoid the twelve-month requirement do not qualify for exemption.

16. For example, Aghnides, *Mohammedan Theories of Finance,* pp. 216–17, lists several items that are either nonproductive or primary necessities: "dwelling-houses; wearing apparel; household utensils; slaves employed as servants; riding animals; arms kept for use; food used by one's self and family; articles of adornment, if not made of gold and silver; gems, pearls, rubies, hyacinths, emeralds, and the like; coins of other than gold and silver, if intended for personal expenditure; books and tools."

17. Cf. ibid., Ch. III, p. 296 ff. For example, the Hanafi school held that gold, silver, and articles of trade were non-apparent property, while livestock and any otherwise non-apparent property taken outside of the city were apparent property, with the obligations on agricultural produce (the tithe) held to be an obligation distinct from *zakat.* On the other hand, the Shafi school included agricultural produce and the output of mines along with livestock as apparent property.

18. *Sura* IX, v. 60. However, there was some dispute among the various schools as to whether religious authorities had the right to make exceptions, deleting or adding specific recipients, or to transfer *zakat* revenues from one region to another.

19. For example, see Aghnides, *Mohammedan Theories of Finance,* pp. 249–50.

20. See ibid., p. 254.

21. Economists term neutral or proportional a tax that strikes all taxpayers with the same impact; a progressive tax is one whose relative burden rises with income or wealth (that is, with the ability to pay), while a regressive tax hits the poor harder, less severely the rich. The levy on the smallest and most common livestock, sheep and goats, was actually somewhat regressive, above minimum flock sizes. A Muslim with forty sheep, for example, owed *zakat* of 2.5 percent, while another with 121 sheep owed about 1.66 percent, and one with 400 sheep 1 percent.

22. For example, see *al-Hidayah,* as quoted in Aghnides, *Mohammedan Theories of Finance,* pp. 367–68.

23. The proportional *kharaj* was thus similar to the tithe. The difference was largely one of location, with land subject to the tithe being for the most part in Arabia proper or land granted to members of the Arab army after its conquest.

24. *Sura* IX, v. 29. The word *jizyah* is derived from *jaza,* meaning compensation or requital for good or evil.

25. Over time, the imposition of *jizyah,* depending as it did upon the specific

terms agreed upon by treaties negotiated by various Muslim political and military leaders with the peoples swept up in the expansion of *Dar al-Islam,* led to many anomalies. For example, some tribes originally agreed to payment of the poll tax and later converted to Islam; without forgiveness of their tax obligations, they assumed the Muslim duty of military service in defense of the community. Other tribes might agree to serve in a military capacity, with no reference to religious conversion, and thus earned exemption from *jizyah.*

26. Various definitions have been given to these general economic classifications; among those cited in Aghnides, *Mohammedan Theories of Finance,* p. 403, a typical one is that the poor are those who must work, the middle class includes those with some wealth (for example, more than 200 dirhams) but who still work, while the rich have enough wealth (above 10,000 dirhams) to be idle. The apparent progressivity of *jizyah* thus clearly is deceptive. For example, under these guidelines, the rich never pay an annual tax exceeding about .05 percent of their wealth, while those in the middle class could pay as much as 12 percent of wealth annually, and the poor even more.

27. This also included levies against discoveries of secreted treasure.

28. The Hanbali school held views similar to the Shafi, and the Maliki school seems to have straddled the issue. Under *zakat* provisions, as indicated above, the levy due would be 2.5 percent; by Shafi interpretations, at least, mines belonging to non-Muslims were exempt from taxation.

29. One tradition attributes to the prophet the dictum that all Muslims are partners in "grass, water and fire"—which could explain the exemptions for coal and well water. At least potentially, this *hadith* could be used to justify an oil policy that exempted the owners of land on which oil was found from taxation (as are the owners of water wells), or conversely, for invoking the guideline of *universal* partnership, in order to keep such land (or at least the mineral rights beneath it) totally within the public domain. In fact, major Muslim oil producers, both in the Middle East and elsewhere (for example, Indonesia, Malaysia, and Brunei), have opted for universal claims over petroleum deposits.

30. Abdul-Hamid Ahmad Abu-Sulayman, "The Theory of the Economics of Islam," *Contemporary Aspects of Economic Thinking in Islam,* proceedings of The Third East Coast Regional Conference of the Muslim Students Association of the USA and Canada, American Trust Publications, April 1968; emphasis added.

31. *Sura* II, v. 275-76. Cf also II, v. 279, III, v. 125, XXX, v. 38.

32. A minority view which maintains that the Quranic ban is on economic exploitation and not on interest *per se,* is found in Fazlur Rahman, "Economic Principles of Islam," *Islamic Studies* 8 (March 1969); but more typical are the anti-interest opinions of Abu-Sulayman, "The Theory of the Economics of Islam," *Contemporary Aspects of Economic Thinking in Islam.*

33. The Islamic Development Bank is discussed by the Authors, in the context of other Middle Eastern economic assistance programs, in *Oil, OECD and the Third World: A Vicious Triangle?* (Austin: University of Texas Press, 1978). This sort of equity situation may well be easier for international institutions that have only a small number of projects to evaluate or where largely political considerations are involved in the lending procedure. Also, over the long run, a society might find itself with a few financial institutions owning huge amounts of equity.

34. In fact, private borrowers in times of inflation do not repay the true value of

their loans if the Quaranic injunctions are strictly adhered to; thus, the borrowers of anything would be exploiting the lender.

35. "The Theory of the Economics of Islam," *Contemporary Aspects of Economic Thinking in Islam,* p. 24.

36. For example, see Ziauddin Ahmed, "Socio-Economic Values of Islam," *Islamic Studies* 10 (December 1971): 351.

37. See M. Najatullah Siddiqi, "Moral Bases of Islamic Personal Law," *Islam and the Modern Age* 5 (November 1979): 85 FF.

38. For example, see *Sura* IV, v. 8, and *Sura* IV, vv. 12–15.

39. *Sura* IV, v. 11. Cf. also IV, vv. 17–18, and LXXXIX, vv. 17–20.

40. Abu Sulayman, "The Theory of the Economics of Islam," *Contemporary Aspects of Economic Thinking in Islam,* p. 480.

41. Ibid., p. 27.

42. *Sura* II, vv. 269 ff. Cf. also VI, vv. 217 ff.

43. *Sura* IX, v. 60.

44. It has been indicated above (cf. Abu-Sulayman, "The Theory of the Economics of Islam," *Contemporary Aspects of Economic Thinking in Islam,* p. 30) that shortages and the resulting hardships must be shared among the faithful. This interpretation clearly emphasizes the importance of the problem of income distribution to Islam's theology of economic morality.

Capitalism's theoretical method for allocating income (summarized in marginal productivity theory) contains no provision for those who for one reason or another are unable to earn enough to support a minimal life style. Islam obviously requires that society place an economic floor under its poorest citizens. Of course, Western societies have themselves foregone strictly capitalist guidelines in this regard. However, Islamic law probably has to be interpreted at least in spirit as imposing a ceiling on income through its clear injunctions on the obligations of the rich to share generously.

45. *Sura* CVII, vv. 2–7.

46. Rodinson, *Islam and Capitalism,* p. 14.

47. *Sura* XXVIII, v. 77.

48. *Sura* II, v. 194.

49. *Sura* LXII, v. 10.

50. See, for example, Rodinson, *Islam and Capitalism,* pp. 16–17.

51. M. Hamidullah, in *Cahiers de l'I.S.E.A.,* supplement no. 120, series v, no. 3, (December 1961), p. 26 ff.

52. Rodinson, *Islam and Capitalism,* pp. 17–18.

53. *Sura* LXXXIII, vv. 1–6; similar sentiments are expressed in *Sura* VII, vv. 7–8 and *Sura* XXIII, vv. 104–5.

54. For example, *Sura* VI, v. 153; *Sura* VII, v. 83; *Sura* XI, v. 85; *Sura* XVII, v. 37; *Sura* XXVI, vv. 181–82; and *Sura* LV, v. 82.

55. Along with cheating weak heirs such as widows and orphans, which, as we have seen above, is subject as well to repeated warning in the Quran.

56. *Sura* II, v. 184.

57. *Sura* II, vv. 282–83.

58. *Sura* II, v. 284 (part): "Unless it be merchandise present that you give and take between you; then it be no fault in you if you do not write it down. And take witnesses when you are trafficking one with another."

59. *Sura* II, v. 284 (part).

60. Which is not to say that there are also differences, in the West, between Christian teaching and modern capitalist practice. To demonstrate such differences exist, it is not necessary to return to medieval debates on the usury question, but only, for example, to refer to nineteenth and twentieth century papal encyclicals. The principles of Leo XIII in *Rerum Novarum* (1891), Pius XI in *Quadragesimo Anno* (1931), and John XXIII in *Mater et Magistra* (1961) and *Pacem in Terris* (1963) have emphasized Catholicism's ongoing problems with Western capitalism. They also reflect the fact that Catholic social doctrines continue to be largely derived from Thomas Aquinas, who wrote during the full flowering of the medieval dialogue between Islam and (Catholic) Christianity. Thus modern Catholic intellectualism has rather consistently avoided any outright endorsement of capitalism. Unlike Protestant Christianity, it has not, in recent years, had to backtrack very far in its considerations of the ramifications of two centuries of capitalist economic and social development. The possibilities for future dialogue in this regard between Christian and Muslim scholars are obviously promising. The authors hope to pursue this point further in their current broader study of Islam and capitalism.

61. This principle is quite similar to that which has governed homestead claims on government land in the U.S. for more than a century.

62. We will leave aside completely theological considerations in discussing Islam and socialism. Obviously Marxist atheism is incompatible with Islam, but atheism is hardly an essential element of basic socialist economic principles—that is, non-private ownership of the means of production, the labor theory of value, a preference for economic planning over the market as society's allocative mechanism, and fairly sharp limits on both the income and wealth of individuals.

63. For example, see the reference quoted above in note 29.

64. All quoted by Hakim Mohammed Said in *The Employer and the Employee — Islamic Concept* (Karachi: Dar al-Fikr al-Islami, 1972), p. 27.

65. Ibid., pp. 29–31, summarizes a lengthy traditional story of Muhammad encountering a strong, healthy beggar. When asked the extent of his possessions, the beggar told the prophet he had only a sheet of cloth and a bowl. Muhammad proceeded to auction these off to the crowd following him for two dirhams and told the beggar to buy with one dirham food for his family and with the other an axe. Muhammad then took the axe, cut some wood, and instructed the beggar to continue at this endeavor for a fortnight and then to return to see him. The beggar did as he was told and at that time reported to Muhammad that he had earned ten dirhams in the meantime, enough to outfit his family properly in clothing and food. The prophet then told the ex-beggar: "This is a blessing on you, and it is far better for you than that you would appear at the Day of Judgment with beggary disfiguring your face."

66. Ironically, while Marxism cannot for ideological reasons allow profit as it is found in capitalist societies and as it has always been allowed in Islam, it does allow the payment of interest. State-owned banks in Soviet-bloc countries serve as a sink for individual savings, and pay (generally modest) returns to their depositors, while lending to a wide range of individual and industrial borrowers at a similarly wide range of interest rates.

67. This *hadith* is from the accounts of Tirmizi, vol 2, and *Majman uz-Zawaid,* vol. 4, as quoted in Said, *The Employer and the Employee,* p. 55.

68. Ibid.

69. This *hadith* is from the account of *al-Arab al-Mufrad,* as quoted in ibid., p. 57.

70. Ibid., p. 59.

71. See note 62.

72. This middle-way approach has been exposed during this century in several Middle Eastern countries, not always in a specifically Islamic context, for example, the statism of Ataturk's Turkish republic, Nasser's Arab socialism, and the programs of the Bath parties of Syria and Iraq.

73. As we have indicated, Muslim practice has conceded to the state some authority over the collection and distribution of *zakat*. However, even in this case, it is up to the individual to declare the extent of his or her wealth that is subject to *zakat*. Not surprisingly, contemporary Muslim countries do not collect much tax revenue from *zakat*. For example, in 1974/75, the most recent year for which disaggregated data are available, the Saudi Arabian government collected only 16 million rials (about $4.5 million) in *zakat,* less than 0.02 percent of all tax revenue and only about 0.4 percent of non-oil related taxes. In the Yemen Arab Republic, *zakat* of 32.5 million rials (about $7.1 million) was reported by the government in 1977/78; this amounted to about 1.7 percent of all tax revenues.

74. It should be pointed out that Islam's problems with interest are not historically unique, but are shared with those religious traditions to which it is closest — Judaism and Christianity. However, unlike the former, Islam never got itself out of the dilemma by distinguishing between interest paid and received *inside* and *outside* the community; to Muslims, the fact of the sin is independent of the religions of the borrowers and lenders. Thus, strictly speaking, the dilemma may even remain when Muslims borrow (at interest) from non-Muslims. This question arose in early 1979, when the Ayatollah Khomeini seemed to indicate that it might be *haram* (forbidden by religious dictum) for Iran to repay loans negotiated by Muhammad Reza Shah's regime from U.S. and European banks — thereby sending severe tremors into banking systems that had lent Iran upwards of $8 to $10 billion in the closing months of the Pahlavi era. Of course, as indicated above, Islamic thought has yet to undergo the convolutions of Christian law that have changed the definition of usury from that of Aquinas, so close to the Quran, to that of modern-day America that sees only rates in excess of 18 percent (or even 24 percent) as possibly usurious.

75. Again, this is not solely an Islamic problem within the context of Mediterranean monotheistic tradition. In recent years, Latin American Christianity has twice emphatically reaffirmed, in Medellin (1958) and Puebla (1978, where a Pope presided) that capitalism cannot be untrammeled *and* Christian. If northern hemisphere capitalist societies have become both post- and un-Christian, this revival in the southern hemisphere recalls vividly the commonality of medieval Catholicism and Islam on many economic issues as they were discussed among that era's academies.

76. As of January 1, 1980, Iran was credited with having more than 19 percent of the world's estimated proved reserves of natural gas. In this respect, it was second only to the Soviet Union, with 35 percent, and far ahead of the third-place United States, with 7.5 percent.

77. Such judgments prescind from perhaps the even more important long-term considerations of possible nuclear accidents. This situation is all the more emphasized when it is recalled that when and if major breakthroughs in solar energy are realized, Iran is one of the planet's most sunshine-blessed countries. Thus we might ask where a few billions of Iran's current oil revenues might better be spent — in nuclear- or solar-powered research?

78. The recent state of Iranian agriculture was discussed in some detail by two of the present authors in *The Middle East Economies in the 1970's: A Comparative Approach* (New York: Praeger, 1976).

79. Though comparative data are in short supply, Shail Jain, in *Size Distribution of Income* (Washington: International Bank for Reconstruction and Development, 1975), gives some idea of how Iran compares with the rest of the world. The authors, in a monograph now being written, will discuss comparative Middle Eastern income distributions in the context of taxation burdens.

80. Despite lurid notices (appearing even in such careful and respectable Western journals as *Le Monde, The Manchester Guardian,* and *The Christian Science Monitor*) about the re-imposition of such harsh penalties, based on Islamic law, as amputation of hand or foot for theft, even rigidly orthodox Islamic thinkers have recently held that such punishments can only be meted out in a state that provides the wherewithal for all its citizens to earn their bread honestly.

81. In 1980 it is still too early to comment on the likely course of Iran's Islamic revolution. However, it is certainly worth noting that Islam provided an alternative framework to Marxism when the country violently rejected what it identified as capitalism — the venal regime of the Pahlavis. Furthermore, the first president of the new Islamic Republic of Iran, Abol-Hassan Bani-Sadr, is an economist educated in Europe whose academic research and publications have mostly been concerned with the concept of an Islamic economy.

82. *Sura* III, vv. 5-6; emphasis most respectfully added by the authors of this paper.

Chapter 3 — THE COURSE OF SECULARIZATION IN MODERN EGYPT

1. Two examples of the first approach are the outstanding studies by Bernard Lewis, *The Emergence of Modern Turkey* (London: Oxford University Press, 1960), and Niyazi Berkes, *The Development of Secularism in Turkey* (Montreal: McGill University Press, 1964). Among the studies on the ideological response of the *ulama* are Malcolm Kerr, *Islamic Reform* (Berkeley: University of California Press, 1966), and Charles C. Adams, *Islam and Modernism in Egypt* (London, 1933).

2. Gabriel Baer has virtually pioneered the field of social history of modern Egypt. Among his works see in particular *Egyptian Guilds in Modern Times* (Jerusalem,

1964), and *Studies in the Social History of Modern Egypt* (Chicago: University of Chicago Press, 1969). Arnold H. Green has offered a careful analysis of the response of the Tunisian *ulama* to modernization in *The Tunisian Ulama: 1873–1915* (Leiden: Brill, 1978).

3. Donald Eugene Smith, *Religion and Political Development* (Boston: Little, Brown, 1970), p. 7.

4. H. A. R. Gibb and Harold Bowen, *Islamic Society and the West*, vol. 1, part II (London: Oxford University Press, 1957), p. 81.

5. Leonard Binder remarked that the *ulama* sought to re-establish their traditional prerogatives in the constitution that was to be written for Pakistan after partition from India. "The core of this agreement was contained in the provision empowering the Supreme Court to invalidate all acts of the legislature which are repugnant to the Quran and the Sunnah." *Religion and Politics in Pakistan* (Berkeley: University of California Press, 1961), p. x.

6. I have argued elsewhere that the higher Egyptian *ulama* ought rightly to be considered part of the ruling élite in the late eighteenth century, rather than mere intermediaries between government and society, as so many works on the subject characterize them. See "The Emergence of the Shaykh al-Azhar as the Pre-Eminent Religious Scholar in Egypt," in the commemorative volume of the 1000th anniversary of the city of Cairo (Berlin, GDR, Akademie Verlag, 1972). Green, *The Tunisian Ulama,* also found that the *ulama* from the capital, with their close ties to the ruling élite, were more reluctant to join the nationalist movement for fear of losing their preeminent social and administrative positions.

7. The *nizamiyah madrasahs* which spread across the Middle East in the eleventh century can likewise be seen as an attempt by the Sunni state to propagate through educational institutions a particular interpretation of Islamic "truth."

8. Professor Smith identifies this as the dominance of the polity over religious beliefs. See Smith, *Religion and Political Development,* p. 86. I will have more to say on this point later.

9. Ali Mubarak Pasha, *Al-Khitat al-Tawfiqiyah al-Jadidah* (Bulaq, 1887), I: 87. Of ninety-five *madrasah*s which he mentions in volume 6, twenty-three were in ruin, two were inactive, thirty-four were functioning, twenty-five had become *zawiyah*s, and forty-one had become mosques. The total is more than ninety-five because some *madrasah*s fit more than one category.

10. Uriel Heyd noted that in the Ottoman Empire the higher *ulama* helped to write and implement the Sultan's reform programs. But their strategy of participation had the same result as the Egyptian *ulama*s policy of isolation. Heyd wrote, "Retrospectively, the support given by the high ulema to the policy of opening the Ottoman Empire to European secular ideas and institutions seems a suicidal policy from the point of view of the interest of their corps." See "The Ottoman Ulema and Westernization in the Time of Selim III and Mahmud II," *Scripta Hierosolymitana* (Jerusalem, Israel) 4 (1961): 76.

11. See my "Non-Ideological Responses of the Egyptian Ulama to Modernization," in *Sufis, Saints and Scholars,* edited by Nikki Keddie (Berkeley: University of California Press, 1972), pp. 15–24.

12. Manfred Halpern, *The Politics of Social Change in the Middle East and North Africa* (Princeton: Princeton University Press, 1963), pp. 15–24.

13. The Dar al-Ulum which opened in 1872 was a preparatory school for teachers. The secular university and the modern school for judges were not opened until 1907–8.

14. *British Sessional Papers* 112 (1899): 1003, 1007.

15. Gabriel Baer, "Social Change in Egypt: 1800–1914," in *Political and Social Change in Modern Egypt,* edited by P. M. Holt (London: Oxford University Press, 1968), p. 160.

16. Leonard Binder, "Pakistan and Modern Islamic Nationalist Theory," *Middle East Journal* 12 (1958): 48.

17. One of the most obnoxious powers the *ulama* enjoyed was the right to censure the writings of Azhar graduates. A board of conservative *ulama* was able to "try" holders of Azhar certificates and to stop the publication and distribution of their work. The three most famous cases of censure involved Taha Husayn, Ali Abd al-Raziq, and Muhammad Bakhit.

18. In a remarkable little book Muhammad Ali Gharib revealed that he was with other students at al-Azhar when someone rushed into the courtyard and announced that students were striking in the streets. He and his companions, all of them villagers, were surprised, he reported, because they did not know what "strikes, revolution or independence" meant. They only knew that the British occupied their country. See Gharib, *Azhariyat* (Cairo, 1962), p. 37.

19. An interesting study of the manner in which the military penetrated all institutions in Egypt is Anouar Abdel-Malek's *Egypt: Military Society,* translated by Charles Lam Markmann (New York: Random House, 1968).

20. Published studies on the *Ikhwan* movement include Richard P. Mitchell, *The Society of the Muslim Brothers* (Ann Arbor: University of Michigan Press, 1970); Christina Phelps Harris, *Nationalism and Revolution in Egypt* (The Hague, 1964); Ishaq Musa Husaini, *The Moslem Brethren* (Beirut: Khayat's, 1956); and J. Heyworth-Dunne, *Religious and Political Trends in Modern Egypt* (Washington, D.C., 1950).

21. For a careful study of *waqf* reform in modern Egypt see the chapter on this subject in Baer, *Social History of Modern Egypt,* pp. 79–92.

22. For a study of how the regime approached the problem of reform for al-Azhar and an analysis of the reform law see my article, "Al-Azhar in the Revolution," *Middle East Journal* (Winter 1966): 31–49. One of my subsequent articles reports the failure of the reform to have the desired effect upon the traditional core of religious studies within the university or upon the *ulama*. See "Al-Azhar: A Millennium of Faithfulness to Tradition," *Mid East* (April 1970): 34–41.

23. Among other things, the *ulama* were accused of medievalism, obstructionism, and of forming within Islamic society a religious aristocracy or priesthood. Even President Nasser joined in the personal attack upon them by declaring "Of course the shaykh does not think of anything except the turkey and the food with which he filled his belly. He is no more than a stooge of reaction, feudalism and capitalism. At that time some shaykhs were trying to deceive us with fatwas of this nature. From the beginning, Islam was a religion of work. The Prophet used to work like everybody else. Islam was never a profession." (Cited in Crecelius, "Al-Azhar in the Revolution," *Middle East Journal* (Winter 1966): 42.

24. The resignation of western-trained scholars to the growing control by the state is reflected in a statement by Mahmud Hubballah, who wrote, "Yet, the state that controls the sinews of life has the right, when it wishes, to interfere in religion itself, which becomes dependent upon the wish of the state." "The Challenge of Modern Ideas and Social Values to Muslim Society," *Islamic Literature* 11 (1959), 35; cited in Crecelius, "Al-Azhar in the Revolution," *Middle East Journal* (Winter 1966): 37.

25. The Charter was in fact to mention Islam only once. When it referred to religious matters it spoke in general terms such as the following: "The eternal spiritual values derived from religions are capable of guiding man, of lighting the candle of faith in his life and of bestowing on him unlimited capacities for serving truth, good and love. In their essence all divine messages constituted human revolutions which aimed at the reinstatement of man's dignity and his happiness. It is the prime duty of religious thinkers, then, to preserve for each religion the essence of its divine message." *The Charter* (Cairo, 1962), p. 85. The Charter also states clearly that the Revolution would not bow to religious pressure. "The freedom of religious belief," it read, "must be regarded as sacred in our new free life."

26. P. J. Vatikiotis, *The Modern History of Egypt* (New York, Praeger, 1969), p. 323. In a perceptive article Ibrahim Abu-Lughod commented on similar anti-secular trends throughout the Arab world in the decade of the 1950s. See "Retreat from the Secular Path? Islamic Dilemmas of Arab Politics," *The Review of Politics* 28 (October 1966): 447–76.

27. *The Charter*, p. 42.

28. An analysis of this trend appears in my article, "Die Religion im Dienste des islamischen Staatssozialismus in Ägypten," *Bustan* 3 (1967): 13–20.

29. Morroe Berger, *Islam in Egypt: Social and Political Aspects of Popular Religion* (Cambridge: At the University Press, 1970), p. 47.

30. The *Minbar al-Islam* contains the single most important attempt by a group of writers to lay out the major concepts of a socialist ideology drawn from Islamic principles. See my "Die Religion in Agypten," *Bustan* 3 (1967).

31. See all Cairo dailies of August 22, 1979.

32. For a thoughtful analysis of some aspects of this new Islamic resurgence see R. Stephen Humphries, "Islam and Political Values in Saudi Arabia, Egypt and Syria," *The Middle East Journal* (Winter 1979): 1–19.

33. Berger, *Islam in Egypt*, p. 128.

34. Smith, *Religion and Political Development*, p. 86.

35. Halpern, *Politics of Social Change*, and C. E. Black, *The Dynamics of Modernization* (New York: Harper & Row, 1966), for instance, refer to the necessity of changing one's psychological system. Smith, *Religion and Political Development*, pp. 113–18, refers to this process as polity-transvaluational secularization.

Chapter 4—VEILING IN EGYPT AS A POLITICAL AND SOCIAL PHENOMENON

1. Cf. Amina al-Said, pp. 373 ff., in E. Fernea and B. Bezirgan, *Middle Eastern Women Speak* (Austin: University of Texas Press, 1977), also pp. 199–200; J. Berque, *The*

Arabs, Their History and Future (London, 1964), pp. 181 ff; and A. al-Quazzaz, *Women in the Middle East and North Africa* (Austin: University of Texas Press, 1977).

2. The new law of personal status has made significant changes. E.g., she must be informed if her husband marries again, and then has the right to sue for divorce, which the judge is obligated to grant her within six months. She also has more security after divorce and longer custody of the children (to age 10 for boys, 12 for girls, and if a court so decides, even longer).

3. This was made current as a phrase in Arabic as early as 1899, when Qasim Amin's famous book of that name was published in Cairo.

4. Cf. Henry Ayrout S. J., *The Peasant of Egypt* (Boston, 1963), p. 157.

5. Edward Lane: *Manners and Customs of the Modern Egyptians* (London, 1908), p. 53.

6. Al-Marghinani, *The Hedaya or Guide, a Commentary on the Mussulman Laws,* translated by Ch. Hamilton, 2nd ed. (Lahore, 1957), p. 598.

7. Literally "a tent," the *chadar* is an enveloping mantle which covers an Iranian woman from head to toe and is often drawn over the face.

8. Cf. Ali Shariati, *On the Sociology of Islam,* translated by Hamid Algar (Berkeley: University of California Press, 1979), p. 23.

9. It should not surprise us that the modalities of fundamentalism are different in Shii and Sunni Islam; in fact, we should expect it. It seems logical to Iranian fundamentalists to follow the *mujahid*; it would be extraordinary for the Muslim Brotherhood in Egypt to rally behind, e.g., the Shaykh al-Azhar. He, however, is a government appointee; a *marjaal-taqlid* is not.

10. *Shar,* "direction," is what is divinely prescribed, e.g., in the Quran. It is used in the sense of "Divine Law." Fiqh, "insight," is the word used for the understanding of the scholars of the various *madhhabs,* or ways of understanding, of the Divine Law and is set forth and argued in explicit manuals.

11. Current statistics, always difficult to obtain, are not the purpose of this paper. Interested readers are referred to "The Balance of People, Land, and Water in Modern Egypt" in John Waterbury's *Egypt: Burdens of the Past, Options for the Future* (Hanover, N.H.: American Field Studies, 1976), from which I have drawn these figures.

12. Since the peace initiative with Israel, fewer of these Arabs come to Egypt, due to their governments' hostility to Egyptian policy.

13. By fall 1979, young men were beginning to appear in significant numbers in the short beard without mustaches that is associated in Egypt with the *sunna* of the Prophet. In this way they have found a functioning visible sign, rather like the *ziyy shari.*

14. As a postscript, the same young woman two years later gave up shari clothes and reverted to international dress. She said that her commitment to Islam was unchanged, but that now that she knew who she was, she no longer felt any need to prove it by distinctive dress.

15. I am much indebted to my friends and colleagues Dr. Adil Sulayman Gamal and Dr. Mohamed al-Nowaihi for astute comments on the original draft of this article. They have helped me to see new aspects of the question, though the conclusions are my own.

16. Among women factory workers (some 12 percent of the factory labor force), desire for greater personal freedom ranked next to economic need as motivation for putting up with the difficulties of working girls. Cf. Mona Hammam, "Egypt's Working Women" in *MERIP Reports No. 82* (November 1979).

Chapter 5 — ISLAM IN PAHLAVI AND POST-PAHLAVI IRAN

1. A. K. S. Lambton, "Quis Custodiet Custodes: Some Reflections on the Persian Theory of Government," *Studia Islamica* 6 (1956).

2. S. Amir Arjomand, "Religion, Political Action and Legitimate Domination in Shiits Iran," *European Journal of Sociology* 20 (1979).

3. Ibid., p. 104.

4. Ibid., p. 95.

5. Scarcia, "Kerman, 1905: La guerra tra Seihi e Balasari," *Annali del Instituto Universitario Orientale di Napoli* 13 (1963): 200.

6. H. Algar, *Religion and State in Iran, 1785-1905: The Role of the Ulama in Qajar Period* (Berkeley and Los Angeles, 1969), p. 20.

7. See Mangol Bayat-Philipp, *Mysticism and Dissent: Socioreligious Thought in Qajar Iran,* forthcoming.

8. Ibid., chap. 6.

9. M. Harri, *Shiism and Constitutionalism in Iran* (Leiden, 1978).

10. R. Mottahedeh, *Loyalty and Leadership in an Early Islamic Society* (Princeton, 1980).

11. *Hukumat-i Islami* (Najaf, 1971).

12. See *Rah-i tayyshuda* (Tehran, 1948); *Islam, maktab-i mubariz va muvalid* (Tehran, 1965); and the minutes of his trial transcribed in 1964.

13. See for instance J. Al-i Ahmad, *Gharbzadigi* (Tehran, 1962).

14. Mangol Bayat-Philipp, "A Phoenix Too Frequent: The Concept of Historical Continuity in Modern Iranian Thought," *Asian and African Studies* (1980); and "Shiism in Contemporary Iranian Politics" in *Iran: Toward Modernity,* edited by Haim and Kedourie (London: 1980). See also Yann Richard, "Ali Shariati, le précurseur," *Les Nouvelles Littéraires* (December 1978). A selection of his writings appear in *On the Sociology of Islam,* trans. by H. Algar (Berkeley, 1979); and R. Campbell, *Marxism and Other Western Fallacies: An Islamic Critique* (Berkeley, 1980). The last two works must be read with caution. The editor, anxious as he is to prove Shariati was not anti-clerical or influenced by Marxism, and that his views are basically not different from Khomeini's or other revolutionary clerics, has selected too carefully some texts, omitting other more representative writings. Such selective omission, however, has not proven any point since even those very works translated contradict the editor/translator's assertions. Notice, for instance, in the Introduction to *On the Sociology of Islam,* the term *mala* (assembly of notables) is wrongly translated as priesthood, whereas in the text on p. 115 it appears as aristocracy. The entire

content of the text "Dialectic of Sociology," pp. 111-18, leads to the definite conclusion that Shariati meant official clergy, whether he used the term *mulla* or *mala*. Similarly, how can official clergy mean anything else than the present ruling clergy (Introduction to *Marxism and Other Western Fallacies,* pp. 10-12)? True, Khomeini has shared Shariati's criticism of those *ulama* who have wrongly understood and wrongly taught religion. Both prepared the Islamic revolution. But from there to claim that Khomeini and Shariati's religious thought are compatible and complementary is to miss the significance of Shariati as a modern, progressive, secular-educated, lay ideologist. It also serves the purpose of perpetuating the fallacious and misleading method of studying Islamic thought in monolithic fashion.

15. *Darsha-yi Islamshinasi* (n.d.), p. 94.

16. Ibid.

17. *Intizar, mazhab-i itiraz* (Tehran, n.d.), pp. 25-29.

18. Ibid., pp. 23-24.

19. Cited in H. Algar, *On the Sociology of Islam,* p. 11.

20. *Bazgasht bi khishtan va niyazha-yi insan-i imruz,* p. 13.

21. *Umat va Imamat* (Tehran, 1968), pp. 5-6.

22. *Az kuja aghaz kunim* (Tehran, n.d.), p. 11.

23. *Bazgasht,* pp. 13-14.

24. Ibid., pp. 39-40.

25. Intizar, pp. 20-21.

26. Ibid., p. 39.

27. Ibid., pp. 33-35.

28. *Umat,* pp. 52-53. *Az kuja,* p. 24.

29. *Bazgasht,* pp. 15-16, 32-33, 38-39.

Chapter 6 — THE ARAB-ISRAELI WARS, NASSERISM, AND THE AFFIRMATION OF ISLAMIC IDENTITY

1. See, for example, *Hawl Bayt Al-Maqdis* published by the High Council for Muslim Affairs (Cairo, 1969). Cf. the proceedings of *The Fifth Conference of the Academy of Islamic Research* published by Al-Azhar (Cairo, 1971) and Fuad Hasanein Ali, *Filastin al-Arabiyyah* (Cairo, 1973), who writes "O Jerusalem, Land of Judgment and Resurrection, O eternal city, warring over thee continues. The wars of the Crusades did not cease on the 9th of December 1917 as General Allenby claimed with pride in front of the Jaffa gate prior to the takeover by International Zionism. It is as though Crusading Britain fought and Zionism reaped the fruit of victory. What befell your holy places at the hands of the Crusades is repeated today in an uglier form, within the sight and hearing of the world, at the hand of the Zionists."

2. See, for example, Muhammad M. Al-Fahham, "The Restoration of Jerusalem," *The Fifth Conference of the Academy of Islamic Research* (Cairo, 1971), where he

writes about the Muslim conquest of Jerusalem: "He conquered it by the most honorable, refined and immortal class of beings, human or angelic, ever known to this world. They met after the first time, under his leadership at the night of Ascension in the region" (p. 38). He goes on to say that there is no trace of the temple of David or Solomon left since it was repeatedly demolished and the Temple of Jupiter was built in its place. Furthermore, "the Muslims have a greater right to Dawood who was a Messenger of God. He preached Islam and like all other Prophets was a Muslim. Dawood according to the Jews is merely a worldly king and has nothing sacred or prophetic about him. How can they ascribe or attach any religious sacredness to him?" (p. 43). And "We need to go into the details of Jewish conspiracy and wilful opposition against the personality of Jesus. It suffices here to state that conspiracy against him and his disciples continued throughout the centuries. The early Christians met with terror, torture and extinction at the hands of the conspiring Jews. During the modern times we find several Jewish publishing houses in New York which are famous for their inclination toward Zionism. They publish material that is of the highest degree of indecency and offense to the person of Jesus" (p. 49).

3. Mahmud al-Abidi, *Qudsuna* (Beirut, 1972), pp. 156ff.

4. Ibid., p. 156, reproduced a Zionist poster showing the Dome of the Rock with Hebrew slogans to the effect that "The Aqsa Mosque in Jerusalem is built on the place of Solomon's Temple. This Mosque is our property."

5. The letter dated August 23, 1969, was written to Muhammad Fawzi, Minister of War of the United Arab Republic. It is quoted in *Hawl Bayt al-Maqdis* (Cairo, 1969), published by the Supreme Council of Islamic Affairs of al-Azhar.

6. Al-Abidi, *Qudsuna*, p. 123, quotes the speech of Abd Allah Salim, foreign minister of Jordan at the United Nations in April 1971, where he said, "There is no peace without Jerusalem."

7. *The Fifth Conference of the Academy of Islamic Research* (Cairo, 1971).

8. "Never did the history of mankind reveal so outrageous a crime, and so glaring an injustice, as the one that had been committed by a religious sect whose members had long been notorious for transgressing Divine Commands, disobeying Prophets, and rebelling against every country they happened to settle in," according to Ishaq Musa al-Husaini, "The Palestinian Question from the Islamic Viewpoint," *The Fifth Conference of the Academy of Islamic Research* (Cairo, 1971), p. 88.

9. Nadim al-Baytar, *Al-Faaliyyah al-Thawriyyah fi al-Nakbah* (Beirut, 1965). Al-Baytar affirms that the loss of Palestine had rendered traditional Arab existence as obsolete and marginal and has opened the way for a radical revolution which will lead to salvation. This revolutionary transformation is inevitable; it follows as a consequence of the experience of loss (pp. 33–34).

10. A case in point is the writings of Sayyid Qutb who early in his career came under the influence of Abbas Mahmud al-Aqqad and became interested in Western thought. Prior to 1948 he published *Qissat al-Ashwak, Muhimmat al-Shair fi al-Hayah, al-Shati al-Majhul* among others. After 1948 he became interested in Islamic topics and joined the Muslim Brotherhood. He repudiated all his pre-1948 works and published a commentary on the Quran as well as works calling on Muslims to repudiate Western influence and return to pristine Islam. See, for example, *Hadha al-Din, Maalim fi al-Tariq,* and *al-Mustaqbal li-Hadha al-Din.*

11. Abd Allah Muhammad Madi *et al., al-Azhar fi Ithnay Ashara Aman* (Cairo, 1964).

12. C. F. Jones, "The New Egyptian Constitution," *Middle East Journal* 10 (1956): 300.

13. *The Draft of the Charter* (Cairo, n.d.), pp. 63 ff.

14. Ibid., p. 12.

15. Ibid., p. 77.

16. Ibid., p. 9, talks about the "unshakable faith in God, His Prophet and His sacred messages which He passed on to man as guide to justice and righteousness."

17. Crecelius, "al-Azhar . . . ," p. 43.

18. Zafer Ishaq Ansari, "Contemporary Islam and Nationalism, A Case Study of Egypt," *Die Welt des Islam* 7 (1961): 11.

19. He referred to it as "my Vietnam" where at one time up to 70,000 Egyptian soldiers were bogged down, even during the 1967 Israeli aggression. Anthony Nutting, *Nasser* (New York, 1972), p. 338.

20. The word *pact* had acquired a derogatory connotation due to relentless anti-Baghdad Pact propaganda in the Egyptian press and media. It was aimed at foiling Dulles' efforts to form a pact among nations that bordered on the southern flank of Russia. Nasser, espousing nonalignment, did not want any of the Arab states to join in what to him was an American imperialist plan.

21. *The Islamic Pact* (Cairo, n.d.), p. 43, published by the Supreme Council of Islamic Affairs and distributed as a gift of *Minbar al-Islam*. The book also included several articles by various Muslim scholars condemning the pact: Shaykh Abd al-Latif Subki compared it to Satan's temptation of Adam and Eve and prayed that God may "protect Islam from any plots made by such irresponsible people" (pp. 62–64). Shaykh Muhammad Muhammad al-Madani compared it to the mosque of the hypocrites where the Prophet Muhammad refused to pray (pp. 56ff). While maintaining that true Islam was the policy followed in Egypt, "they are afraid of the Great Wall which is sponsored by the United Arab Republic, and which springs from the teachings of Islam and aims at helping the oppressed Muslims. . . . A sincere call for liberation and for maintaining Islamic dignity is now made from the land of al-Azhar" (p. 60).

22. Ibid., p. 32.

23. The conferees agreed that "the Islamic world forms one collectivity united by the Islamic doctrine. . . . The political and intellectual attacks on the Muslim world necessitate that Muslims cooperate and aid one another in forming a world collectivity to provide pride and strength to defend and protect its doctrines and interests, and to participate in establishing world peace and the progress of human life toward a better condition. In order for this collectivity to be a reality, it is necessary that allegiance will be to the Islamic doctrine and the interests of the Muslim *Ummah* in its totality above the allegiance to nationalism or other isms. It is also necessary for the Muslim countries to establish relations with one another in the different fields of politics, economics, and education." *Majallat Rabitat al-Alam al-Islami* (July 1965), year 13.

24. And in a speech in Suez on March 22, 1966, he said, "Reactionism was never of God's law. The law of God is always the law of justice and the law of justice, o brothers,

is socialism" (*al-Akhbar,* March 23, 1966, cited by al-Munajjid, *al-Tadamun,* p. 68). "This pact renders Islam inoperative in its highest principles and stabs it in its most forthright teachings" (Shaykh Zakariyya al-Bardisi, *Minbar al-Islam* [April 1966], p. 243, cited by al-Munajjid, p. 87).

25. See Morroe Berger, *Islam in Egypt Today* (Cambridge, 1970).

26. *Al-Mulhaq al-Dini, al-Jumhuriyyah* 30 (July 15, 1966) reports that "it has been decided to hold weekly meetings for the religious leaders and the imams of the mosques in the Office of Religious Affairs in the Headquarters of the Socialist Union."

27. Muhammad Wasfi, Director of Religious Affairs, announced that these meetings were part of "a complete revolutionary plan to prepare the leaders of al-Azhar to perform their positive role in the battle of construction and progress. . . . It will bring together imams of religion, the leaders of al-Azhar, the preachers, and the Arab Socialist Union on the basis of total amalgamation with the progress of society and revolutionary interaction with the people," *al-Mulhaq al-Dini, al-Jumhuriyyah* 28 (July 1, 1966).

28. *Al-Mulhaq al-Dini, al-Jumhuriyyah* 26 (June 17, 1966), reported that instructions were given to the imams to prepare their sermons in writing. They had to deal with contemporary issues and follow the guidelines of the ministry of *awqaf.*

29. Muhammad Mazhar Said, *Minbar al-Islam* (July 1966), p. 68.

30. Kamal al-Din Rifat, Secretary of the Dawah and Thought in the Socialist Union, said: "There is no contradiction at all between Islam and socialism; for Islam since its genesis had advocated socialism, and socialism is one of the principles of Islam," *al-Mulhaq al-Dini, al-Jumhuriyyah* 28 (July 1, 1966).

31. Muhammad Ata in ibid., 27 (July 1, 1966), cited by Salah al Din al Munajjid, *Balsharat al-Islam* (Beirut, 1966), p. 80.

32. Muhammad Mahmud Alwain in *Mulhaq* 27 (June 24, 1966) is reported to have said, "All Sufism is socialism. The pioneer of socialism in Islam is Abu Dharr al-Ghifari. The history of Sufism at different periods is nothing but the best image of socialism" (cited by Munajjid, *Balshafat,* p. 82).

33. Jamal Al-Din al-Ramadi, *Mulhaq* (July 23, 1966). In the same issue Abd al-Halim Dawakhli wrote an article, "Al-Islam thawrah wa-quwwah"; Hasan Habashi wrote "al-Islam Thawrah" in *Minbar al-Islam* 11 (year 33), p. 152.

34. Mustafa Bahjat Badawi, *Mulhaq* (July 22, 1966), cited in *Balshafat,* p. 49.

35. Musa Sharaf in *Mulhaq* (July 22, 1966), cited in *Balshafat,* p. 50.

36. Nasser in a speech reported in *al-Ahram,* July 23, 1966, cited in *Balshafat al-Islam,* p. 52. In a speech on June 25, 1962, Nasser said: "Socialism is sufficiency and justice; it is social justice . . . liberation from political, economic, and social exploitation. Socialism in this sense is the law of justice . . . the law of God. . . . Islam in its early days was the first socialist nation. He was the first to implement the policy of nationalization [*tamin*]." Abdallah Imam, *al-Nasiriyyah* (n.p., n.d.), pp. 366–67. In a speech on April 25, 1964, in Sana, Yemen, before religious leaders, Nasser said, "Islam was not only a religion. It was a religion that organized social justice in this world, It organized equality and provided equal opportunity. . . . All this we have expressed to you in one word — socialism" (p. 368). In a speech before *Majlis al-Ummah* on November 12, 1964, Nasser said: "Our socialism is a scientific socialism based on science and knowledge. We have not said that it

was a materialistic socialism. . . . We did not say that it was Marxist socialism. . . . We did not say that we have departed from religion . . . but we said that our religion is a social-ist religion and that Islam in the Middle Ages fulfilled the first socialist experiment in the world" (p. 369).

37. Mahmud Shalabi, *Ishtirakiyyat Muhammad* (Cairo, 1962).

38. Mahmud Shalabi takes Khadijah as a model of cooperative socialism be-cause she hired men and shared the profit with them. He goes on to say: "Thus before the world knew socialism, the Arabs knew it and they implemented it as a healthy drop that emanated from the depth of the holy heart of an Arab woman," cited by al-Munajjid, *al-Tadlil al-Ishtiraki* (Beirut, 1965), p. 67.

39. Mahmud Shalabi, *Ishtirakiyyat Umar* (Cairo, 1964–65).

40. Mahmud Shalabi, *Ishtirakiyyat Abu Bakr* (Cairo, 1963).

41. *Al-Islam Din al-Ishritakiyyah* (Cairo, n.d.), which included the texts of radio and television speeches by the *ulama* on socialist topics including Shaykh Muhammad al-Madani, "Socialist Principles in Islam and Social Integration"; Shaykh Ghazali, "Con-cerning Means of Acquiring Property and Limitations Placed Thereon"; Shaykh Ahmad al-Sharabasi. "Money and Socialism in Islam," which talks about Muhammad, Umar I, and Umar II as good socialists; Shaykh Muhammad Abu Zahra, who says that the misuse of property was the cause of seizure in Islam.

42. One of those who proposes an Islamic solution to the question of the ascen-dancy of Israel is Abd al-Halim Uways, in his *Tariquna ila al-Quds: Ruya Islamiyyah* (Cairo, 1974). "To proceed from Islam . . . besides the assurance of help from God there is the affirmation of the road one reaches at the end. . . . It is the assurance of victory. Can God's will be overcome—His will which is all-powerful—could it be overcome by a missile launcher, an aircraft carrier, radiation or bombs?" (p. 28). The basic principle of the new renaissance, says Uways, must be the rallying cry of Islam (*wa-Islamah*). This is especially crucial at this time because the world today is struggling among contradictory ideologies. Israel appears to get stronger with religious zeal and commitment to the Zionist ideology. The Arab world has for some time been in the middle of the cold war between capitalism and Marxism. The appropriation of Islam as a motivating ideology will ensure the support of the masses and guarantee the utmost effort, zeal, and sacrifice. This ideology must be bolstered by a historical awareness which is closely linked to it. It provides the theoretical principles that undergird the civilization, serving to ground the authentic heritage of the people and guarantee freedom from dependence on imported ideologies and doctrines. It thus offers the opportunity for leadership and eliminates "followership" and imitation of others. Crucial to a renaissance and the liberation of occupied territory is the availability of arms, says Uways. These must be manufactured locally to ensure constant supply and free the nation from dependency on others for survival. Destiny must be appropriated through constant struggle, *jihad*. Uways sees Islamic history as a successive effort at "defensive" *jihad* against enemies who seek to eliminate Islam. Thus constant vigilance and a "continu-ing revolution" are the "proper response to the conspiracies that are hatched day and night against our Arab Muslim *Ummah*" (p. 73).

43. See, for example, Muhammad Hafiz Yaqub, *Al-Takhalluf al-Arabi wa-al-Taharrur al-Arabi* (Beirut, 1977), pp. 86 ff. He writes, "The June defeat has revealed the disintegration, deterioration, and the incapacity of Arab existence; it emphasized the neces-sity to overturn it and change it" (p. 86).

44. Muhammad Abd al-Rahman Baysar, *al-Mutamar al-Khamis li-Majma al-Buhuth al-Islamiyyah* (Cairo, 1970), p. 13.

Chapter 7 – THE ROLES OF ISLAM IN SAUDI ARABIA'S POLITICAL DEVELOPMENT

1. John Lewis Burckhardt, *Notes on the Bedouins and Wahabys, Collected During His Travels in the East* (London: Henry Colburn and Richard Bentley, 1831), II: 117.

2. Sheikh Hafiz Wahba, *Arabian Days* (London: Arthur Barker Limited, 1964), pp. 107–8. It is interesting to note that a little over two centuries later, after Abd al-Aziz's conquest of al-Hijaz in 1925-26, the *ikhwan* objected to and prohibited the carrying of the *mahmal* into Makka by the Egyptians. See H. St. John Philby, *Arabian Jubilee* (New York: John Day, 1953), pp. 89–90.

3. For greater historical detail, see the source of most of our knowledge on the Sauds, the works of H. St. John Philby, particularly his *Saudi Arabia* (Beirut: Librairie du Liban, 1968).

4. The figures vary considerably. See John S. Habib, *Ibn Saud's Warriors of Islam: The Ikhwan of Najd and Their Role in the Creation of the Saudi Kingdom* (Leiden: Brill, 1978), pp. 71–75; and compare David G. Edens, "The Anatomy of the Saudi Revolution," *International Journal of Middle Eastern Studies* 5 (1974): 57, fn. 2.

5. Despatch No. 20, American Vice-Consul, Aden to Secretary of State, October 7, 1924, in *Documents on the History of Saudi Arabia,* edited by Ibrahim al-Rashid (Salisbury, N.C.: Documentary Publications, 1976), I: 168.

6. Letter no. 138, Colonel Knox to British Secretary of State for the Colonies, March 30, 1924, India Office and Library Records, London, file R/15/5/71.

7. Report by Dr. Harrison to British Political Agent, Bahrain, September 1, 1917, India Office and Library Records, file R/15/5/27.

8. For information on the *ikhwan* generally, see Phoenix, "A Brief Outline of the Wahhabi Movement," *Journal of the Central Asian Society* 17, part 4 (October 1930): 413-16; Hafiz Wahba, Jazirat al-Arab fi al-Qarn al-Ishrin (Cairo: Maktabat al-Nahda al-Misriyya, 4th ed. 1961), pp. 293–312.

9. See, for example, George Linabury, "The Creation of Saudi Arabia and the Erosion of Wahhabi Coservatism," *Middle East Review* 11, no. 1 (Fall 1978): 5–12; and Helen Lackner, *A House Built on Sand; A Political Economy of Saudi Arabia* (London: Ithaca Press, 1978), pp. 215-18.

10. George Rentz, "Saudi Arabia: The Islamic Island," *The Journal of International Affairs* 19, no. 1 (1965): 83.

11. See Faysal's statement in *The Middle East Journal* 17, nos. 1 and 2 (Winter-Spring 1963): 161-62.

12. Fouad al-Farsy, *Saudi Arabia: A Case Study in Development* (London: Stacey International, 1978), pp. 89–98, p. 126, fn. 1.

13. *Atab News,* May 12, 1975 (Jamad al-Ula 1, 1395), p. 1.

14. *Al-Jazira,* 22 Safar 1400 (10 January 1980), p. 8.

15. *Arab News,* 19 March 1980 (Jamad al-Awwal 2, 1400), p. 1.

16. The various non-judicial roles of the *qadi* were spelled out by Mr. William Tewell, a former ARAMCO lawyer at a Harvard Law School lecture, Cambridge, Mass., April 2, 1980. For information generally on the legal system see George M. Baroody, "The Practice of Law in Saudi Arabia," in *King Faisal and the Modernisation of Saudi Arabia,* edited by Willard A. Beling (London: Croom Helm, 1980), pp. 113–24.

17. See the relevant documents in *The Middle East Journal* 18, no. 3 (Summer 1964): 351–54.

18. Soliman A. Solaim, "Saudi Arabia's Judicial System," *The Middle East Journal* 25 no. 3 (Summer 1971): 407.

19. *Quran* VI: 159.

20. *Nadwat Ilimiyya Hawla al-Sharia al-Islamiyya wa Haquq al-Insan fi al-Islam* (Beirut: Dar al-Kitab al-Lubnani, 1973), pp. 39–40.

21. These figures were culled from an unpublished paper by Sirhan al-Utaybi, "Development of Manpower in Saudi Arabia" (April 26, 1976).

22. See Richard F. Nyrop *et al., Area Handbook for Saudi Arabia,* 3rd ed. (Washington, D.C.: USGPO, 1977), pp. 104–109.

23. See Ministry of Planning, *Second Development Plan, 1395–1400 A.H.* (al-Riyad, 1976).

24. *Arab News,* May 16, 1975 (Jamad al-Ula 5, 1395), p. 1.

25. See the announcement of the al-Rajhi establishment in *Al-Jazira,* 6 Rabi Awwal 1400 (24 January 1980), p. 1.

26. *Saudi Report* 1, no. 27 (April 21, 1980): 1.

27. Commentary by Muhammad Umar al-Amudi, *al-Madina,* 18 Rabi al-Thani 1400 (March 5, 1980), p. 16.

28. *The Economist* 264, No. 6985 (July 16, 1977): 62.

29. *Al-Jazira,* 22 Safar 1400 (January 10, 1980), pp. 1, 10–11.

30. For example, see *The Times* (London), June 17, 1978, pp. 4, 13.

31. *The Times* (London), 18 June 1978, p. 6.

32. *Al-Jazira,* 6 Jumada al-Thani 1400 (21 April 1980), p. 1. The statement was made by Prince Majid, Governor of the Makka region.

33. *Arab News,* April 26, 1980 (Jamad al-Thani 11, 1400), p. 1.

34. For a strongly worded editorial on the clash of values between the British and Saudi kingdoms see *al-Nadwa,* 9 Jumada al-Thani 1400 (April 24, 1980), p. 1.

35. Letter of Abd al-Rahman to Abd al-Aziz, 3 Rajab 1342 or February 8, 1924, India Office and Library Records, file R/15/5/70.

36. *Al-Jazira,* 19 Rabi Awwal 1400 (February 6, 1980), p. 4.

37. William A. Eddy, "King Ibn Saud: 'Our Faith and Your Iron'," *The Middle East Journal* 17, no. 3 (Summer 1963): 258.

38. Hamad Sadun al-Hamad, "The Legislative Process and the Development of Saudi Arabia," Ph.D. diss. (University of Southern California, 1973), p. 187.

39. Ahmad Zaki Yamani, *Islamic Law and Contemporary Issues* (Jidda: Saudi Publishing House, 1388), pp. 8–9.

40. For more information generally see Motleb A. Nafisa, "Law and Social Change in Saudi Arabia: Directive Legal Rules" (LL.M. thesis, Harvard Law School, May 1972), especially pp. 17–21.

41. *Nizam al-Taminat al-Ijtimaiyya,* issued under Royal Decree No. M/22 of 6 Ramadan 1389 (Makka: Matbaat al-Hukuma, first printing 1389/1970), p. 10.

42. *Foreign Capital Investments Regulation* of 1383 (1964) (al-Riyad: Industrial Studies and Development Centre, mimeo, n.d.), p. 4.

43. Ministry of Justice, "The Saudi Report on the Legal System in the Kingdom of Saudi Arabia" (mimeo, n.d.), p. 2.

44. Letter No. 35, American Minister, Jidda to Secretary of State, December 4, 1944, National Archives, Washington, D.C., Record Group 59, State Decimal Files 1940–44, unnumbered box.

45. *Al-Riyad,* 6 Muharram 1400 (25 November 1979), p. 3.

46. R. Stephen Humphreys, "Islam and Political Values in Saudi Arabia, Egypt, and Syria," *The Middle East Journal* 33, no. 1 (Winter 1979): 9.

47. Editorial comments by Turki Abd Allah al-Sudayri, *al-Riyad,* 9 Muharram 1400 (28 November 1979), p. 1. It is interesting to note that shortly after this he resigned his position.

Chapter 8 – PAKISTAN: QUEST FOR ISLAMIC IDENTITY

1. For a detailed discussion of this period cf. Aziz Ahmad *Islamic Culture in the Indian Environment* (London: Oxford University Press, 1964). A useful general history of Islam in Pakistan is provided by Freeland K. Abbott, *Islam and Pakistan* (Ithaca: Cornell University Press, 1968).

2. Jamil-ud-din Ahmad, ed., *Speeches and Writings of Mr. Jinnah,* (Lahore: Muhammad Ashraf, 1952), I: 177–78.

3. H. Malik, "Problems of Regionalism in Pakistan" in *Pakistan in Transition,* edited by W. H. Wriggins (Islamabad, Pakistan: University of Islamabad Press, 1975), p. 65.

4. Cf. Wayne A. Wilcox "Ideological Dilemmas in Pakistan's Political Culture" in *South Asian Politics and Religion,* edited by D. E. Smith (Princeton: Princeton University Press, 1966), pp. 339–51.

5. Cf. Leonard Binder, *Religion and Politics in Pakistan* (Berkeley: University of California Press, 1961); E. I. J. Rosenthal, *Islam in the Modern National State* (Cam-

bridge: Cambridge University Press, 1965), pp. 181–281; Fazlur Rahman, "Islam and the Constitutional Problems of Pakistan," *Studia Islamica* 32, 4 (December 1970): 275–87; W. C. Smith "Pakistan, an Islamic State" in *Islam in Modern History* (Princeton: Princeton University Press, 1957), pp. 206–55.

6. *Constitution of the Islamic Republic of Pakistan* (Government of Pakistan, March 1956), Preamble.

7. Ibid., Part I, Art. 1.

8. Ibid., Preamble.

9. Ibid., Part IV, Art. 32.

10. Ibid., Part XII, Art. 197.

11. Ibid., Art. 198.

12. Cf. Rahman "Islam and the Constitutional Problems of Pakistan," *Studia Islamica* 32, 4 (December 1970) for an analysis from this point of view.

13. *Report of the Court of Inquiry constituted under Punjab Act II of 1954, to inquire into the Punjab Disturbances of 1953* (Lahore, 1954), pp. 231 ff.

14. As quoted in M. Ahmed "Islamic Aspects of the New Constitution of Pakistan," *Islamic Studies* 2, no. 2, (June 1963): 262.

15. For a detailed study of the Islamic character of the 1962 Constitution cf. Ahmad, ibid., pp. 249–86.

16. Ahmad, ibid., Appendix C, p. 283.

17. For a detailed study of this problem cf. John L. Esposito "Muslim Family Law Reform in Pakistan" *Journal of Malaysian and Comparative Law* (December 1977), especially pp. 299–303, 307–10. In 1963 the West Pakistan Provincial Assembly voted to repeal the *Muslim Family Law Ordinance.* A similar move in the National Assembly was defeated but only with a coordinated effort of women's organizations, the press, and the government. Moreover, the Council of Islamic Ideology in 1979 recommended amending the Ordinance in several areas in which its reforms have been deemed to be un-Islamic.

18. Maulana Abul Ala Maududi (1903–79) has been a major figure in the history of Pakistan. Through his writings he has provided a systematic interpretation of Islam which has received attention both in South Asia and the Middle East. His religious organization/party has been dedicated to the dissemination and implementation of Maududi's Islamic ideology. Cf. Charles J. Adams "The Ideology of Maulana Maududi" in *South Asian Politics and Religion,* (Princeton: Princeton University Press, 1966), pp. 371–97 and Aziz Ahmad *Islamic Modernism in India and Pakistan 1857–1964* (London: Oxford University Press, 1967), pp. 208–23. Among Maududi's writings, the most relevant for this study are *Islamic Law and Constitution* (Karachi: Jamaat-i-Islami Publications, 1955), *First Principles of the Islamic State* (Lahore: Islamic Publications, 1960), and *Political Theory of Islam* (Lahore: Islamic Publications, 1960), a revision of an earlier version which appeared in *Islamic Law and Constitution.*

19. Cf. Philip E. Jones "Islam and Politics Under Ayub and Bhutto: A Comparative Analysis," unpublished manuscript (Madison: Seventh Conference on South Asia, November 1978).

20. *Forum* (Dacca), vol. 1, no. 16 (March 7, 1970): 5 as cited in Jones, "Islam and Politics Under Ayub and Bhutto," pp. 16–17.

21. *Criterion* 5, no. 4 (1970): 62–63, as cited in H. Mintjes "The Debate on Is-lamic Socialism in Pakistan" *al-Mushir* (Rawalpindi) 20, no. 4 (Summer 1978): 70.

22. "I, _____, do solemnly swear that I am a Muslim and believe in . . . the Prophethood of Muhammad (peace be upon him) as the last of the Prophets and that there can be no Prophet after him." *The Constitution of the Islamic Republic of Pakistan* (Islam-abad: 1973), third Schedule, p. 153.

23. William L. Richter, "The Political Dynamics of Islamic Resurgence in Paki-stan," *Asian Survey* 19, 6 (June 1979): 547–57.

24. Cf. part of the published proceedings in Waheed-uz-Zaman, ed., *The Quest for Identity* (Islamabad: University of Islamabad Press, 1973).

25. *Pakistan Times,* April 18, 1977.

26. *Pakistan Times,* July 7, 1977, p. 8.

27. *Measures to Enforce Nizam-i-Islam: Address to the Nation by President General Zia-ul-Haq* (Islamabad: Ministry of Information and Broadcasting, December 1978).

28. *Introduction of Islamic Laws: Address to the Nation by President General Zia-ul-Haq* (Islamabad: Ministry of Information and Broadcasting, February 1979).

29. *Measures,* p. 3.

30. Many of the *ulama* wanted the state to compel the public observance of the prayer periods by all Muslims. Zia argued that enforcement of such a law would be impos-sible and thus persuasion rather than compulsion was chosen. However, there is a qualifica-tion which may prove significant in the future. "But for the time being we want to rely on persuasion rather than compulsion." Ibid., p. 4.

31. *Introduction of Islamic Laws,* pp. 3 and 4. Further emphasis on national identity may be seen in recent attempts to introduce wearing of the traditional garb as a school uniform. Moreover, Justice Hamoodur Rahman, former Chief Justice of the Su-preme Court and Presidential Advisor on Constitutional Affairs, commenting on the call for simplicity in dress in the *Introduction of Islamic Laws* (p. 22) has advocated introduc-tion of a national dress "a simple uniform dress." Interview with Justice Hamoodur Rah-man, Islamabad, August 29, 1979.

32. There are many Quranic references to *zakat*—Quran II: 43, XXXVII: 14, and others. Cf. Chapter 2, "Islam and Modern Economic Change," of this volume for a more detailed discussion.

33. *Measures,* p. 12.

34. *Introduction of Islamic Laws,* p. 16.

35. Ibid., pp. 17–18.

36. Interview with Dr. Mohammad Uzair, Economic Consultant to the ICP and author of *Interest Free Banking* (Pakistan: Royal Publisher, 1978).

37. Flogging has been applied with regularity. Amputation has occurred very rarely; no one has been sentenced to stoning for adultery.

38. King Abdul Aziz University in Saudia Arabia and Cairo's al-Azhar Univer-sity were major consultants.

39. While there are many political factors involved, this analysis will be restricted to the Islamic aspects.

40. *Measures,* p. 2.

41. The problematic nature of this artificial resolution adopted by most Muslim countries has, of course, emerged quite demonstrably with the so-called Islamic resurgence in a number of Muslim countries.

42. For a provocative study of this problem and its causes Cf. F. Rahman "Islamic Modernism: Its Scope, Method and Alternatives" *International Journal of Middle East Studies,* vol. 1 (1970): 317-33.

43. Rahman, "Islam and the Constitutional Problems of Pakistan," *Studia Islamica* 32, 4 (December 1970): 285.

44. *Munir Report,* pp. 210-13.

45. W. C. Smith, "Pakistan, an Islamic State" in *Islam and Modern History,* p. 228. Smith's study is perhaps the most insightful analysis available. Not only does it shed light on the first decade of Pakistan's history, but many of his comments continue to have relevance today.

46. Ibid., p. 224.

Chapter 9 – ISLAMIC RESURGENCE IN MALAYSIA

1. See K. J. Ratnam, *Communalism and the Political Process in Malaya* (Kuala Lumpur: University of Malaya Press, 1965); and G. Means, *Malaysian Politics* (London: Hodder and Stoughton, 1976).

2. For descriptions of the role of the Chinese in Malaysia see D. W. Chang, "Current Status of Chinese Minorities in Southeast Asia," *Asia Survey* 8 (June 1973): 586-603; V. Purcell, *The Chinese in Southeast Asia* (London: Oxford University Press, 1951).

3. D. Noer, "Islam in Indonesia and Malaysia: A Preliminary Study," *PIMA* 9 (July–December 1975): 50-70. One Malaysian expressing a wider recognition of current trends is Chandra Muzaffar, President of Aliran, see his *The Universalism of Islam* (Penang: Aliran, 1979).

4. For description of this period see W. R. Rolf, *Origins of Malay Nationalism* (Kuala Lumpur: University of Malaya Press, 1967); Ratnam, *Communalism and the Political Process in Malaya*; R. K. Vasil, *Politics in a Plural Society* (Kuala Lumpur: Oxford University Press, 1971).

5. See the *Asian Survey* annual Malaysia country reviews for the development of the National Front.

6. See G. Means, "Special Rights as a Strategy for Development," *Comparative Politics* 5 (October 1972): 29-61; and F. von der Mehden, "Communalism, Industrial Policy, and Income Distribution in Malaysia," *Asian Survey* 15 (March 1975): 250-65.

7. Quoted in E. Rosenthal, *Islam in the Moslem National State* (Cambridge:

Cambridge University Press, 1965), pp. 291–92. This provides a good review of the legal position of Islam in Malaysia. Also see G. Means, "The Role of Islam in the Political Development of Malaysia," *Comparative Politics* 1 (January 1964): 264–84.

8. During the latter years of the rule of Tun Mustapha, Sabah's Chief Minister, there were regular allegations of pressure and payments used to achieve conversions to Islam. Although considerable publicity and active missionary work is involved in present conversions of Chinese, the same allegations have not been made regarding campaigns in Peninsula Malaysia. See M. Roff, *The Politics of Belonging* (Kuala Lumpur: Oxford University Press, 1974), pp. 111–13 for a discussion of Mustapha's Islamic campaign.

9. There are various versions of the May 13th Affair: See Tenkgu Abdul Rahman, *May 13, Before and After* (Kuala Lumpur: Malaya Utusan, 1969); F. Gagliano, *Communal Violence in Malaysia: The Political Aftermath* (Athens: Ohio University, 1970); and J. Slimming, *Malaysia: Death of a Democracy* (London: John Murray, 1969).

10. F. von der Mehden, "Religion and Politics in Malaya," *Asian Survey* 3 (December 1963): 609–15. Tenkgu stated that it was "impossible to apply the Islamic religion in every way to the administration of the country."

11. Ibid.

12. For example, during the tension prior to the withdrawal of Singapore from Malaysia, Malay papers reportedly stated that, to be true citizens of Malaysia, people should convert to Islam. G. Means, "The Role of Islam in the Political Development of Malaysia," *Comparative Politics* 1 (January 1964): 347.

13. *The Star* (Penang), March 20, 1979.

14. Mazaffar, *The Universalism of Islam.*

15. T. S. Chee, "Literacy Responses and the Social Process," *Southeast Asia Journal of Social Science* 3 (1975): 89.

16. Interviews with Datuk Asri and Anwar Ibrahim, June 1979.

17. This reaction is not altogether new as students returning from the Middle East in the 1950s were described as having an "almost unbelievable narrowness of religious feeling and Malay chauvinism," D. Moore, "The United Malays National Organization and the 1959 Malayan Elections," Ph.D. diss. (University of California, 1960.)

18. *Watan* (Kuala Lumpur), March 1 and 11, 1979. As one religious leader stated, "the success of Muslims in Iran is a success against tyranny and denial," saying it was a victory for an Islamic nation "which is just and prosperous in every sense of the word," while a PAS politician claimed inaccurate reporting of events in Iran as an "anti-Islam mass media."

19. *Far Eastern Economic Review* 105 (February 9, 1979).

20. See "Of Khalwat and the Constitution," *Asiaweek*, June 29, 1979, pp. 22, 27. Any reading of Malaysian newspapers will provide numerous examples of alleged instances of Khalwat and religious and political discussions of what shall be done.

21. "The Spectre of Kerling," *Asiaweek*, June 8, 1979, pp. 16–17.

22. Sharon Siddique of the Institute of Southeast Asian Studies, Singapore, a careful observer of Dakwah movements divides them into two types, the outward-looking organization such as PERKIM that seeks conversion and the inward-looking such as ABIM which attempts to revise Islam within the Moslem community. Interview, July, 1979.

23. Interview with Anwar Ibrahim, June 1979.

24. *Watan,* March 11, 1979.

25. Moore, "The United Malays National Organization and the 1959 Malay Elections," Ph.D. diss. (University of California, 1960).

26. *Straits Times,* May 19, 1959.

27. Ibid., May 1, 1959.

28. For discussions of PAS see *Kelantan: Religion, Society and Politics in a Malay State,* edited by W. Roff (Kuala Lumpur: Oxford University Press, 1974); N. Funston, "The Origins of Parti Islam Se Malaysia," *Journal of Southeast Asian Studies* 7 (March 1976): 58-73; and C. Kessler, *Islam and Politics in a Malay State: Kelantan, 1838-1969* (Ithaca: Cornell University Press, 1978).

29. Malaya, *Radio Malaya Press Statement,* Director of Information (July 1959), 181.

30. Interview, June 1979.

Chapter 10 — ISLAM AND NATIONAL INTEGRATION THROUGH EDUCATION IN NIGERIA

1. This paper is a revised and enlarged version of one presented at the Annual Meeting of the American Academy of Religion, New Orleans, November 18-21, 1978. I am grateful for the valuable assistance of Dr. I. Ukeje, J. Kamara, R. Ilechukwu, R. Salah, and Dr. A. Smedley.

2. Thomas Hodgkin, *Nigerian Perspectives: An Historical Anthology* (London, 1960), pp. 67-69.

3. One of the most prominent Maliki theologians and jurists of the late fifteenth century was the North African Muhammad b. Abd al-Karim al-Maghili (d. 1504); he visited the Hausa towns of Kano and Katsina.

4. For recent studies on the life and career of Usuman Dan Fodio, see Mervyn Hiskett, *The Sword of Truth: The Life and Times of the Shehu Usuman Dan Fodio* (London, 1973); Ismail A. B. Balogun, *The Life and Works of Uthman Dan Fodio* (Lagos, 1975); B. G. Martin, *Muslim Brotherhoods in Nineteenth-Century Africa* (Cambridge, 1976); Alhaji Shehu Shagari and Jean Boyd, *Uthman Dan Fodio: The Theory and Practice of His Leadership* (Lagos, 1978).

5. Martin, *Muslim Brotherhoods,* p. 28.

6. H. F. Backwell, ed., *The Occupation of Hausaland 1900-1904, Being a Translation of Arabic letters found in the House of the Wazir of Sokoto* (Bohari, 1903; London, 1927), pp. 13-14.

7. Some of the best works on early Nigerian political parties are B. J. Dudley, *Parties and Politics in Northern Nigeria* (London, 1968); Richard L. Skalar, *Nigerian Political Parties: Power in an Emergent African Nation* (Princeton, 1963); and C. S. Whitaker, Jr., *The Politics of Tradition, Continuity and Change in Northern Nigeria 1946-1966*

(Princeton, 1970). A very good general work on the history of Nigeria is Michael Crowder's, *The Story of Nigeria* (London, 1978). Balewa was a commoner and northern school teacher who spent a year at the London University Academy for Teachers.

8. Dudley, *Parties and Politics,* pp. 314-15.

9. Crowder, *Story,* p. 224.

10. Wilfred Cartey and Martin Kilson, eds., *The Africa Reader: Independent Africa* (New York, 1970), p. 85.

11. Crowder, *Story,* pp. 273-74.

12. For information on recent party activity, the elections, and the return to civilian rule, see various issues of *West Africa, New African* and *Africa: An International Business, Economic and Political Magazine, 1978-79.*

13. *West Africa,* August 21, 1978, p. 1629.

14. See A. Fajana, "Some Aspects of Yoruba Traditional Education," *ODU, University of Ife Journal of African Studies* 3, 1 (July 1966):16-28; J. A. Majasan, "Traditional System of Education in Nigeria," *Nigeria Magazine* nos. 119, 120, and 121 (1976):23-29, 44-48, 25-30; Godfrey N. Brown and Mervyn Hiskett, eds., *Conflict and Harmony in Education in Tropical Africa* (Cranbury, N.J.: 1976), part I.

15. See Hiskett, "Islamic Education in the Traditional and State Systems in Northern Nigeria," in Brown and Hiskett, *Conflict and Harmony,* pp. 134-42.

16. Some excellent studies on missionary activity in Nigeria are J. F. Ade Ajayi, *Christian Missions in Nigeria 1841-1891: The Making of the New Elite* (Evanston, 1965) and E. A. Ayandele, *The Missionary Impact on Modern Nigeria 1842-1914: A Political and Social Analysis* (New York, 1967).

17. Helen Kitchen, ed., *The Educated African: A Country-by-Country Survey of Educational Development in Africa* (New York, 1962), p. 365.

18. James S. Coleman, *Nigeria: Background to Nationalism* (Berkeley and Los Angeles, 1958), pp. 134, 138.

19. A. Babs Fafunwa, *History of Education in Nigeria* (London, 1974), pp. 71-72.

20. Ayandele, *Missionary Impact on Modern Nigeria,* p. 286. Concerning late nineteenth- and early twentieth-century Christian attitudes toward Islam, Ayandele writes: "Anti-Islamic feelings were aroused among the Christian missions in Britain and in the United States when the Madhi and his successor, the Khalifa, won more and more successes [in the Sudan]. The long imprisonment of the French Catholic priests by the Khalifa, the retreat of Emin Pasha before his victorious force and the abandonment of Emin Pasha's province, all inflamed Christian ardour" (p. 118).

21. Coleman, *Nigeria,* p. 113.

22. Alhaji Sir Ahmadu Bello, *My Life* (London, 1962), pp. 24-25.

23. See Fafunwa, *History of Education,* p. 65.

24. T. G. O. Gbadamose, *The Growth of Islam among the Yoruba 1841-1908* (1978), pp. 167-69.

25. See J. S. Trimingham, *Islam in West Africa* (London, 1959), Appendix IV; *Encyclopaedia of Islam,* 2nd ed., s.v. "Ahmadiyyah"; J. Humphrey Fisher, *Ahmadiyya: A Study in Contemporary Islam on the West African Coast* (London, 1963).

26. F. H. El-Masri, "Religion in Ibadan: Islam," in *The City of Ibadan,* edited by P. C. Lloyd, A. L. Mabogunje, and B. Awe (London, 1967), p. 225 n.1.

27. Fisher, *Ahmadiyyah,* p. 175; A. R. I. Doi, "Islam in Nigeria: Changes since Independence," *Islam in the Modern Age* 6, no. 3 (August 1975):44–45.

28. Fafunwa, *History of Education,* pp. 168, 174; Fisher, *Ahmadiyyah,* pp. 174–75.

29. Fafunwa, *History of Education,* p. 174.

30. Gbadamosi, *Growth of Islam,* pp. 145–46.

31. Bello, *My Life,* p. 31.

32. See Coleman, *Nigeria,* p. 134.

33. A Nigerian doctoral student at a well-known American university recently mentioned to me that he intends to resume Arabic and Quranic studies with a *mallam* upon his imminent return to Zaria; he has not had formal lessons for more than ten years.

34. See John N. Paden, *Religion and Political Culture in Kano* (Berkeley, 1973), pp. 59–60.

35. Paden, *Religion,* pp. 206–207, S. A. Dawodu, "Youth and Islam in Nigeria," *Nigerian Journal of Islam* 1, no. 2 (January–June 1971):30. The MSSN's annual organ, the Muezzin, is published in English.

36. Fafunwa, "Conference of Muslim Lecturers and Administrative Staff of Nigerian Universities: Appeal for Funds," *Nigerian Journal of Islam* 1, no. 2 (January–June 1971):43–44. The *Journal* is the organization's official publication. Dr. Fafunwa, a Yoruba, also founded the Muslim Association of Nigeria in 1959. He obtained his higher education in the United States, and has held academic, administrative, and consultative posts in various Nigerian, Sierra Leonian, and Liberian institutions and associations, as well as in UNESCO and the UN.

37. After independence, the Sardauna began a campaign for northern Islamic unity which necessitated neutralizing some of the brotherhoods and championing his own, the Usmaniyya, as the true successor to the Islamic legacy of Usuman Dan Fodio. All northern Muslims automatically became members, active or inactive: non-Muslim northerners were to be proselytized; he personally led this effort, but with meager success. Further, the Northern Region was to establish direct relations with the international Muslim world spearheaded by his 1963–64 visits (financially supported by Saudi Arabia and Kuwait) to countries of West and North Africa, Pakistan, Iraq, and Jordan. He is said to have suggested a modification of the Arab League, headquartered in Cairo, to include African Muslim lands; see Paden, *Religion,* pp. 178–89; Walter Schwarz, *Nigeria* (New York and London, 1968), pp. 248–49.

38. *Nigerian Herald,* April 20, 1979.

39. Paden, *Religion,* pp. 119–20.

40. See, for example, *Nigerian Herald,* April 20, 1979, and May 18, 1979, *New Nigerian,* July 5, 1979.

41. *Nigerian Herald,* May 18, 1979.

42. *African Development* (December 1976): 1285.

43. *The Constitution of the Federal Republic of Nigeria* (Apapa, 1978).

44. See, for example, F. H. El-Masri, "The Role of Imams in the New Nigeria," *Nigerian Journal of Islam* 1, no. 1 (June 1970):24; Dawodu, "Youth and Islam," *idem.* 1, no. 2 (January–June 1971): 31–32; *idem.,* letter of Alhaji T. S. Akonni, pp. 49–50.

45. *Federal Republic of Nigeria National Policy on Education* (Lagos, 1977), p. 3.

46. Ibid., pp. 5–9 *passim.*

47. Ibid., pp. 11–12.

48. Kano, Sule, and Shagari graduated from Daduna College in the 1940s and pursued careers in education and politics. Amini Kano, a socialist, has held several governmental posts, including that of Federal Commissioner for Communications (1967–71) and Health (1971–74). He is an accomplished author (in Hausa) and regularly delivers public talks on Quranic exegesis. Mallam Maitama Sule was the Chief Whip of the NPC (1955–59), Federal Commissioner of Mines and Power (1959–66), and State Commissioner for Kano (1967–74). He, too, gives public religious addresses. President Shehu Shagari, a native of Sokoto and an early science teacher, has served as Federal Minister of Economic Development (1959–70) and Federal Commissioner for Finance (1971–75).

49. *West Africa,* January 3, 1977, p. 2.

50. Ibid., December 20, 1976, p. 1939. See, also, the remarks of the Waziri of Sokoto, Alhaji Junaidu, in Brown and Hiskett, *Conflict and Harmony,* pp. 467–71.

Chapter 11 – RELIGION AND MODERNIZATION IN SENEGAL

1. See Godfrey and Monica Wilson, *The Analysis of Social Change* (Cambridge: Cambridge University Press, 1968), pp. 24–44; Robert Holt and John E. Turner, *The Political Basis of Economic Development* (Princeton: Van Nostrand, 1966); Joseph Kahl, *The Measurement of Modernization* (Austin: University of Texas Press, 1968), pp. 133–51; Alex Inkeles, "Making Men Modern: On the Causes and Consequences of Individual Change in Six Developing Countries," *American Journal of Sociology* 76 (November 1970):339–425.

2. See Lucy Creevey (Behrman), "Patterns of Religious and Political Attitudes and Activities During Modernization: Santiago, Chile," *Social Science Quarterly* 53 (December 1972):520–33; David Horton Smith and Alex Inkeles, "The OM Scale: A Comparative Socio-Psychological Measure of Individual Modernity," *Sociometry* 29 (December 1966):353–77; Peter Berger, *The Sacred Canopy* (Garden City: Doubleday, 1969); Charles Y. Glock and Rodney Stark, *Religion and Society in Tension* (Chicago: Rand McNally, 1965), pp. 85, 287–88; and J. Milton Yinger, *The Scientific Study of Religion* (New York: Macmillan, 1970), pp. 32–40.

3. Snaiberg, *AJS* 76 (November 1970): 399–425.

4. Lucy Creevey (Behrman), "Political Development and Secularization in Two Chilean Urban Communities," *Comparative Politics* (January 1972): 269–70; and L. Cree-

vey (Behrman) "The Political Impact of Catholic Priests in Chile," in *Religion and Modern-ization,* edited by Donald Smith (Princeton: Princeton University Press, 1972).

5. See Daniel Lerner, *The Passing of Traditional Society* (New York: The Free Press, 1958).

6. See Lucy E. Creevey and Ruth Schachter Morgenthau, "Modern Political History of Francophone Tropical Africa," in *Modern Political History of Africa,* edited by Michael Crowder (Cambridge: Cambridge University Press, forthcoming).

7. See Lucy Creevey, "Urbanization and Planning."

8. Ministere des Finances et des Affaires Economiques, *Situation Economique du Senegal, 1974* (Dakar, 1975), pp. 6, 110.

9. Changes occur but gradually and not always consistently. See the classic study by A. E. Epstein, *Politics in an Urban African Community.*

10. Ibid., pp. 68, 71.

11. See ILO, *Employment, Incomes and Equality; A Strategy for Increasing Productive Employment in Kenya* (1972), and Colin Leys, *Underdevelopment in Kenya, the Political Economy of Neocolonialism 1964-1971* (1972).

12. *Situation Economique,* 1974 (Dakar, 1975).

13. See Lucy Creevey (Behrman), "Muslim Politics and Development in Sene-gal," *The Journal of Modern African Studies* 15, 2 (1977): 261-77, and *Jeune Afrique* (1978).

14. For a discussion of politics in Senegal, see Edward J. Schumacher, *Politics, Bureaucracy and Rural Development in Senegal* (Berkeley, 1975); Francois Zuccarelli, *Un Parti Politique Africain: l'union Progressiste Senegalaise* (Paris, 1970); and Lucy Creevey (Behrman), *Muslim Brotherhoods and Politics in Senegal* (Cambridge, 1970).

15. See Creevey (Behrman), *Muslim Brotherhoods,* pp. 18-33.

16. Among many studies on Islam in West Africa and specifically in Senegal, see: Alphonse Gouilly, *L'Islam dans l'Afrique Occidentale Francaise* (Paris: Editions Larose, 1952); J. C. Froelich, *Les Musulmans d'Afrique Noire* (Paris: Editions de l'Orante, 1962); M. Chailley et al., *Notes et Etudes sur l'Islam en Afrique Noire* (Paris: Calmann-Levy, 1960); Marcel Cardaire, *l'Islam et le Terroir Africain* (Koulouba: Imprimerie du Gov-ernement, 1952); Vincent Monteil, *L'Islam Noir* (Paris: Editions du Seuil, 1964); Paul Marty, *Études sur l'Islam au Senegal,* vols. I & II (Paris: Ernest Leroux, 1917); Lucy Cree-vey (Behrman), "L'Islamization of the Wolof in the End of the Nineteenth Century," *African Historical Studies* (1966).

17. See Marty, *Études sur l'Islam,* and Paul Marty and Jules Salenc, *Les Ecoles Maraboutiques du Senegal; La Medersa de Saint-Louis* (Paris: Ernest Lerous, 1914).

18. Creevey (Behrman), *Muslim Brotherhoods,* p. 10.

19. Octave Depont and Xavier Coppolani, *Les Confreries Religieuses Musul-manes* (Algiers: Adolphe Jourdan, 1897); Edouard Montet, *La Culte des Saints Musulmans dans l'Afrique du Nord* (Geneva: Librairie Georg, 1909).

20. Ibid., pp. 157-80.

21. Schumacher, *Politics,* pp. 23-43, Zuccarelli, *Un Parti Politique,* pp. 188-89.

22. Creevey, *Muslim Brotherhoods,* pp. 107–55.

23. In 1966 the census listed 5,060 as marabouts. See Creevey, *Muslim Brotherhoods,* p. 64.

24. See reports in *Le Soleil* (Dakar), March 1976.

25. Ibid., December 18, 1975.

26. Ibid.

27. Ibid., January 22, 1976.

28. In January 1980, Abdoulaye tried to establish a Muslim political force in Senegal. It is too soon to know what kind of influence this group will have although it is not likely to be very powerful, because Abdoulaye is not. His efforts are an echo—albeit a faint one—of his father's activities in the forties and fifties.

29. *Le Soleil,* March 1976.

30. Ibid., June 14, 1976.

31. For more information on this survey see Lucy Creevey, "Social and Political Behavior and Attitudes in Dakar," unpublished manuscript, 1979. Surveying in Dakar means an entire courtyard of interested listeners. Efforts to obtain other than the head of household's opinion are relatively pointless as his advice is sought in any case. However, in this survey heads of household were deliberately chosen because they were opinion leaders.

32. See Abdoulaye Diop, *Societe Toucouleur et Migration; Enquete sur la Migration Toucouleur a Dakar* (Dakar: IFAN, 1965).

INDEX

ISLAM AND DEVELOPMENT

was composed in 10-point Compugraphic Times Roman and leaded two points
by Metricomp Studios,
with display type in Merganthaler Linoterm Lydian,
by Joe Mann Associates, Inc.;
printed on Warren 50-pound acid-free Antique Cream paper,
Smyth-sewn and bound over boards with Columbia Bayside Linen,
also adhesive-bound with Wyomissing Corvon 22 covers,
by Maple-Vail Book Manufacturing Group, Inc.;
and published by

SYRACUSE UNIVERSITY PRESS
SYRACUSE, NEW YORK 13210